HAMBLEN COUNTY TENNESSEE

TOMBSTONE RECORDS

WPA Records

Heritage Books
2024

HERITAGE BOOKS
AN IMPRINT OF HERITAGE BOOKS, INC.

Books, CDs, and more—Worldwide

For our listing of thousands of titles see our website
at
www.HeritageBooks.com

A Facsimile Reprint
Published 2024 by
HERITAGE BOOKS, INC.
Publishing Division
5810 Ruatan Street
Berwyn Heights, MD 20740

Originally published 1938

International Standard Book Number
Paperbound: 978-0-7884-8800-9

TABLE OF CONTENTS

HAMBLEN COUNTY
CEMETERY RECORDS

CHURCH RECORD

WPA RECORDS

The WPA Records are, for the most part, carbon copies of the original
that was typed on onion skin paper during the Depression. Since these
records were typed on poor machines by people who did not type well
either and read by persons not always sure of the older handwritten
material, the results are often less that perfect.

We have made every attempt to make as good a copy as can be made from
these older papers. Sometimes there are water stains and burned edges
around the paper.. This is the results of a fire at the home of one of
the workers, Mrs. Penelope Allen, who was over most of the project.

The WPA Records are now very scattered between the State Archives, various
Public and Private Libraries and other collections. Some day, there is
a hope that all of these can be collected and stored in one place. In
spite of their many mistakes and problems, these are still the most com-
plete collection of Tennessee records found anywhere.

HAMBLEN COUNTY

CEMETERY RECORDS

INDEX

(Note: Index for Bethesda Cemetery at end of this index)

A

Flagg, H. G., 32
Flagg, J. H. G., 26
Flagg, J. S., 26
Flagg, John M., 26, 32
Flagg, Mattie A., 36
Fleenor, H. R., 25
Fleenor, Lillia Mae, 25
Foster, Larkin, 136
Foster, Lizzie, 136
Foster, Sallie A., 136
Foster, Sparrel, 128
Foster, Thomas, 136
Fox, Ethel, 170-a
Fox, O. P. R., 170-a
Fox, Pearl C., 170-a
Fox, William, 113
Francisco, C. F., 223
Francisco, Thersie, 223
Franklin, Dorcus R. T., 105
Franklin, E. O., 118
Franklin, John H., 105, 118
Franklin, J. W., 26
Franklin, Mary T., 105
Franklin, William C., 119
French, George D., 102
French, J. R., 219
French, Sophia H., 102
Frye, Annis, 121
Fry, Mahala, 224
Fuller, C. E., 65
Fuller, Nina Lee, 65
Fullington, Della M., 222
Fulton, Coy E. W., 136
Fulton, Eliza J., 136

G

Gaines, A. B., 36
Gaines, Jeanette, 36
Galbraith, Anna D., 165
Galbraith, J. L., 165
Galbraith, James L., 165
Galding, William R., 164
Gallaher, Carrie W., 51
Gallaher, Frank, 51
Gallaher, Nellie M., 93
Gallaher, R. O., 93
Gamble, Edna, 119
Gammon, Nannie A., 170-b
Gandler, Dannie, 51
Garcia, Helen M., 88
Garcia, Joseph, 88
Garrett, Sarah, 40
Garretson, A. M., 155
Garretson, Alice M., 155
Garretson, D. R., 155

Garretson, Ellen, 155
Garretson, J. A., 151
Garretson, Jacob, 153
Garretson, Job, 153
Garretson, John, 154
Garretson, Leatha, 151
Garretson, Rebecca, 155
Garretson, Roy Reed, 155
Garretson, Sarah, 154
Garretson, T. C., 155
Garretson, Wilbur R., 151
Garretson, Winifred P., 153
Garrison, Thomas, 125
Garson, Tinna, 66
Gary, Pearl Hefner, 180
Gass, Amanda, 217
Gass, Charles G., 102
Gass, Coy S., 102
Gass, Sadie S., 102
George, Jessie G., 90
Gentry, Clint, 142
Gentry, James S., 109
Gentry, Lethia, 200
Gentry, Temmie, 200
Gentry, W. L., 63
Gibbs, Nannie, 100
Gibson, Berta, 138
Gibson, J. E., 138
Gibson, Katherine, 45
Gibson, Lewis, 45
Gibson, Mary, 45
Gibson, Myrtle J., 138
Gilbert, Thomas, 26
Gilchrist, Lucie H., 170-b
Gilchrist, Joy, 170-b
Gilchrist, Stephen I., 170-b
Gill, Annie C., 112
Gill, James S., 112
Gill, Nannie, 119
Gill, Samuel, 119
Gill, Thomas H., 112
Gilliam, Carrie Belle, 146
Gillum, John W., 221
Gillum, Joseph, 221
Gillum, Martha, 221
Glenn, J. M., 162
Goan, Alice L., 223
Goan, Alley H., 66
Goan, E. H., 220
Goan, J. J., 219
Goan, L. M., 127
Goan, Lyda Mae, 37
Goan, Minnie L., 97
Goan, Morris L., 127
Goan, Nellie E., 127
Goan, William M., 66

Jenkins, H. M., 137
Jenkins, James D., 127
Jenkins, John, 46, 133
Jenkins, Maggie, 127
Jenkins, Monroe, 187
Jenkins, Nellie P., 46
Jenkins, Phebe A., 133
Jenkins, Rhoda, 133
Jenkins, Sidney E., 137
Jenks, Charlie, Jr., 179
Johns, Mollie, 80
Johns, J. T., 80
Johns, Joseph E., 160, 60
Johnson, A. D., 27
Johnson, Ada, 118
Johnson, Bettie A., 140
Johnson, E. C., 51
Johnson, Elbert W., 27
Johnson, Ella, 168
Johnson, Ethel, 179
Johnson, Fannie Vic., 51
Johnson, J. C., 140
Johnson, James C., 134
Johnson, John H., 191
Johnson, June H., 140
Johnson, Lewis T., 90
Johnson, Mack C., 110
Johnson, Mary A., 98
Johnson, Mollie, 128
Johnson, Sara A., 191
Johnson, Sue J., 144
Johnson, Syd C., 93
Johnson, W. C., 179
Johnson, W. F., 118
Johnson, W. H., 51
Johnson, W. M., 98
Johnston, Abbie L., 164
Johnston, Andrew, 164
Johnston, Axelia, 164
Johnston, Laura, 138
Johnston, Mary, 164
Johnston, Nancy A., 164
Jellay, Mary E., 73
Jellay, M. R., 73
Jones, Charles, Jr., 220
Jones, Ester E., 82
Jones, Hannah, 192
Jones, Ida J., 223
Jones, John, 139
Jones, L. S., 77
Jones, Levinia, 149
Jones, Margaret V., 124
Jones, Mary E., 82
Jones, Miranda I., 77
Jones, P. J., 82
Jones, Repts, 192

Jones, Robert, 45, 106
Jones, R. M., 148
Jones, S. D., 61
Jones, Thomas M., 148, 149
Jones, Vina, 166
Jones, William E., 60, 107
Jones, W. S., 208

K

Kanode, Fain A., 109
Kellerd, Hannah M., 122
Kelly, Susie Burchell, 141-a
Kenipe, Lucy J., 209
Kenley, Eliza S., 137
Kenley, H. C., 137
Kenley, W. F., 139
Kennedy, Frances B., 170
Kennedy, John H., 170
Kenner, Elizabeth, 161
Kerba, Elsa, 132
Kesterson, C. K., 53
Kesterson, James L., 23
Kesterson, Nellie, 53
Keyes, Jack, 127
Kilgore, Beulah, 121
Kilgore, Emma, 121
Kilgore, Mollie, 121
Kimbrough, Dortha Lee, 133
Kimbrough, Eula, 133
King, Hiram, 81
King, Leander M., 113
King, Oliver C., 113
King, Penelope M., 113
Kinskie, Mary D., 93
Kirk, William B., 124-b
Kirkpatrick, A. B. M., 100
Kirkpatrick, Anne, 24
Kirkpatrick, Granville, 95
Kirkpatrick, Harriet, 42
Kirkpatrick, H. L. W., 31
Kirkpatrick, Hugh, 100
Kirkpatrick, J. B. M., 175
Kirkpatrick, J. M., 32
Kirkpatrick, Jessie O., 32
Kirkpatrick, John Roger, 175
Kirkpatrick, Laura C., 32
Kirkpatrick, Marion, 42
Kirkpatrick, Martha, 37, 42
Kirkpatrick, Mary, 37, 95
Kirkpatrick, Naoma, 24
Kirkpatrick? P. M., 42
Kirkpatrick, Virgie, 175
Kirkpatrick, Wilkins, 37
Kirkpatrick, William, 24
Kistler, James, 139

Medlin, J. W., 128
Medlin, Malinda Jane, 177
Medlin, Matilda Noe, 177
Medlin, Phoebe, 128
Medlin, Samuel C., 177
Mefford, Harry, 137
Mefford, Harvey, 156
Mefford, James H., 105
Mefford, Rowena, 134
Mefford, Sallie N., 105
Mefford, Sarah E., 105
Melton, Annie, 49
Melton, Joe H., 176
Melton, Temple, 49
Messick, Josephine, 56
Messick, W. L., 56
Michael, Columbia J. L., 161
Michael, Elijah, 161
Michael, Mary Kate, 161
Michell, E. F., 138
Michell, Eliza F., 138
Michell, George W., 138
Michell, J. C., 138
Michell, James C., 130, 138
Michell, K. E., 138
Michell, Mary R., 138

Michell, Mildred N., 138
Michell, Sarah L., 71
Michell, Tommie C., 138
Michell, W. F., 138
Midkiff, Augusta, 129
Midkiff, E., 129
Midkiff, J. W., 129
Midkiff, Lizzie, 129
Milan, John L., 130
Miller, Alice A., 130
Miller, Annie E., 155
Miller, Bertie P., 156
Miller, Bess H., 137
Miller, Charlie T., 156
Miller, D. R., 82, 83
Miller, D. S., 155
Miller, E. D., 168
Miller, E. L., 81
Miller, Earl E., 156
Miller, George W., 155
Miller, Elihah E., 191
Miller, Grace, 81
Miller, H. M., 130
Miller, H. R., 155
Miller, Harvey S., 37
Miller, Henry R., 154
Miller, Hope Woodson Taylor, 189

Miller, J. B., 208
Miller, J. D., 130
Miller, J. E., 113
Miller, J. L., 41
Miller, Jackson, 187
Miller, James O. B., 187
Miller, John, 94, 189, 190, 208
Miller, Joseph V. S., 191
Miller, L. H., 208
Miller, Laura, 156
Miller, Lucian H., 130
Miller, Lucy Cox, 190
Miller, M. A., 155
Miller, M. B., 81
Miller, M. E., 138
Miller, M. P. E., 155
Miller, Margaret, 97, 208
Miller, Mary B., 113
Miller, Mary Rachel, 55
Miller, Martha, 187, 189, 190
Miller, Mollie, 130, 154
Miller, N. E., 83
Miller, Nancy, 191
Miller, Nettie, 208
Miller, Orlena, 94
Miller, R. N., 208
Miller, Rachel, 155
Miller, Robert Henry, 111, 156
Miller, S., 187
Miller, Sallie, 190
Miller, W. M., 190
Miller, Walter, 190
Miller, William R., 154
Milligan, Allie Ruth Inman, 193
Milligan, Ema N., 77
Milligan, Francis, 193
Milligan, Leland D., 192
Milligan, M. W., 77
Milligan, Marjorie, 193
Milligan, W. H., 77
Mills, Charles P., 97
Mills, Edith M., 209
Mills, Ethel J., 103
Mills, G. A., 209
Mills, M. J., 209
Mills, Mary, 97
Mills, Rosa P., 93
Mims, J. M., 135, 136
Mims, Jervis, 134
Mims, Margarette, 134
Mims, S. J., 135
Mims, Walter D., 135
Mims, Willie C., 135

Parker, Ella Neal, 210, 211
Parker, Gertie B., 167
Parker, John B., 210, 211
Parker, Maggie Mae, 210
Parker, Margaret B., 210, 211
Parker, Martha, 207
Parker, Mary R., 166
Parker, Sibbie S., 210
Parker, W. G. W., 210
Parker, William H., 211
Parrish, David, 172
Parrish, Elizabeth, 173
Parrish, Fred, 172
Parrish, Horace, 172
Parrish, Ida Collette, 173
Parrish, J. C., 172
Parrish, Mack, 172
Parrish, Mary B., 172
Parrish, Mattie, 172
Parrish, Thomas, 172
Parrish, William R., 172
Parrott, Hugh, 226
Parrott, John H., 103
Parrott, Lou J., 103
Parvin, Elmira, 55
Parvin, Nancy, 23
Parvin, Robert, 30
Parvin, V. H., 30
Paschal, S. W., 207
Patchen, Arthur D., 118
Patterson, Mildred A., 206
Patton, G. W., 21
Patton, Mollie, 21
Paxton, Tessie, 173
Payne, David B., 110
Payne, Helen J., 110
Payne, Reed, 148
Payne, T. J., 138
Pearce, Roy, 170-b
Pearson, Dorman, 99
Pearson, L. T., 207
Peck, E. A., 115
Peck, J. F., 115
Pence, David, 87
Pence, Mary, 87
Pendergrass, Kathern, 51
Pendergrass, Lucy, 52
Pendergrass, W. A., 51, 52
Penland, Clifford, 194
Penland, Hazel, 194
Penland, J. T. W., 198
Penland, Minnie, 194
Penland, W. A., 194
Peoples, Clara W., 227
Peoples, Henry, 219

People, Joe Morgan, 96
Peoples, Lou J. C., 227
Peoples, P. J. C., 227
Peoples, S. N., 225
Perrow, Charles H., 103
Perrow, Leon G., 103
Perrow, Sue G., 103
Perryman, Armanda, 81
Perryman, Malinda, 81
Perryman, Sterling, 81
Peters, Mary Elizabeth, 113
Pettigrew, Alice, 162
Pettigrew, Charles, 162
Pettigrew, Claude H., 124
Peoples, J. Nat, 228
Peoples, L. B., 228
Peoples, S. M., 227
Pettigrew, J. W., 124
Pettigrew, Julia, 124
Pettigrew, Lee Roy, 162
Pettigrew, Lewis, 162
Pettigrew, Mollie, 162
Pettigrew, Myrtle D., 124
Pettigrew, Nannie H., 129
Pettigrew, Robert, 162
Pettigrew, Sallie, 162
Pettigrew, Samuel E., 129
Pettigrew, William C., 106
Petty, J. B., 137
Petty, Margaret, 137
Phillips, Luther I., 35
Phipps, A. B., 132
Phipps, Josie, 132
Phipps, M. A., 132
Pierce, Cordelia, 189
Pierce, J. H., 189
Pierce, James W., 189
Porter, George S., 102
Portrum, A. N., 129
Portrum, Addie, 126
Portrum, Anna H., 108
Portrum, Charley J., 130
Portrum, James, 129
Portrum, John, 129
Portrum, Lula C., 107
Portrum, Samuel, 94
Portrum, Susan K., 107
Portrum, T. W., 107
Poston, Peter H., 68
Potter, A. E., 187
Potter, B. G., 187
Potter, Ben, 46
Potter, Daven, 46
Potter, Ethel Ruth, 187
Potter, Evan, 187

Rayle, E. G., 146
Rayle, Elisha G., 137
Rayle, James R., 138
Rayle, Lula E., 168
Rayle, Sarah J., 138
Rauscher, Mary J., 93
Read, Arthur T., 55
Read, C. R., 73
Read, Effie Mae, 55
Read, F. M., 55
Read, Garret L., 52
Read, J. S., 55
Read, Jessie K., 56
Read, Margaret E., 57
Read, Wiley, 134
Reagen, Muriel A., 236
Reams, Charity A., 310
Reams, Dorthula, 199
Reams, George W., 210
Reams, John W., 199
Reams, Obediah, 196
Reams, Thomas, 210
Rector, John, 106
Rector, Malinda, 106
Rednour, Ada, 175
Rednour, Charles Alvie, 175
Rednour, E. M., 175
Reeve, Effie, 88
Reeve, Katharine R., 88
Reeve, M. P., 88
Reinhardt, Sallie V., 109
Reynolds, George T., 132
Reynolds, Lue P., 153
Reynolds, William M., 153
Rhea, Bobbie, 172
Rhea, David, 31
Rhea, E., 172
Rhea, Ellen, 172
Rhea, Ezekiel, 172
Rhea, Inaz J., 31
Rhea, J. R., 121
Rhea, J. S., 31
Rhea, Jesse, 172
Rhea, John, 89, 90
Rhea, L. B., 171
Rhea, Lee, 172
Rhea, Lewis G., 170-b
Rhea, Lora I., 89
Rhea, Lucretia, 24
Rhea, M. E., 31
Rhea, Maggie Beckner, 175
Rhea, Mary H., 90
Rhea, Minerva H., 31
Rhea, Nancy J., 30
Rhea, Nannie E., 205
Rhea, Odesall, 171

Rhea, Robert, 24, 172, 175
Rhea, S. S., 171
Rhea, Sam, 171
Rhea, Vance, 171
Rhea, William A., 90
Rhoades, Charles D., 66
Rhodes, Dortha I., 66
Rhoades, Ethel Almeda, 66
Rhoades, James, 48
Rhoades, Jane V., 48
Rhoton, Martha M., 161
Rice, B. M., 209
Rice, Catharine C., 163
Rice, Cora, 163
Rice, Edwin A., 224
Rice, E. L., 209
Rice, Harriet A., 163
Rice, J. M., 132
Rice, James, 163
Rice, John, 132
Rice, Lorena, 209
Rice, Lynn D., 163
Rice, Rufus E., 163
Rich, Mary B., 94
Rich, William D., 94
Richards, Lizzie E., 156
Richards, Lloyd E., 205
Richards, Marie, 209
Richards, Nancy A., 156
Richards, Newton, 156
Richards, W. B., 156
Richardson, B. F., 148
Richardson, Elijah, 118
Richardson, Martha, 118
Ridley, Cornelius, 72
Ridley, Isabella, 72
Ridley, Susan J., 72
Riggs, Arthur S., 143
Riggs, C. D., 129
Riggs, F. P., 154
Riggs, H. E., 154
Riggs, Jane, 194
Riggs, Jesse, 184
Riggs, Lewis, 85
Riggs, Mary, 184, 224
Riggs, Nancy E., 85
Riggs, Rebecca, 197
Riggs, Samuel, 184, 197
Riggs, Willie K. Carmicahel, 143
Rightsell, C. D., 197
Rightsell, Cecil P., 68
Rightsell, Effie, 197
Rightsell, J. E., 69
Rightsell, L. M., 68
Rightsell, Robert W., 197
Rightsell, William, 192

Riley, J. D., 119
Riley, Mary J., 117
Riley, Thomas W., 117
Rines, Ida J., 206
Rines, J. C., 206
Rines, J. Lee, 206
Rines, John H., 206
Rines, Mary E., 206
Rines, T. E., 206
Rines, Wade, 206
Rines, Walloe, 206
Rippetoe, Alice M., 103
Rippetoe, Clarence H., 92
Rippetoe, Elizabeth C., 42
Rippetoe, George W., 42
Rippetoe, Hattie Mae, 105
Rippetoe, J. W., 42
Rippetoe, Jessie D., 92
Rippetoe, Joseph F., 104
Rippetoe, Martha F., 104
Rippetoe, Mary L., 103
Rippetoe, W. I., 42
Rippetoe, W. P., 105
Rippetoe, William P., 42
Ritchie, Alice C., 81
Roberson, Alice, 201
Roberson, Charles, 202
Roberson, Ethel, 202
Roberson, Hugh F., 201, 202
Roberson, Maggie, 202
Roberson, Mary, 202
Roberson, Nannie, 202
Roberson, T. L., 202
Roberson, T. M., 201
Roberson, Tennessee, 202
Roberts, F. M., 134
Roberts, Lena, 210
Roberts, M. A., 210
Roberts, M. J. B., 119, 161
Roberts, Mary C., 134
Roberts, Sallie, 161, 183
Roberts, Samuel C., 210
Robertson, Andy J., 130
Robertson, Anna, 153
Robertson, Annie, 154
Robertson, Charley T., 137
Robertson, Curtis E., 91
Robertson, D. A., 60
Robertson, Daniel J., 130
Robertson, Derrby, 60
Robertson, Dorshea, 91
Robertson, Eliza, 128, 134
Robertson, Elmetta P., 47
Robertson, Elizabeth, 152, 153
Robertson, Emma, 128
Robertson, Hampton S., 91

Robertson, Homer, 130
Robertson, Howard, 114
Robertson, J. C., 60
Robertson, J. E., 90
Robertson, James, 154
Robertson, John, 60, 153, 154
Robertson, Laura B., 99
Robertson, Lennie, 137
Robertson, Lizzie T., 91
Robertson, Marion G., 60
Robertson, Mary, 60
Robertson, Nancy, 60, 90
Robertson, Obediah, 60
Robertson, Otho L., 181
Robertson, Pauline Freelove, 181
Robertson, Rachael S., 130
Robertson, Robert M., 90
Robertson, Rufus K., 137
Robertson, Sampson H., 181
Robertson, Sarah I., 130
Robertson, Thomas, 134
Robertson, T. N., 45
Robertson, William, 60, 154
Robinson, Alex, 164
Robinson, Maggie, 92
Rockwell, James C., 92
Rockwell, Kiffin Y., 92
Roddie, Annie, 132
Roddie, Nancy, 132
Roddie, W. B., 132
Roddy, B. M., 35
Roddy, E. E., 35
Roddy, Elizabeth, 41
Roddy, Ella J., 41
Roddy, Isabel F., 35
Roddy, John R., 35
Roddy, Lydia N., 41
Roddy, P. N., 121
Roddy, Thomas, 41
Roddy, Walter Thomas, 35
Roddye, James, 19
Rogers, Chesley, 153
Rogers, George Washington, 153
Rogers, H. F., 62
Rogers, Harvey M., 205
Rogers, Robert M., 107
Rogers, W. F., 160
Rose, James C., 106
Rose, Virginia J., 106
Ross, Alexander, 101
Rouse, Ezra S., 236
Rouse, Kenneth, 235
Rouse, Rachael, 236
Rouse, Sarah E., 235
Rouse, W. E., 34
Routh, W. E., 34

Sunderland, W. W., 201
Sunderland, Wendell, 202
Susong, Adolphus, 65
Susong, E. W., 66
Susong, Eunice, 67
Susong, Eva, 66, 67
Susong, Fannie, 64
Susong, George L., 64
Susong, Harriet, 64, 108
Susong, Henry D., 173
Susong, Joseph, 64
Susong, Mary E., 66
Susong, Nannie, 173
Susong, Wm. E., 66, 67
Susong, W. M., 64
Sutton, B. R., 66
Sutton, Helen K., 66
Sutton, S. K., 66
Swaim, Charles T., 139
Swaim, Lou L., 139
Swaim, M. P., 139
Swaim, H. P., 217
Swaim, W. P., 217
Swan, Lucinda, 140
Swatts, Maggie L., 129

T

Tadlock, Ema L., 203
Tadlock, John, 203
Tadlock, W. L., 203
Talbott, Allie B., 201
Talbott, Alma M., 202
Talbott, John M., 201
Talbott, Judith, 201
Talbott, Nannie J., 201
Talbott, Oscar, 201
Talbott, Ross, 201
Talbott, Temperance, 201
Talbott, W. R., 201
Talley, Arlie T., 176
Talley, A. T., 197
Talley, Bertha, 54
Talley, Henry C., 176
Talley, James, 212
Talley, Julia A., 197
Talley, Kate, 46
Talley, M. D., 198
Talley, Mary S., 197
Talley, Mattie E., 197
Talley, Nannie, 176
Talley, Pleasent M., 212
Talley, Sallie J., 36
Talley, Sarah, 197
Talley, T. A., 46
Talley, T. J., 36

Talley, Wilbur, 54
Talley, Wm. Joseph, 46
Tarter, Alpha, 39
Tarter, Andrew, 39
Tarter, Elizabeth, 38
Tarter, H., 39
Tarter, Rosannah, 91
Tate, Belle D., 106
Tate, Caroline, 170-c
Tate, Carrie, 170-c
Tate, Edward O., 170-c
Tate, Frank D., 106
Tate, Harriet, 170-c
Tate, John H., 106
Tate, Margaret J., 170-c
Tate, Samuel B., 170-c
Tate, Stephen W., 170-c
Tate, William, 170-d
Taylor, A. G., 154
Taylor, A. M. P., 140
Taylor, Ada B., 106
Taylor, Alice G., 154
Taylor, Azzie Lee, 99
Taylor, B. A., 57
Taylor, B. F., 38
Taylor, Bessie, 139
Taylor, Caroline, 92
Taylor, Charles M., 39
Taylor, Cora, 98
Taylor, Daniel Jones, 147
Taylor, Edwin F., 106
Taylor, Emma, 39
Taylor, Erastus S., 178
Taylor, E. W., 98
Taylor, Franklin, 94
Taylor, George E., 139
Taylor, Herbert R., 178
Taylor, H. W., 154
Taylor, James A., 92
Taylor, Katharine, 139
Taylor, Lola, 117
Taylor, Lula W., 21
Taylor, M. M., 33
Taylor, M. V., 21, 28
Taylor, Margaret Jane, 147
Taylor, Mary, 92, 106
Taylor, Milton S., 21
Taylor, Minnie E., 33
Taylor, N. G., 154
Taylor, Nannie, 33, 39
Taylor, Nancy W., 28, 141
Taylor, Ora, 28
Taylor, R. F., 21
Taylor, Redden, 28, 141
Taylor, Richard F., 154

Taylor, Robert J., 141
Taylor, Rufus, 106
Taylor, Susannah, 33
Taylor, Virginia M., 140
Taylor, N. G., 231
Taylor, N. L., 33
Taylor, W. M., 57
Taylor, Wayne F., 115
Templin, James G., 110
Thacker, Cornelia, 76
Thacker, Eli, 76
Thacker, Olivia, 124
Thomas, Carrie, 207
Thomas, Elizabeth, 25, 195
Thomas, Isaac A., 195
Thomas, J., 34
Thomas, Jacob, 25, 152
Thomas, Jerry, 34
Thomas, L., 34
Thomas, Laura, 34
Thomas, Lucy J., 152
Thomas, Minnie, 171
Thomas, Nettie G., 197
Thomas, W. P., 207
Thomas, Walter, 34
Thomason, Emely H., 50
Thomason, George N., 213
Thomason, H., 50
Thomason, James, 176, 213
Thomason, Sarah R., 213
Thompson, Alice I., 200
Thompson, Anne, 139
Thompson, B. M., 130
Thompson, C. B., 64
Thompson, Catherine, 67
Thompson, Clinton K., 129
Thompson, D. A., 139, 140
Thompson, Dickie, 165
Thompson, Dora Ann, 140
Thompson, Edith Pearl, 140
Thompson, Emily, 64
Thompson, Geneva, 130
Thompson, Gideon, 137
Thompson, H. N., 129
Thompson, H. Rice, 137, 138
Thompson, Hazel, 64
Thompson, Hylda, 64
Thompson, J. E., 140, 141
Thompson, J. C., 165
Thompson, J. W., 64
Thompson, James, 137, 129, 141
Thompson, Janet, 141
Thompson, John, 67, 129
Thompson, Joseph, 200
Thompson, Josephine, 140
Thompson, Jesse J., 200

Thompson, Juliette, 137
Thompson, Katherine, 129
Thompson, Laura R., 129
Thompson, M. J., 130
* Thompson, Mel, 64
Thomson, Joanah, 64
Thomson, Luke, 64
Three Springs, 51
Tidwell, Mattie M., 170
Tidwell, R. S., 170
Tomlinson, Clem, 100
Tomlinson, Lizzie M., 100
Tomlinson, Oscar, 114
Tomlinson, Thomas G., 21
Toupson, Margaret, 194
Toney, Ben M., 110
Toney, Guy, 111
Toney, J. A., 166
Toney, Jodie, 166
Toney, John M., 110
Toney, Minnie P., 166
Toney, Nancy, 110, 111
Toney, Paul E., 110
Toney, Robert, 111
Toney, S. A., 162
Toney, W. R., 166
Toney, Wilburn, 166
Townsend, Charles L., 162
Townsend, Freddie, 162
Townsend, J. A., 162
Townsend, James A., 160
Townsend, S. S., 162
Townsend, Willie, 162
Trammel, W. D., 105
Travis, C. H., 206
Travis, Ella H., 119
Travis, Estella H., 206
Travis, Lloyd H., 206
Travis, W. T., 119
Treece, A. L., 205
Treece, Daniel R., 143
Treece, Jane, 143
Treece, John R., 144
Treece, Sallie, 146
Treece, Sarah J., 143
* Thompson, Oscar, 51
Thompson, R. A., 64
Thompson, Sallie, 138
Thompson, Sarah, 127, 137
Thompson, Wm. F., 200
Thompson, W. M., 129
Thompson, W. N., 185
Thompson, Viola, 165
Treece, W. S., 142
Trent, America R., 117
Trent, C. C., 46

TOMBSTONE RECORDS

HAMBLEN COUNTY

(Pg. 1)

BETHESDA CEMETERY
INDEX

TOMBSTONE RECORDS

HAMBLEN COUNTY

(Pg. 2)

BETHESDA CEMETERY

Crouch, Kattie, Moffett, 3
Crouch, Mary Scott, 3
Crouch, M. S. 3
Crouch, R. C. 3
Crouch, Robert C. 3
Church, Hospital, 1
Church, New Hopewell Presbyterian, 1.
Church, Organization, 1
Church, Russellville, Presbyterian, 1, 2
Church, St. Pauls Presbyterian, 1.
City, Johnson, 1
College, Maryville, 1
County, Hawkins, 13
County, Rockbridge, Va. 2

D

Daugherty, J. F. 4
Daugherty, Myrtle Shaw, 4
Davis, Burtie H. 11
Davis, Emory Authur, 5
Davis, John L. 8
Davis, John W. 7
Davis, Joseph Patton, 5
Davis, J. P. 5
Davis, Katharine Kelly Wheeler, 5
Davis, R. L. 8
Davis, T. M. 8
Deaver, Dora 17
Deaver, Lois, 17
Deaver, Shepard, 17
Deaver, W. T. 17
Doak, Katharine Nenney, 4
Doak, W. H. 4
Dodson, Emma L. 9
Dodson, Flossy C. 8
Dodson, James Elisha 9
Donaldson, Celia, 15

Donaldson, Charles Eckel, 4
Donaldson, John 2
Donaldson, Joseph Eckel Jr. 4
Donaldson, Miss Maria, 1
Dougherty, Isaac, 8
Dougherty, William Allen, 8
Drinnon, Elizabeth Seal, 5
Drinnon, Lelia K. 7
Drinnon, M. L. 6
Drinnon, Ruby Glenn, 6
Drinnon, T. C. 6
Drinnon, U. S. 7
Drinnon, W. B. 5
Duff, Emmett C. 15
Dunbar, Elihu, 11
Dyer, Barbara Jean,
Deed, Church, 2
Deed, Land, 1

E

Eagleton, Rev. George 1
Eckel, Joseph, 13
Eckel, Mary J. 13
Edens, Charles B. 9
Evans, Louise Rochelle 14
Evans, Rev. T. J. 14
Elders 1,

F

Fields, Annie Allen, 10
Fields, Zack C. 10
Fisher, Amelia, 16
Fisher, Daniel, 16
Fisher, Hattie S. 16
Fleenor, John H. 9
Ford, John S. 7
Ford, J. S. 7
Ford, Nackey E. Slemons, 7
Forgey, Ellen Folsom, 13

Forgey, Irene, 13
Forgey, James R. Jr. 18
Forgey, James Reynolds, 13
Forgey, Jas. R. 2
Forgey, J. R. 13
Forgey, L. K. 18
Forgey, Louise K. 18
Fuller, Eugene F. 10

G

Gilbert, James Oda, 10
Gilmer, Andrew M. Jr. 17
Gore (?) G. A. 16
Green, Isaac R. L. 8
Green, Lillie 8
Greene, Minnerva, 11
Griffith, Rev. 1

H

Hale, E. B. 14
Hale, Eliza J. 13
Hale, William Chamberlain, 14
Hansell, Mary Elvira, 7
Hardbarger, Mrs. E. J. 4
Harrell, Charles R. 6
Harrell, Livia M. 6
Harris, A. W. 11
Harris, Francis, 11
Harris, Franklin P. 11
Haun, Ruby 8
Hayes, Sallie Bewley, 4
Hayes, James F. 4
Hays, Lennie C. 4
Hays, Lucy, 4
Holley, Beatrice H. 16
Holley, Edna B. 16
Holley, Emmett P. 16
Holley, Ira D. 6, 16
Holley, James T. 16

Holley, Karl B. 16
Holley, M. A. 6
Holley, Mary A. Craig, 6
Holley, William T. 6
Holley, Willie J. 16
Holley, W. T. 6
Hood, Rev. Nathaniel, 1
Horner, James D. 9
Horner, K. 9
Horner, Kattie A. McCarver, 9
Horner, Rebecca A. 9
Horner, Thomas N. 9
Horner, T. N. 9
Hughes, Marshall J. 13
Hughes, Sarah J. 13

J

Jack, Linda Kyle, 15
Jack, Sam W. 15
Jackson, Nora M. 9
Jarnagin, Mary E. 15
Jarnagin, Sara A. 15
Jetrick, J. W. 17
Johnson, Linnie, 14
Johnson, Walter, 2

K

Kesterson, Charles M. 5
Kesterson, Mary E. 5
Kyle, Linda, 15
Kyle, Lyda, 15

L

Lane, I. A. Jr. 3
Lane, Isaac A. 4
Lane, John B. 3
Lane, Lennie C. Hays, 4
Lawson, Bonnie M. 8

BETHESDA CEMETERY

Lawson, John A. 8
Lawson, Laura 5
Lawson, Mary K. 6
Lawson, Ona L. 8
Lawson, Sallie C. 8
Leming, Frances Victoria,
   Rufty, 10
Leming, James A. 10
Lewis, William Lyons, 13
Long, Col. Wm. P. 14
Long, E. L. 11
Long, Eliza V. 14
Long, F. M. 14
Long, Gawen Leeper, 18
Long, Henry W. 2
Long, J. F. 6
Long, John Robert, 15
Long, Kattie Taylor, 11
Long, Margaret, 17
Long, Mary K. 6
Long, Priscilla, 14
Long, Priscilla Shields, 14
Long, Thos T. 6
Long, William H. 14
Long, W. P. 14
Lynch, J. B. 13

M

Mace, Eliza Riggs, 8
Mace, James Pless, 8
Marshall, Cordelia L. 7
Marshall, James Lafaette 7
Marshall, J. L. 7
McAlister, Armanda Brown, 17
McAlister, Thomas, 17
McCarty, John, 37
McCarver, Lou E. Howery, 9
McCarver, Ida Silvia 8
McCarver, J. T. 9
McCarver, Nannie S. 8

McCarver, Salamis Louis, 8
McCord, John B. 3
McCord, Nellie B. 3
McGhee, C. H. 6
McGhee, Cordelia 6
McGhee, Fannie E. 6
McGhee, Geo. W. 6
McGhee, J. L. 7
McGhee, J. W. 6
McGhee, Julia C. Bewley, 7
McGhee, Robert S. 6
McGhee, Thiressa A. Bewley, 6
McGhee, William M. 10
McQueen, (?) 13, 14
Miller, Ida Dell Pullen, 4
Miller, Lucy Hays, 4
Miller, Stuart N. 4
Miller, William S. 4
Millis, Martha Alice Vampler, 7
Millis, W. W. 7
Mills, Fannie 5
Minnis, Rev. Wm. 1
Moore, Dosser, 15
Moore, E. H. 3
Moore, Mrs. Mary 2
Morris, Robert 4
Moffett, Louisa S. 4
Moffett, William W. 4

N

Nackey, Roberta Goode, 7
Nelson, Mary Lou Trantham, 15
Newman, Rev. C. C. 1
Noe, Willard, 3
Nusbaum, David, 14
Nusbaum, Frank, 14
Nusbaum, Jennie 7
Nusbaum, Warren, 15

O

Orr, Mary A. 13
Orrick, E. J. 15
Orrick, Ella Pearl, 15
Orrick, Nellie E. Long, 15
Orrick, Willis L. 15
Orrick, Z. E. 15
Owens, K. R. 8
Owens, Minnie May Williams, 8

P

Pangle, Clarice Sanders, 10
Pangle, Dr. H. G. 2
Pangle, Lewis N. 9
Pennell, Clinard C. 10
Pullen, Will P. 4

R

Rayl, Leanner, Cox 12
Rayl, Tom N. 12
Rayl, William J. 12
Read, Laura Ann, 10
Reed, H. W. 7
Reed, Mattie Elizabeth, 7
Riggs, C. D. 14
Riggs, Isabella Long, 14
Robertson, Edward, 17
Robertson, Eliza J. 17
Robertson, Ellen Shannon, 18
Robertson, Joseph, 17
Robertson, Marilda, 17
Robertson, Nina Belle, 17
Robinson, Mrs. Ellen Shannon, 2
Rogan, Hugh Graham, 16
Rogan, Maggie Margaret,
    Callaway, 16
Rogan, Maria Louisa, Graham 16
Rogan, Mary Katharine, 16

Rogan, Theophilus, 16
Rogan, W. Williams, 16
Runyon, Elsie Brown, 5
Rymer, J. V. 12
Rymer, Lizzie Bishop

S

Sautelle, Rev. Eli N. 1
Sawyer, Earl M. 10
Sawyers, J. Frank, 10
Sawyer, Mollie Moore, 10
Seal, Elizabeth, 5
Seavers, Florence E. 17
Shannon, Armanda J. 14
Shannon, Mrs. Eleanor, 1
Shannon, James H. 14
Shannon, James P. 14
Shannon, John M. 14
Shannon, Joseph 1
Shannon, Joseph A. 14
Shannon, Mary Ann, 15
Shannon, Mr. & Mrs. Joseph, 2
Shannon, Mrs. Joseph 1
Shannon, William, 15
Shaw, Thomas N. 4
Shelton, Anderson, 11
Sheppard, William H. 12
Shields, Catharine B. 12
Shields, James 12
Shields, Joanna Lee, 12
Shields, John Blair, 12
Shields, Mary, 12
Shields, Mary Cobb, 12
Shields, Mary Elizabeth, 12
Shields, Priscilla, 14
Shields, Samuel, W 12
Shields, Sarah Jane, 3
Shipley, Eliza J. 6
Shipley, W. T. 6
Shoun, Dora B. 10

BETHESDA CEMETERY

Shropshire, C. J. 11
Sikes, Willie Ross, 9
Silvers, Argent A. McAlister, 11
Silvers, Crockett A. 7
Silvers, J. Herbert, 11
Silvers, Thirza J. 7
Silvers, Walter F. 5
Slavers, Florence E. 7
Sloat, Edna Mae Brown, 7
Sloat, J. E. 5
Sloat, L. S. 7
Sloat, Mary Francis Byers 5
Sloat, Mary R. 7
Smith, Mrs. Carrie L. 11
Snapp, John Patton, 6
Southern, Jessie E. 9
Southern, John M. 9
Southern, Martha J. 9
Stapleton, Darsley Lamar, 17
Stapleton, Nancy Jane, 17
Starnes, Anna R. 13
Starnes, J. J. 13
Sexton, Church, 2
State, Georgia, 13, 14
State, Texas, 1
State, Va. 2

T

Tam, Hannah E. 14
Tam, J. D. 14
Tam, Joshua D. 14
Taylor, Catherine B. Shields 12
Taylor, C. B. 12
Taylor, C. V. 13
Taylor, Dr. Rufus, 3
Taylor, Eliza J. 13
Taylor, F. W. 13
Taylor, James Calvin, 3
Taylor, J. C. 2
Taylor, Jennie Shields, 13
Taylor, Kattie Susanna, 3

Taylor, Mamie E. 13
Taylor, M. E. 13
Taylor, Minnie Lee, 12
Taylor, R. L. 12
Taylor, Robert L. 12
Taylor, Rufus, 12
Taylor, Sarah Jane Shields, 3
Taylor, Sam Milton, 13
Taylor, Thomas R. 12
Thomason, Joe D. 10
Thomason, Vina M. 10
Todd, W. J. 12
Tranthem, Anna Mae, 15
Tranthem, J. J. 15
Tranthem, Lee M. 15
Tranthem, L. X. 15
Trent, Certie P. 17
Turley, J. F. 3
Turley, John Frank, 3
Turley, Kattie Susanna Taylor, 3
Tuttle, James Gilmore, 11
Town, Atlanta, 13
Town, Bristol, 3
Town, Dandridge, 1
Town, Lowland, 1
Town, Madison, 14
Town, Morristown, 2, 3,
Town, New Market, 1
Town, Russellville, 2
Town, Whitesburg, 1

Utsman, Laura Fisher, 16

V

Valley, Abbs, 2
Valley, Lee, 13

W

Walker, Kenneth D. 10
Wall, F. W. 6

TOMBSTONE RECORDS

HAMBLEN COUNTY

(Pg. 7)

BETHESDA CEMETERY

Wall, Julia Paralee Johns, 5
Wall, Lola Mae, 10
Wampler, A. A. 5
Wampler, Arnold Hillard, 5
Wampler, Dortha E. Chandler 5
Wampler, H. C.
Wampler, Louisa A. Rasnick 5
Weems, Kidwell, 5
Wheeler, George Burton 5
Wheeler, Mary J. Baker 5
Wheeler, M. J. 5
Wheeler, Samuel V. 5
Wheeler, S. B. 5
Williams, Crockett P. 8
Williams, John R. 8

Williams, J. R. 8
Williams, Minnie May, 8
Williams, Nellie J. 8
Williams, N. J. 8
Wilson, Frank L. 6
Wilson, G. W. 6
Wilson, Melvina Shipley, 6
Witt, A. Moore, 9
Witt, R. M. 9
Wright, Elmer A. 9
Wright, Jessie E. Southern 9
Wright, Mary Bewley, 17
Wright, W. H. 17

Y

Young, Rev. W. C. 1

BETHESDA PRESBYTERIAN CHURCH

Copied from Morristown Gazette And Mail

Saturday August 25, 1934

The following interesting facts concerning Bethesda Presbyterian church were given by Rev. W. C. Young, pastor of the Presbyterian church at Whitesburg, at the centennial celebration commemorating the one hundredith anniversary of the establishment of the church held Thursday.

"Bethesda Presbyterian church was organized in 1832 by the pastor of New Hopewell Presbyterian church near Dandridge, Tenn. On August 23rd, 1834, Joseph Shannon -- an elder of St. Paul's Presbyterian church near Lowland - and his wife, Mrs. Eleanor Shannon gave a deed to three and three-quarter acres of land for the church and cemetery, (the present location), but the deed was not witnessed until the spring of 1835.

"Among the charter members of the church were Mr. and Mrs. Joseph Shannon, Mr. and Mrs. Obadiah Boaz, and Miss Maria Donaldson. Miss Donaldson later became the wife of Murphy Barten, and their daughter, Miss Eliza Barton of Johnson City, and a member of the Russellville Presbyterian church, is the only living child of a charter member of Bethesda church.

"For some time after the church was organized, the preaching services were held irregularly because of the scarcity of available ministers, and due to the fact that the roads were so difficult to travel. Among those serving the church in a ministerial capacity up to 1842 were Rev. Wm. Minnis, pastor of the St. Paul Presbyterian church; Rev. Nathaniel Hood, thought to be the assistant of Rev. Minnis, and Rev. Isaac Anderson from Maryville College. Rev. Nathaniel Hood was the pastor from 1842 to 1845; Rev. Eli N. Sautelle, 1857 to 1859; Rev. C. C. Newman, 1859 to 1860; Rev. George Eagleton, 1860 to 1863, the latter minister removing to Texas, where he succumbed several years later.

"In 1862, the minutes of St. Paul church record a delegate sent to Presbyterian held at Bethesda church.

"During the war, when church activities were some what lessened by the terrible conflict, and the church building was used as a general hospital, and for a short time as a smallpox hospital.

"In 1867, Rev. Mr. Griffith became pastor of a group of Presbyterian churches composed of those of New Market, Dandridge, and Bethesda, and remained their pastor until 1869.

"Since 1869 there has been no regular pastor serving the church, but only occasional preaching by the pastor of the Russellville Presbyterian church and other ministers.

"From Bethesda church, members went out to organize the Morristown Presbyterian church in 1871, and the Russellville Presbyterian church in 1875.

"The church property was deeded to five trustees and their assigns, or successors, the present trustees being Dr. H. G. Pangle of Russellville, Jas. R. Forgey and Henry W. Long of Morristown, J. C. Taylor of near Morristown, and E. H. Moore of Russellville.

"Several years ago, Mrs. Ellen Shannon Robinson, a granddaughter of Mr. and Mrs. Joseph Shannon, bequeathed a legacy of $15,000 to be used for the upkeep of the cemetery at the church. After receipt of this legacy, the trustees erected a sexton's home and employed Walter Johnson to take care of the church and cemetery.

"Among the old markers found in the church cemetery is one reading "Dr. Luther Brown - 1817 - 1851, Rockbridge county, Virginia; son of Mrs. Mary Moore of Abb's Valley." John Donaldson, the son of a Revolutionary soldier, lies buried in the church cemetery, as also do the remains of Rev. Isaac Barton, a pioneer East Tennessee Baptist minister."

HAMBLEN COUNTY
BETHESDA CEMETERY
(Page 1)

The church yard of Bethesda Presbyterian Church, located about one fourth of a mile to the left of the highway leading from Morristown to Bristol, four miles east of Morristown.
The cemetery is well kept and accessible.
Copied by Willard Noe, Morristown, Tennessee
April 26, 1937

T. E. Brown
Dec. 9, 1865

L. J. Brown
Born May 1, 1870
Died July 26, 1914

Fannie L. Brown
Born Nov. 20, 1878
Died Mar. 27, 1915
"Safe in the arms of Jesus"

J. Y. C. Brown
Born Jan. 27, 1838
Died June 15, 1912

His Wife
Rebecca J. Brown
Born July 15, 1844
Died Jan. 4, 1924

Sturm W. Carson
1867 - 1932

Maggie B. Carson
1874 - 1901

Nellie B. McCord
1869 - 1933

John B. McCord
1860 - 19

James Calvin Taylor
Born Feb. 21, 1857
Died May 10, 1936

His Mother
Sarah Jane Shields, Wife of
Dr. Rufus Taylor
Born Sept. 4, 1830
Died Feb. 11, 1920

Kattie Susanna Taylor, Wife of
J. F. Turley
Born July 21, 1860
Died Sept. 29, 1908
"None could appreciate her worth, more than he who mourned her loss."

John Frank Turley
Born Sept. 3, 1856
Died May 4, 1922

Robert C. Crouch
Born Apr. 14, 1844
Died May 2, 1931

Mary Scott, Wife of
R. C. Crouch
Born Nov. 28, 1853
Died June 3, 1910

Kattie Moffett, only child of
R. C. & M. S. Crouch
Born June 8, 1882
Died June 29, 1901

I. A. Lane Jr.
Born Apr. 5, 1904
Died Aug. 4, 1904

John B. Lane
Born Apr. 5, 1904
Died Aug. 1, 1904

HAMBLEN COUNTY
BETHESDA CEMETERY
(Page 2)

Isaac A. Lane
May 24, 1857
Feb. 14, 1934

His Wife
Lennie C. Hays
July 10, 1857
June 8, 1907

Julia Alice Hays
Died Jan. 4, 1935
Age 76 yrs. 7 mo.

Robert Morris
1898 - 1931

Ida Dell Pullen, Wife of
Stuart N. Miller
June 30, 1873
Oct. 24, 1908

Charles Eckel Donaldson
Born June 6, 1885
Died Oct. 21, 1903

Joseph Eckel Donaldson Jr.
Born Feb. 14, 1904
Died Aug. 20, 1904

Will P. Pullen
Born Sept. 28, 1864
Died Feb. 3, 1907
"Died among strangers, but
sleeps at home."

James F. Hayes
July 24, 1833
Jan. 21, 1917

His Wife
Sallie Bewley
Feb. 4, 1839
Oct. 2, 1914

William S. Miller
1853 - 1921

His Wife
Lucy Hays
1862 - 1914

Maria Donaldson, Wife of
William M. Barton
Born June 27, 1814
Died Apr. 14, 1911

Katherine Kenney Doak
1844 - 1923

W. H. Doak, M. D.
1840 - 1904

Myrtle Shaw, Wife of
J. F. Daugherty
Born July 23, 1844
Died Aug. 13, 1909

Thomas N. Shaw
June 6, 1859
Mar. 12, 1914

Barbara Jean Dyer
June 18, 1935
Age 5 mo. 13 da.

William W. Moffett
Oct. 22, 1855
Dec. 15, 1903

Louisa S. Moffett
Feb. 10, 1858
Mar. 10, 1918

Mrs. E. J. Hardbarger
Died Dec. 8, 1905
Age about 74 yrs.
"Jesus said, In my fathers house
are many mansions."

John R., Son of
J. Y. C. & R. J. Brown
Born Apr. 20, 1882
Died Jan. 15, 1879

Mary E., Wife of
B. A. Creech
Born Apr. 30, 1848
Died Apr. 20, 1911

HAMBLEN COUNTY
BETHESDIA CEMETERY
(Page 3)

Bettie Brown
Feb. 9, 1908

Elsie Brown Runyon
Sept. 15, 1890
Dec. 2, 1918

Walter F. Silvers
July 5, 1877
Dec. 17, 1918

His Wife
Fannie Mills
Apr. 20, 1881

Katharine Kelly Wheeler, Wife of
J. P. Davis
Nov. 3, 1868
Jan. 15, 1935

Joseph Patton Davis
Jan. 21, 1858
Aug. 25, 1918

J. H. Sloat
Born Aug. 26, 1854
Died May 4, 1929

His Wife
Mary Francis Byers
Born Sept. 26, 1854
Died Dec. 22, 1917

Emory Authur Davis
July 19, 1887
Feb. 27, 1930

George Burton Wheeler, Son of
S. B. & M. J. Wheeler
Born Dec. 2, 1877
Feb. 12, 1907

Samuel V. Wheeler
Apr. 15, 1838
Feb. 4, 1 925

His Wife

Mary J. Baker
Oct. 25, 1842
May 25, 1921

Charles M. Kesterson
Mar. 11, 1855
Oct. 26, 1908

Mary E. Kesterson
Apr. 15, 1875

Kidwell Weems
1882 - 1922

Laura Lawson
Born Nov. 26, 1893
Died Sept. 9, 1917

Julia Paralee Johns Wall,
Wife of F. W. Wall
Oct. 30, 1859
Apr. 13, 1910

Louisa A. Rasnick, Wife of
A. A. Wampler
Sept. 12, 1875
Jan. 1, 1922

Dortha E. Chandler, Wife of
H. C. Wampler
Born Dec. 7, 1837
Died July 27, 1910

Arnold Hillard, Son of
A. A. & L. A. Wampler
July 22, 1909
Nov. 17, 1909

W. B. Drimon
Born Aug. 18, 1834
Apr. 18, 1913

His Wife
Elizabeth Seal
Born Dec. 27, 1839
Nov. 29, 1909

HAMBLEN COUNTY
BETHESDIA CEMETERY
(Page 4)

Ruby Glenn, Dau. of
T. C. & M. L. Drinnon
June 12, 1908
July 29, 1908

Mary E. Lawson
Sept. 17, 1871
Apr. 13, 1923

John Patton Snapp
Aug. 11, 1861
Mar. 12, 1930

Henrietta Espran Bewley
Apr. 8, 1841
Mar. 12, 1914

Mary E., Wife of
J. F. Long
Born Oct. 25, 1852
Died Aug. 11, 1885

Livia M., Wife of
Charles R. Harrell
Jan. 31, 1876
Aug. 14, 1894

Thos. T. Long
July 12, 1844
Aug. 17, 1887

Cordelia Mc Ghee
Feb. 19, 1874
Nov. 20, 1930

C. H. Mc Ghee
Born May 14, 1832
Died Nov. 17, 1908

William T. Holley
Sept. 28, 1855 -

His Wife
Mary A. Craig
Mar. 5, 1859
Apr. 27, 1915

W. W. Barton
1837 - 1903

James Craig
Born July 28, 1799
Died June 10, 1884

Ira D., Son of
W. T. & M. A. Holley
Born July 7, ——
Died Oct. 31, 1880

Frank L. Wilson
Jan. 16, 1935
Age 53 yr.

G. W. Wilson
June 16, 1841
Feb. 20, 1938

Melvina Shipley, Wife of
G. W. Wilson
Born Nov. 3, 1850
Died Nov. 1, 1914

Eliza J., Wife of
W. T. Shipley
Born June 2, 1854
Died Dec. 11, 1899

Geo. W. Mc Ghee
Nov. 16, 1827
Aug. 23, 1883

His Wife
Thiress A. Bewley
Sept. 30, 1828
Jan. 10, 1906

Robert S. Mc Ghee
Died May 8, 1876
Age 20 years

Fannie E., Wife of
J. W. Mc Ghee
Born Feb. 3, 1857
Died Sept. 29, 1884

HAMBLEN COUNTY
BETHESDIA CEMETERY
(Page 5)

W. W. Millis
Born Feb. 8, 1853
Died Aug. 21, 1913

Martha Alice Wampler, Wife of
W. W. Millis
Born Dec. 28, 1861
Died June 16, 1928

Mackey Roberts Goode
Jan. 6, 1912
Sept. 21, 1917

Florence E. Slavers
Born Apr. 6, 1860
Died Dec. 2, 1924

John S. Ford
Born Mar. 4, 1845
Died Apr. 21, 1913

Mackey E. Slemons, Wife of
J. S. Ford
June 13, 1846
Nov. 18, 1918

Julia C. Bewley, Wife of
J. L. McGhee
Feb. 16, 1869
June 22, 1925

Mattie Elizabeth, Wife of
H. W. Reed
Born Aug. 22, 1854
Died Apr. 14, 1905

Cordelia L., Wife of
J. L. Marshall
Born June 30, 1860
Died May 20, 1903

James Lafaette Marshall
Born Nov. 15, 1858
Jan. 13, 1894

Jennie Nusbaum
Oct. 22, 1850
Jan. 21, 1921

Mary R. Sloat
May 28, 1921
June 3, 1921

Edna Mae Brown, Wife of
L. S. Sloat
May 19, 1885
Dec. 24, 1924

Will Buchanan
1879 - 1915

John W. Davis
Nov. 3, 1851
Apr. 1, 1934

Eliza Davis
June 27, 1859
Feb. 28, 1917
"Gone but not forgotten."

U. S. Drinnon
Nov. 11, 1879
Dec. 5, 1915

His Wife
Lelia E. Drinnon
Aug. 13, 1885

Crockett A. Silvers
Oct. 12, 1843
Dec. 19, 1925

His Wife
Thirza J. Silvers
Jan. 17, 1858
Feb. 23, 1933

"At Rest"
Mary Elvira Hansell
Born Feb. 13, 1855
Died Mar. 31, 1938

HAMBLEN COUNTY
BETHESDA CEMETERY
(Page 6)

Isaac Dougherty
Dec. 11, 1844
Apr. 20, 1916

William Allen Dougherty
Mar. 14, 1877
Apr. 8, 1921

Salamis Louis Mc Carver
Nov. 6, 1879
July 18, 1916

Ida Silvia Mc Carver
Died Dec. 17, 1930
Age 22yr.

Crockett P. Williams, Son of
J. R. & N. J. Williams
Jan. 7, 1907
June 22, 1927

John R. Williams
June 29, 1873

Nellie J. Williams
May 25, 1881
Sept. 1, 1917

Ruby Haun
May 11, 1905
Dec. 18, 1936

John L., Son of
R. L. & T. M. Davis
Born July 11, 1922
Died Jan. 31, 1928

Ben A. Creech
Jan. 28, 1881

His Wife
Nannie S. Mc Carver
Dec. 15, 1886
Apr. 25, 1919

K. R. Owens
1883 -

His Wife
Minnie May Williams
1885 - 1920

Isaac R. L. Green
Sept. 23, 1866
Mar. 21, 1922

His Wife
Lillie Green
Oct. 22, 1874

Sallie C. Lawson
Jan. 6, 1877
May 21, 1924

Bonnie M. Lawson
Sept. 2, 1897
Mar. 22, 1934

"Father"
John A. Lawson
Apr. 18, 1878
Sept. 5, 1912

Oma L. Lawson
Sept. 11, 1907
Aug. 15, 1912

Eliza Riggs Mace
Nov. 27, 1870
Aug. 2, 1924

James Pless Mace
Mar. 17, 1886
May 19, 1925

Flossy C. Dodson
Aug. 5, 1884
Nov. 30, 1890

James Elisha Dodson
Feb. 27, 1863
Feb. 2, 1924

His Wife
Emma L. Dodson
Nov. 30, 1861

Kattie A. Mc Carver, Wife of
T. N. Horner
July 30, 1857
Dec. 6, 1924

Thomas N. Horner
Mar. 23, 1855
Dec. 1, 1929

Rebecca A., Dau. of
T. N. & K. Horner
Sept. 26, 1883
July 15, 1925

Nora M. Jackson
May 3, 1863
Dec. 2, 1936

A. Moore, Wife of
R. M. Witt
May 29, 1839
Feb. 3, 1905

R. M. Witt
June 27, 1845
Mar. 31, 1925

Lewis N. Pangle
Nov. 15, 1861
Jan. 31, 1927

Grant Greene
Jan. 4, 1879
Mar. 11, 1927
"An honest man's the noblest
work of God."

Charles B. Edens
Nov. 8, 1886
Nov. 1, 1925

Willie Ross Sikes
Died May 31, 1936
Age 4 days

Sarah Anne Anderson
Died Mar. 1, 1935
Age 65 yr.

John H. Fleenor
Nov. 23, 1858
Nov. 2, 1926

Martha J. Southern
Feb. 9, 1854
Apr. 30, 1936

John M. Southern
Jan. 26, 1842
Nov. 13, 1902

Elmer A. Wright
Jan. 26, 1889

His Wife
Jessie E. Southern
Apr. 1, 1892
Sept. 26, 1927
"We shall meet again."

J. T. Mc Carver
Mar. 3, 1854
Mar. 12, 1934

Lou E. Howery, Wife of
J. T. Mc Carver
Sept. 18, 1852
May 10, 1928

James D. Horner
Feb. 4, 1885
Feb. 7, 1929

HAMBLEN COUNTY
BETHESDA CEMETERY
(Page 8)

Dyce Drinnon
Sept. 9, 1911
Dec. 5, 1 927

James Oda Gilbert
Died Aug. 15, 1935
Age 51 yr. 9 da.

Beulah Barnard
Died Dec. 24, 1935
Age 22 yr.

Zack C. Fields
1850 - 1935

His Wife
Annie Allen
1862 - 19-
"At Rest"

George P. Crockett
Aug. 11, 1874
July 4, 1934

Joe D. Thomason
Nov. 24, 1871
Apr. 24, 1934

Vina M. Thomason
Aug. 21, 1869
Feb. 10, 1933

Lola Mae Wall
Died Nov. 30, 1936
Age 26 yr. 6 mo. 8 da.

Dora B. Shoun
Died Mar. 22, 1933
Age 43 yr. 11 mo. 15 da.

Frances Victoria Rufty, Wife of
1865 - 1930
James A. Leming M. D.

D. H. Anderson
Feb. 19, 1872 - May 4, 1931
"Gone but not forgotten."

Charlie C. Barnard
1896 - 1931

Earl M. Sawyer
May 10, 1879
Oct. 30, 1932

J. Frank Sawyer
Nov. 27, 1840
Oct. 30, 1911

Mollie Moore Sawyer
Mar. 26, 1843
May 18, 1904

William M. Mc Ghee
Nov. 6, 1867
Oct. 11, 1931

Eugene F. Fuller
Jan. 4, 1882
Sept. 2, 1932

Clinard C. Pennell
Died Mar. 1, 1937
Age 26 yr. 11 mo.

Laura Ann Read
Died Jan. 17, 1937
Age 87 yr. 10 mo. 9 da.

Clarice Sanders Pangle
Sept. 4, 1895
Apr. 30, 1936

Jaromiah M. Broyles
Died Mar. 24, 1935
Age 76 yr. 4 mo. 24 da.

Kenneth D. Walker
Mar. 16, 1916
July 25, 1936

Laura B. Robertson, Wife of
Ed. Burgin
Born Sept. 22, 1883
Died July 14, 1910

HAMBLEN COUNTY
BETHESDIA CEMETERY
(Page 9)

James Gilmore Tuttle
Born Oct. 21, 1839
Died Nov. 24, 1906
Co. 9 17 Mich. Infty.

Argent A. McAlister, Wife of
J. Herbert Silvers
Jan. 31, 1902
Feb. 17, 1924
"Gone but not forgotten."

Minnerva Greene
Born Mar. 12, 1849
Died Dec. 26, 1918

John Greene
Born Sept. 27, 1848
Died Jan. 26, 1892
"Gone but not forgotten."

Eliha Dunbar
Born June 4, 1849
Died Dec. 3, 1895

Burtie H. Davis
Aug. 30, 1875
Aug. 11, 1901

Mrs. Carrie L. Smith
Died July 26, 1901
Age 38 yr.

O. K. Capps
Born Apr. 30, 1831
Died Mar. 3, 1910

Martha A. Capps
Born May 29, 1839
Died June 21, 1913

Franklin P. Harris, Son of
A. W. & Francis Harris
Born Apr. 7, 1871
Died Mar. 26, 1899

Anderson Shelton
Born Feb. 16, 1828
Died Sept. 23, 1901

Kattie Taylor, Wife of
H. L. Long
Born Sept. 7, 1844
Died Sept. 17, 1888

H. L. Long
Born Oct. 27, 1842
Died Aug. 11, 1915

Rosa M. Anderson
Born May 10, 1880
Died June 25, 1898

Harriet V., Wife of
O. G. Anderson
May 9, 1844
May 15, 1918

J. M. Anderson
July 10, 1865
Mar. 28, 1912

Ellen A., Wife of
John W. Bewley
Born Apr. 26, 1836
Died Jan. 2, 1897

John W. Bewley
Born Nov. 26, 1826
Died Mar. 10, 1896

In Honor of the 17 Soldiers who
died in 1863 in Defence of the
Southland, the names of only are
known—
W. R. Brooks
G. J. Shropshire
1st Georgia Cavalry

HAMBLEN COUNTY
BETHESDA CEMETERY
(Page 10)

W. J. Todd
Sept. 7, 1865
July 3, 1922
"At Rest"

Catharine B. Shields, Wife of
R. L. Taylor
Born May 26, 1834
Died Jan. 20, 1908

Robert L. Taylor
Born May 22, 1834
Died Mar. 8, 1906

Minnie Lee, Dau. of
C. B. & R. L. Taylor
Born July 12, 1868
Died Feb. 17, 1887

Thomas R., Son of
C. B. & R. L. Taylor
Born Oct. 25, 1861
Died Aug. 28, 1886

Rufus Taylor
Born Sept. 19, 1825
Died Sept. 25, 1861

Jeanna Lee, Dau. of
James & Mary Shields
Born Mar. 9, 1836
Died July 28, 1861

Mary Elizabeth, Dau. of
James & Mary Shields
Born May 20, 1832
Died May 15, 1881

Mary Cobb, Wife of
James Shields
Born Dec. 31, 1802
Died Sept. 25, 1863

James Shields
Born Nov. 8, 1797
Died July 7, 1882

John Blair, Son of
James & Mary Shields
Born Nov. 5, 1828
Died July 28, 1882

Samuel W. Shields
Born May 12, 1841
Died Jan. 31, 1910

Lizzie Bishop Rymer, Wife of
J. V. Rymer
Dec. 18, 1878
Mar. 29, 1905

Lucretia G., Dau. of
F. P. & A. M. Bishop
Born Aug. 19, 1881
Died May 25, 1900

"Devoted husband and loving
     Father"
Francis P. Bishop
Born Aug. 27, 1837
Died Sept. 25, 1894

William H. Sheppard
Died Mar. 21, 1871
Age 29 yr. 11 mo. 11 da.

William J. Rayl
1820 - 1906

Leanner Cox Rayl
1823 - 1900

Tom N. Rayl
1862 - 1930

J. B. Lynch
1855 - 1918

Oscar S. Bishop
Sept. 22, 1873
Feb. 15, 1930

HAMBLEN COUNTY
BETHESDA CEMETERY
(Page 11)

Sarah J., Wife of
Marshall J. Hughes
Born Aug. 26, 1843
Died May 10, 1894

Marshall J. Hughes
Born Mar. 8, 1841
Died Feb. 28, 1895

William Lyons Lewis
Feb. 16, 1866
Jan. 14, 1932

Sam Milton Taylor
Died in Atlanta Geo.
Oct. 20, 1875
Age 33 yr. 9 mo. 15 da.

Eliza J. Taylor
Born Oct. 13, 1821
Died Dec. 9, 1897

F. W. Taylor
Born Nov. 16, 1810
Died Mar. 16, 1886

C. V. Taylor
Jan. 13, 1860
Apr. 22, 1904

Mamie M. Taylor
Mar. 9, 1864
May 19, 1913

Jennie Shields, Dau. of
C. V. & M. M. Taylor
Aug. 8, 1884
Aug. 6, 1904

Ellen Folsom, Dau. of
J. R. & L. K. Forgey
Born Aug. 4, 1888
Died Nov. 18, 1895

Irene, Dau. of J. R. & L. K. Forgey
Dec. 31, 1883
Aug. 28, 1909

James Reynolds Forgey
Died Apr. 16, 1936
Age 82 yr. 1 mo. 4 da.

Frank A. Brown
Died Mar. 7, 1928
Age 70 yr.

Mary Ann, Wife of
Rev. I. C. Brown
Born in Lee Valley Hawkins Co.
   Tenn. Nov. 27, 1880
Fell asleep in Jesus June 21, 1887

Redell C. Brown
Born in Lee Valley Hawkins Co.
   Tenn. July 27, 1817
Died Dec. 30, 1898

Mary A. Orr
Jan. 23, 1857
Jan. 19, 1917

J. J. Starnes
Jan. 16, 1843
Jan. 16, 1922

   His Wife
Anna R. Starnes
Nov. 6, 1843

Joseph Eckel
May 8, 1817
Oct. 24, 1899

   His Wife
Mary J. Eckel
Nov. 9, 1820
Jan. 25, 1883
"Until the day dawn, and the
   shadows flee away."

Eliza J. Hale
Born Mar. 21, 1850
Died Dec. 12, 1919

HAMBLEN COUNTY
BETHESDA CEMETERY
(Page 12)

E. B. Hale M. D.
Born Dec. 14, 1837
Died Feb. 20, 1893

William Chamberlain Hale
Died Feb. 14, 1937
Age 74 yr. 1 mo. 5 da.

Col. Wm. P. Long
Born Aug. 16, 1811
Died May 31, 1897

Eliza V., Wife of
W. P. Long
Born Oct. 26, 1815
Died Nov. 2, 1889

James M. Crocket
Born Nov. 16, 1831
Died Oct. 17, 1888

His Wife
Adelia S. Crockett
Born Jan. 24, 1845
Died June 28, 1908

Robert A. Crockett
Born Oct. 12, 1868
Died Sept. 24, 1896

Hannah H., Wife of
J. D. Tam
Born July 31, 1825
Died Nov. 15, 1898

Joshua D. Tam
Born July 4, 1811
Died Mar. 2, 1899

William H. Long
Mar. 7, 1840
May 29, 1921

His Wife
Priscilla Shields
Sept. 13, 1844
Feb. 3, 1900

Priscilla, Dau. of
H. W. & F. M. Long
Dec. 18, 1911
Feb. 22, 1912

Linnie Johnson
Born Jan. 6, 1883
Died Aug. 9, 1908
"Asleep in Jesus."

Isabella Long, Wife of
G. D. Riggs
Born Feb. 12, 1834
Died May 12, 1904

Louise Rochelle, Wife of
Rev. T. J. Evans
1840 - 1893
Born at Madison Ga.

Armanda J. Shannon, Wife of
James H. Shannon
Born May 1, 1863
Died Jan. 4, 1902

Joseph A. Shannon
Born Apr. 6, 1834
Died Apr. 18, 1900

James P. Shannon
Born Nov. 30, 1831
Died Mar. 17, 1905

John M. Shannon
Born Apr. 20, 1868
Died Apr. 19, 1902
"A kind husband and a loving
father."

Frank Nusbaum
Dec. 16, 1872
Nov. 16, 1881

David Nusbaum
May 25, 1837
Oct. 2, 1883

HAMBLEN COUNTY
BETHESDA CEMETERY
(Page 13)

Warren Nusbaum
Jan. 25, 1870
Feb. 24, 1932

Infant son of
J. J. & L. K. Trantham
Jan. 29, 1916

Anna Mae Trantham
May 17, 1909
Jan. 2, 1926

Mary Lou Trantham Nelson
Jan. 6, 1911
Dec. 2, 1928

Emmett C. Duff
Born Apr. 25, 1871
Died June 7, 1915
"Gone but not forgotten."

Sam W. Jack
Mar. 16, 1847
Apr. 25, 1919

His Wife
Linda Kyle
Sept. 14, 1854
Sept. 1, 1931

Infant dau. of
R. T. & Sallie Anderson
Apr. 30, 1915

Nellie E. Long, Wife of
Willie L. Orrick
Dec. 2, 1900
Apr. 5, 1933

Ella Pearl, Dau. of
E. J. & Z. E. Orrick
Born & Died Nov. 18, 1923

Lee M. Trantham
Apr. 10, 1847
Mar. 16, 1914

His Wife

L. E. Trantham
Jan. 14, 1850

Dosser Moore
July 18, 1885
Dec. 29, 1913

John D. Couch
Dec. 27, 1861
Oct. 19, 1930

Lillie Wall Couch
Dec. 17, 1863
Apr. 10, 1936

Mary E. Jarnagin
Sept. 13, 1841
July 8, 1927

Lara A. Jarnagin
Jan. 1, 1850
Jan. 15, 1917

Celia Donaldson
Born Jan. 14, 1798
Died Jan. 2, 1865

The Grave of
John Robert Long
Sept. 8, 1844
Departed this life
Aug. 20, 1866

Mary Ann Shannon
Born July 28, 1802
Died Oct. 2, 1840

William Shannon
Born June 11, 1795
Died Dec. 6, 1855

Celia J. Craig
Born July 25, 1816
Died June 10, 1877

HAMBLEN COUNTY
BETHESDA CEMETERY
(Page 14)

Willie J. Holley
Nov. 5, 1894

James T. Holley
Mar. 6, 1897

Ira D. Holley
July 7, 1860
Oct. 31, 1880

Edna B. Holley
Nov. 5, 1881

Beatrice H. Holley
Sept. 3, 1883

Karl B. Holley
May 12, 1886

Emmett P. Holley
June 28, 1889

Martha Matilda Jackson, Wife of
J. A. Cassidy
July 4, 1834
Dec. 10, 1872

Mary Elizabeth Cassidy
Sept. 2, 1856
Nov. 26, 1859

Jesse Barton
Born May 25, 1837
Died Mar. 13, 1862

Rebecca Long, Wife of
D. Barton
July 2, 1864
Sept. 4, 1912

David Barton
Born Nov. 13, 1838
Died Sept. 4, 1912

C. J. Barton
Aug. 28, 1841
Mar. 18, 1923

Eliza Barton
Oct. 17, 1846

Maria Louisa Graham, Wife of
Theophilus Rogan
1833 - 1910

Maggie Margaret Callaway Rogan
1858 - 1863

W. Williams Rogan
Nov. -, 1873
Dec. -, 1873

Hugh Graham Rogan
1860 - 1915

Mary Katharine Rogan
1856 - 1932

Theophilus Rogan
July 20, 1825
Sept. 23, 1904

Hattie S. Fisher, Dau. of
Daniel & Amelia Fisher
Oct. 15, 1843
Dec. 24, 1915

Laura Fisher Utsman
June 5, 1855
July 21, 1926

G. A. Core
July 4, 1852
Nov. 9, 1912

17

HAMBLEN COUNTY
BETHESDA CEMETERY
(Page 15)

Lois Deaver, Dau. of
W. T. & Dora Deaver
Nov. 12, 1895
Aug. 11, 1912

Shepard Deaver
Sept. 7, 1844
Apr. 11, 1933

His Wife
Dora Deaver
Jan. 17, 1862
Sept. 23, 1930

Nannie L. Brown, Dau. of
J. Y. C. & R. J. Brown
Born Aug. 21, 1873
Died May 2, 1904

John R., Son of
J. Y. C. & R. J. Brown
Born Apr. 1882
Died Jan. 1897

Clinton A., Son of
J. Y. C. & R. J. Brown
Oct. 1867
Sept. 17, 19(?)

Hughes W. Gough
1857 - 1934

Florence H. Seavers
Apr. 6, 1860
Dec. 3, 1924

Mary Bewley Wright
Jan. 11, 1881
Feb. 9, 1918

W. H. Wright
Born Dec. 9, 1889
Died May 30, 1916

Darsley Lamar Stapleton
Sept. 6, 1908
Dec. 16, 1918

Nancy Jane Stapleton
Born July 6, 1884
Died Mar. 1, 1923

Nina Belle, Dau. of
Edward & Marilda Robertson
Born Apr. 8, 1908
Died Aug. 9, 1917

Amanda Brown, Wife of
Thomas McAlister
Apr. 9, 1848
Died Nov. 21, 1913

Margaret Long
Nov. 4, 1936
Age 19 yrs.

Eliza J. Robertson
Dec. 31, 1847
Mar. 26, 1926

HAMBLEN COUNTY
BENT CREEK CEMETERY
(Page 1)

Located near Whitesburg on the old pike leading from Whitesburg to Morristown. It was the church yard of Bent Creek Baptist Church, which was organized prior to 1794 by Isaac Barton, Caleb Witt, and James Roddye. Caleb Witt and James Roddye are buried in this cemetery. James Roddye was a Revolutionary soldier. Many years ago the old church was torn down and a new brick church built in Whitesburg.

There are approximately 600 graves marked with field stones.

Copied by, Mrs. Margaret H. Richardson, Miss Ada Ruth Noe, Mrs. Arile Turner, and Miss Rebecca Colyer. May 7, 1937

R. H. Campbell
Died Mar. 23, 1936
Age 50 yrs.

William Campbell
Died Nov. 12, 1929
Age 47 yrs. 1 mo. 11 da.

Mary J. Smith
Dec. 16, 1846
Dec. 13, 1914
"Farewell dear sister sweet thy rest"

(Double)
   Smith
Arizona Smith
May 26, 1868
Jan. 4, 1932

James M. Smith
Dec. 15, 1851
May 16, 1932

Leannah E. Harris
April 18, 1844
Jan. 19, 1919
"Gone but not forgotten"

W. J. Harris
Born Mar. 39, 1838
Died June 20, 1908
"Resting in Peace."

Son of B. A. & E. M. Mc Ferrin
Dec. 23, 1881
Mar. 14, 1896
"At Rest"

Edgar, Son of G. M. & M. M. Lane
Born Oct. 20, 1891
Died Aug. 20, 1896
Age 4 yrs. 10 mo. 18 da.
"Suffer little children and forbid them not to come unto me for of such is the Kingdom of Heaven"

"Gone to be an angel"
Infant son of,
E. C. & Mollie Rader
Born Sept. 4, 1890
Died Oct. 7, 1890

Cornelius A. Rader
Sept. 24, 1862
Oct. 23, 1924

 His Wife
Loulia Belle Moore
Jan. 9, 1866
Mar. 4, 1922
"They have done what they could"

J. P. Haren
Mar. 26, 1818
Dec. 19, 1898

HAMBLEN COUNTY
BENT CREEK CEMETERY
(Page 2)

(Double)
        Walker
C. M. Walker
Oct. 28, 1848
March 20, 1926

        His Wife
Elizabeth M. Haun
Feb. 3, 1847
Mar. 2, 1915

Milburn Haun
Died Jan. 20, 1889
Age 29 yr. 11 mo. 27 da.
"We need thee dear darling in our
home we miss thee where thou art
we soon shall come and live forever
there."

Joseph D. Mooney
Born July 10, 1837
Died Dec. 26, 1913

        His Wife
Mary Haun
Born Aug. 6, 1838
Died Jan. 17, 1921
"Blessed are the dead which die in the
Spirit, that they may rest from their
labors and their works do follow them."

Dr. Joel Smith
Born Oct. 4, 1848
Died Sept. 25, 1883
"A light from our household is gone, a
voice that we loved is still, a place is
vacant in our heart, that can never be
filled."

George R. Smith
Born Mar. 11, 1856
Died Apr. 14, 1879

In Memory of Elizabeth, Wife of
Samuel Smith
Born April 4, 1823
Died Feb. 13, 1896
"She died as she lived a Christian"

Samuel Smith
Born Aug. 16, 1819
Died Apr. 16, 1900
"Weep not he is at Rest"

(Double)
L. H. Charles
Sept. 16, 1844
Apr. 2, 1918
(Soldier)

        His Wife
Barsha M. Charles
Feb. 4, 1853
Apr. 15, 1926

Martha E. Harris
Born Nov. 4, 1861
Died Jan. 9, 1881

James Harris
Born Jan. 6, 1808
Died May 17, 1865

Elizabeth, Wife of
Jameson White
Born May 16, 1816
Died Sept. 7, 1871

Johnie P., Son of
T. L. & L. A. Williams
Born July 29, 1879
Died Mar. 16, 1882

Dederick N. Horner
June 15, 1850
Dec. 6, 1920

        His Wife
Julia A. Horner
Sept. 26, 1880
Died -

Lovona J. Dorris, Wife of
D. N. Horner
Born Mar. 29, 1862
Died July 11, 1906

HAMBLEN COUNTY
BENT CREEK CEMETERY
(Page 3)

Matt M., Wife of A. E. Hale
Born Mar. 9, 1848
Died July 7, 1877
"Blessed are the dead which
die in the Lord."

Thomas G. Tomlinson
Born Sept. 20, 1873
Died May 17, 1893

Ronena Thomlinson Colyer
Burried by her first husband.

Mollie P., Dau. of
L. & G. W. Patton
Born Oct. 6, 1875
Died Jan. 27, 1878

J. C. Lane, Son of
Garrett & Sarah Lane
Born Sept. 22, 1884
Died Feb. 24, 1906
"Through all pains at times he
smiled a smile of heavenly birth and when
the angels called him home he smiled
farwell to earth."

Mollie E., Dau. of
Garrett & Sarah Lane
Born Dec. 12, 1872
Died Aug. 22, 1902
"Farwell sister peace be thy silent rest;
Slumber sweetly God knew best when to call
thee home to rest."

Wilson D. Murdoch
Born May 6, 1832
Died April 6, 1859

In Memory of Milton S. Taylor
Born Feb. 20, 1850
Died July 11, 1873
Age 23 yrs. 4 mo. 21 da.

Sammuel F. Smith
Born July 23, 1868
Died Nov. 13, 1883
"He had given his heart to
God though young, He was a
soldier of the cross."

Reddene T. Smith
Born June 9, 1855
Died Dec. 22, 1855
"Budded on earth to bloom in
Heaven."

Thomas M. Smith
Born June 15, 1866
Died Nov. 10, 1867
"Jesus took little children
in his arms and blessed them."

"Budded on earth to bloom in
Heaven"
Lula W., Infant Dau. of
R. F. & M. V. Taylor
Born Aug. 14, 1873
Died May 3, 1874
Age 6 mo. 17 da.

Sarah Jane Smith
Born Feb. 15, 1852
Died May 11, 1869
"She was a devoted Christian
girl, serving the Lord all
her days."

Devalson D. White
Born Mar. 5, 1866
Died Nov. 24, 1868

William Howard Davis
Died June 26, 1936
Age 38 yr. 2 mo.

"Asleep in Jesus"
Earl Barton, Son of
William & Jennie Davis
Born Aug. 24, 1894
Died April 11, 1904
"Suffer little children to come unto
me and forbid them not for such is
the Kingdom of God."

(Double rock)
Julia A. Davis
Born March 13, 1837
Died April 15, 1896

Pleasant J. Davis
Born Sept. 9, 1826
Died June 8, 1887
"With aching hearts we place them here,
Father and Mother we love so dear, we
hope to meet them by and by on that
mansion beyond the sky."

In Memory of an Infant Dau. of
Dr. B. C. & K. T. Weesner
May 15, 1904
Nov. 13, 1905
"A Joy on earth, a hope in Heaven"

Julia Wanta, Dau. of
Dr. B. C. & K. T. Weesner
Born July 26, 1909
Died June 28, 1910
"Suffer the little ones to come unto me."

In Memory of an Infant Dau. of
P. J. & Julia A. Davis
Born Sept. 20, 1858
Died Dec. 11, 1859
Age 1 yr. 2 mo. 21 da.

William J. Horner
Born Dec. 22, 1816
Died Aug. 16, 1870

        His Wife

Sarah L. Horner
Born Jan. 6, 1825
Died Mar. 27, 1902
"Our parents are gone but
not forgotten."

In Memory of James Haun
Born June 1, 1812
Died Dec. 11, 1870
Aged 68 yr. 6 mo. 10 da.
"Be ye also ready."

In Memory of Francis Haun
Born Feb. 12, 1802
Died Jan. 15, 1856

Lucy J. Haun
Born Mar. 14, 1841
Died June 4, 1910
"Earth has no sorrow that
Heaven cannot heal."

Rebecca, Wife of P. Horner
Born Feb. 7, 1813
Died Aug. 28, 1879

Rev. P. Horner
Born Nov. 5, 1813
Died Oct. 29, 1884

L. F., Son of P. & R. Horner
Born Dec. 13, 1837
Died April 3, 1853

M. A., Dau. of P. & R. Horner
Born May 3, 1841
Died Sept. 30, 1844

E. J., Dau. of P. & R. Horner
Born Feb. 11, 1838
Died Sept. 28, 1844

W. A., Son of P. & R. Horner
Born Nov. 18, 1836
Died Aug. 10, 1838

HAMBLEN COUNTY
BENT CREEK CEMETERY
(Page 5)

Eleannor Moore
Born Jan. 9, 1817
Died Dec. 11, 1833
Age 56 yr. 11 mo. 2 da.

Eliza Moore, Wife of John Moore
Born April 7, 1837
Died April 14, 1903

John Moore
Born Feb. 1804
Died April 29, 1897

Nancy Parvin
Born Dec. 3, 1833
Died Mar. 11, 1894
"We will meet thee again."

G. C. Pangle
Born Mar. 11, 1809
Died April 29, 1897

Elizabeth Pangle, Wife of
G. C. Pangle
Born May 8, 1812
Departed this life
Dec. 24, 1855
"Blessed are they that die in the Lord."

Susan Jane, Dau. of G. C. & E. Pangle
Born June 18, 1848
Departed this life July 2, 1849

George White

Mary White
Born Feb. 23, 1799
Died Sept. 2, 1853

Leanah White
Born Oct. 28, 1820
Died April 12, 1900

William White
Born July 31, 1813
Died June 14, 1834

William R. Horner
July 16, 1856
May 26, 1923

Dara M. Horner
Nov. 26, 1863

In Memory of Sammuel White
Born in Lendon County Va.
Aug. 26, 1780
Died April 10, 1854

William R. Horner
Born Oct. 11, 1834
Died Mar. 3, 1899

Elizabeth Lane, Wife of
William R. Horner
Born Mar. 11, 1838
Died May 25, 1916
"Blessed are they that die in
the Lord." "A Golden link has
been removed from out our chain
but sometime we'll reach the
meaning of our tears, Then oh,
then we'll understand."

Sergt. Elbert Horner
Co. C. 8 Tennessee Cav.

James L. Kesterson
Born Aug. 28, 1854
Died June 21, 1915

Richard White
Born May 17, 1790
Died Oct. 10, 1849

Hannah E., Wife of
Richard White
Born Sept. 8, 1779
Died Oct. 12, 1839

J. W. Weaver
Co. C. 4th Tenn.

HAMBLEN COUNTY
BENT CREEK CEMETERY
(Page 6)

"Gone Home"
Mary A. Pangle
Aug. 30, 1845
Feb. 16, 1917

In Memory of James Pangle
Born Aug. 4, 1832
Died Nov. 5, 1835

Mary Roddy Day
June 9, 1832
June 22, 1919

Walker
Hugh C. Walker
1869 - 1925

Mattie D. Walker
1870 - 19-

Muriel Walker
1902 - 1902

Adriel Walker
1902 - 1902

Issac P., Son of
S. M. Myder
Born Mar. 17, 1869
Died Aug. 18, 1884
Aged 15 yr. 5 mo. 1 da.

Joe F. Dyer
Born Mar. 29, 1866
Died Jan. 5, 1887
Age 20 yr. 9 mo. 6 da.

Edward Carmack Dyer
Died June 25, 1924
Age 18 yr. 1 mo. 22 da.

Charley Dewey, Son of
J. N. & S. E. E. Dyer
Born June 4, 1898
Died Sept. 27, 1911

Cobda Bell, Dau. of
L. & M. A. Rader
Born April 28, 1867
Died Nov. 10, 1868
Aged 18 mo. 12 da.

Anne, Dau. of
W. M. & N. Kirkpatrick
Born Oct. 16, 1849
Died Nov. 28, 1850

William Kirkpatrick
Born Dec. 12, 1807
Died May 13, 1867
Age 59 yr. 6 mo.
"God's finger touched him and
he left."

Nacme, Wife of
William Kirkpatrick
Born Feb. 23, 1817
Died Jan. 10, 1894
"No one knew thee but to love
thee, all thy ways were just and
kind. Blessed art thou for thy
doingings, is said by all left
behind."

Rebecca M., Consort of
S. M. Dennison
Died Mar. 23, 1862
Age 32 yr. 2 mo.
"Alas she has left us her spirit
has fled, Her body now slumbers
along with the dead, Her Savior
has called her to him she has
gone Be ye last today To follow
her soon."

Robert Rhea
Born Nov. 27, 1821
Died May 13, 1902

Lucretia Rhea
Born Oct. 1, 1827
Died April 2, 1889

HAMBLEN COUNTY
BENT CREEK CEMETERY
(Page 7)

Mother
Lillie Mae, Wife of
H. R. Fleenor
Nov. 24, 1889
Feb. 10, 1934
"Asleep in Jesus"

George Mitchell Haun
Born Sept. 23, 1857
Died -
"Asleep in Jesus."

Mary Isabelle Charles
Born Jan. 23, 1868
Married to George M. Haun
Dec. 20, 1883
"Asleep in Jesus."

James Cox
May 23, 1821
May 23, 1891

Edna Lane Cox
Jan. 17, 1830
Oct. 8, 1873

W. D. Cox
Born July 23, 1854
Died Nov. 12, 1861

Sacred to the Memory of
S. E. Magnolian, Infant Dau. of
J. B. & M. J. Bass
Died April 25, 1860
"Her smiles filled two hearts with
joy."

Lucy Annis, Beloved wife of,
Gustane Murmann
July 20, 1861
April 9, 1892
"Her blessed and her husband and her
children also, arise and call."

J. T. Courtney
Co. D. 4th Tenn. Soldier
Born Sept. 2, 1828
Died Nov. 12, 1895

Allie M., Wife of M. Natt
Born June 2, 1859
Died Dec. 30, 1884
"She died as she lived trusting
in the Lord."

Vernita, Dau. of
M. C. & A. M. Mynatt
Born & Died Dec. 25, 1884
"God bless us an early death
and takes the Infant to him
self."

Robert Shannon, Son of
Wm. & Rachel Shannon
Born Oct. 28, 1846
Died Oct. 18, 1861
"He took thee from a world of
care in everlasting bliss to
share."

Elizabeth J., Wife of
Jacob Thomas
Born Nov. 22, 1837
Died Sept. 8, 1878

In Memory of Allie, Dau. of
T. J. & C. L. Erwin
Born July 6, 1893
Died Mar. 18, 1897

Ann, Wife of J. L. Wice
Born Aug. 7, 1825
Died April 16, 1888

J. L. Wice, Co. M. 9th Tenn.
Born Dec. 5, 1821
Died Jan. 11, 1897
Soldier

Joseph C. Long
Born Nov. 29, 1859
Died July 12, 1903

James H. Long
Died July 10, 1893
Age 79 yr.

HAMBLEN COUNTY
BENT CREEK CEMETERY
(Page 8)

His Wife
Rutha J. Fieldon
Died Mar. 30, 1899
Age 66 yr.
"Gone but not forgotten"

James L. Beck
Born Oct. 29, 1881
Died July 29, 1901
"Thy gentle voice is hushed,
Thy worn true heart is still,
Safe in the arms of Jesus."

G. P. Haun
Born Sept. 21, 1854
Died Jan. 10, 1909
"Prepare to meet thy God."

Dollie, Wife of G. P. Haun
Born May 2, 1857
Died Aug. 1, 1899
"Beloved one farewell."

Clara Ethel Fields
May 1, 1893
Feb. 14, 1901

Henry Fields
Jan. 29, 1853
April 28, 1899

To A Heavenly Home
Lillard Clemment
Nov. 10, 1895
May 19, 1922
"Darling we miss Thee."

Marion Rader
Born 1902
Died 1923

Elizabeth N., Wife of
H. C. Seaner
Mar. 19, 1844
Apr. 25, 1915

EvelynCox, Dau. of
R. S. & P. R. Rader
Sept. 25, 1910
Feb. 22, 1915

Fred P., Son of
J. A. & Rohenna Nicholes
Born Aug. 31, 1892
Died June 13, 1911

Mary Kate Pruitt
Died Nov. 30, 1836
Age 54 yr. 3 mo. 2 da.

Elizabeth Lorena, Dau. of
Mr. & Mrs. Clarence Colyer
Sept. 2, 1912
Mar. 26, 1915
"We miss thee ever day."

Infant Dau. of Mr. & Mrs.
Clarence Colyer
Nov. 24, 1914
Nov. 25, 1914
"Gone to be an angel."

Rev. Thomas Gilbert
Born Oct. 27, 1825
Died Feb. 11, 1902

Lavina Mason
Born April 5, 1821
Died July 16, 1902

Amelia D., Dau. of
J. H. G. & Mattie A. Flagg
Wife of J. W. Franklin
Born Jan. 8, 1865
Died Mar. 11, 1907
"In God We Trust."

Col. J. S. Flagg, Son of
Dr. John M. & Elizabeth R. Flagg
Born Sept. 2, 1823
Died July 11, 1900

HAMBLEN COUNTY
BENT CREEK CEMETERY
(Page 9)

Father
Henry Horner
Mar. 2, 1858
May 27, 1929

Hattie L. Horner
June 19, 1860
Oct. 2, 1902

"Our Darling"
Ruth, Dau. of John & Laura Hurst
Born Aug. 29, 1899
Died Sept. 3, 1899

Florence J. Drake
Nov. 16, 1868
Dec. 8, 1909

"Our Darling"
Blanche R., Dau. of W. S. & L. B. Ott
June 26, 1894
Sept. 18, 1897

Mother
Betty Drake Ott
May 6, 1869
Feb. 17, 1929

"Gone Home"
Elbert W., Son of A. D. & L. Johnson
Born June 14, 1863
Died Dec. 14, 1887
"Stop youth as you pass by as you are
now so once was I, as I am now, So you
must be prepare for death and follow me."

"A bud of love."
Infant of J. Y. & Nola Brown
Feb. 8, 1903

Maude Bernice Quillen
Oct. 12, 1893
Sept. 25, 1897

Bell, Dau. of J. L. & E. B. Quillen
Born June 2, 1875
Died June 11, 1876

Moore
J. H. Moore
Born Dec. 17, 1828
Died Jan. 1, 1912

His Wife
Maldanota Gobble
Born Nov. 6, 1834
Died April 24, 1879
"Gone to be with Jesus."

Father
Lemuel Rader
Born May 25, 1832
Died Sept. 23, 1899

Mother
Melvina Kirkpatrick, Wife of
Lemuel Rader
Born Oct. 5, 1834
Died Sept. 4, 1911
"Weep not children for us
For we are waiting in Glory
for thee."

Angie, Dau. of N. M. &
M. A. Cooper
Born Jan. 5, 1871
Died Jan. 1, 1872

Pangle
Lillian C. White, Wife of
J. W. Pangle
July 26, 1897
Sept. 9, 1918
"A beautiful Christian characte r"

Pangle
Sallie N. Howery, Wife of
Jacob W. Pangle
Born Feb. 28, 1875
Died July 24, 1916
"A consecrated Christian,
devoted wife and a loving
mother."

28

HAMBLEN COUNTY
BENT CREEK CEMETERY
(Page 10)

"Little Sweetheart"
Lewis Folk, Son of
J. W. & S. N. Pangle
June 20, 1909
Dec. 30, 1909

Harriet Vivian, Infant Dau. of
J. W. & Hattie Pangle
Born & Died Nov. 20, 1921
"A little bud of love to bloom
with God above."

Pangle
"Come Ye Blessed"
H. L. Pangle
Feb. 8, 1835
July 24, 1913
"I am the Resurrection and the Life."

Jas. A. Courtney
Age 8 yrs.

"She Has Gone Home To Rest."
Mary, Wife of A. M. Trolinger
Born Nov. 20, 1843
Died May 8, 1874

Mary Emma, Dau. of
L. & M. Rader
Born Mar. 3, 1872
Died Aug. 11, 1892
"Thou art gone but not forgotten."

Murdock
W. M. Murdock
Jan. 8, 1829
Aug. 8, 1916

His Wife
Elizabeth J. Murdock
Sept. 4, 1839
April 7, 1924

Taylor
"Father"
Redden S. Taylor
Born Oct. 9, 1809
Died Sept. 1, 1884
Aged 74 yrs. 10 mo. 22 da.

"Mother"
Nancy W., Wife of R. S. Taylor
Born Sept. 22, 1817
Died May 22, 1892
Aged 74 yrs. 8 mo.

Murdock
I. C. Murdock
Born May 6, 1844
Died Sept. 25, 1905

His Wife
Nancy A. Murdock
Born Jan. 13, 1851
Died May 31, 1924

Murdock
J. M. P. Murdock
Born Nov. 23, 1830
Died Oct. 1, 1907
"My trust is in God."

Ora V., Dau. of
B. F. & M. V. Taylor
Born Feb. 5, 1880
Died May 14, 1884
Age 4 yr. 3 mo. 9 da.
"A sleep in Jesus"

Lewis
Thomas J. Lewis
Born Dec. 1, 1856
Died June 15, 1902
"Having fulfilled his mission
he fell asleep."

HAMBLEN COUNTY
BENT CREEK CEMETERY
(Page 11)

His Wife
Louetta Shields, Dau. of
T. J. & Dora G. Lewis
Born July 11, 1883
Died Jan. 8, 1888
"Of such is the kingdom of Heaven."

Mahlon Gobble
Born Aug. 18, 1841
Died Nov. 10, 1900

M. L. E. Gobble
Born Jan. 13, 1853
Died Aug. 18, 1887

Florah M., Dau. of M. & M. E. L. Gobble
Born Sept. 2, 1876
Died Aug. 18, 1877

Robert Patterson Moore
Born Dec. 27, 1827
Died Dec. 22, 1884
Age 56 yr. 11 mo. 25 da.

"At Rest"
Ruth Ann Wood
Died July 7, 1877
Age 44 yrs.
Was married to Andrew Moore Oct. 6, 1853.
"Rest mother rest in sweet sleep
While friends in sorrow over thee weep."

In Memory of Mary, Wife of Wm. Pangle
Born July 22, 1819
Died Feb. 3, 1872

In Memory of Catharine Pangle
Born June 1, 1804
Died June 16, 1882
Age 54 yr. 15 da.

In Memory of I. F. Pangle, Son of
Wm. & Catharine Pangle
Born Oct. 3, 1841
Killed in Battle at Raytown, Tenn.
Oct. 11, 1863

In Memory of Caty L. Pangle
Born June 25, 1858
Died Feb. 1, 1862

"Asleep in Jesus"
Lutetia A., Wife of
Isaac N. Pangle
Born Apr. 10, 1847
Died Dec. 19, 1907
"Farewell dear Mother, sweet thy
rest."

Isaac N. Pangle
Born Oct. 30, 1830
Died Nov. 30, 1908
"Behold ye passers by,
As you are now so once was I,
As I am now so you must be,
Prepare for death and follow me."

William Pangle
Born May 5, 1803
Died Oct. 13, 1894

Linda L., Dau. of E. F. &
L. A. Pangle
Born Mar. 31, 1902
Died Oct. 25, 1908

Charlsie Pangle, Wife of
H. W. Creech
1896 - 1922
"At Rest".

Dudley Randle, Son of
J. C. & M. J. Gorden
Born Oct. 5, 1887
Died Sept. 2, 1888

Haun
W. A. Haun
Born Sept. 13, 1825
Died Jan. 25, 1907
"How desolate our home bereft
of thee."

HAMBLEN COUNTY
BENT CREEK CEMETERY
(Page 12)

"Gone Home"
Nancy J. Rhea
Born Aug. 25, 1836
Died June 18, 1894
Aged 57 yr. 9 mo. 23 da.

Matildea, Wife of W. A. Dean
Born Mar. 28, 1838
Died Jan. 14, 1886
"She now sleeps in that peace
Which the world can not give or
take away."

"Gone Home"
Mattie L., Wife of E. M. Grim
Born June 7, 1860
Died Nov. 15, 1879

Elizabeth Haun
Born June 16, 1836
Died Jan. 15, 1848

James M. Moore
Born Sept. 7, 1819
Died Apr. 9, 1853

Minerva Moore, Dau. of
Robert & Jane Moore
Born 1826
Died 1854

Robert Moore
1774 - 1852

Jane Howard, His Wife
1796 - 1843

Lane
William Lane
Feb. 14, 1843
Feb. 14, 1922

His Wife
Mary A. Pangle
Feb. 18, 1842
Sept. 24, 1903

Robert Clyde, Son of
R. E. & V. H. Parvin
Born Jan. 20, 1894
Died July 19, 1896

In Memory of Robert Parvin
Born July 5, 1851
Died Dec. 26, 1905

J. C. White
Born Dec. 18, 1834
Died Jan. 28, 1896

Mac H., Son of L. & L. Horner
Born Feb. 14, 1895
Died Feb. 26, 1896
"Gone but not forgotten."

"Gone So Soon"
Loula Verbena, Infant Dau. of
S. M. & M. T. White
Born & Died Apr. 18, 1890
"Sleep sweet babe and take thy
rest, twas God called thee he
thought best."

White
"Budded on Earth to Bloom in
Heaven"
Cornelia Azlee, Dau. of
S. M. & M. T. White
Born Nov. 5, 1883
Died Sept. 15, 1889

Wife
Mary T. White
Jan. 25, 1864
"Asleep in Jesus, blessed sleep
from which how ever wake to weep."

Husband
Samuel M. White
Mar. 23, 1839
Jan. 6, 1913
"Blessed are the dead which die
in the Lord, that they may rest
from their labors and their works
do follow them."

HAMBLEN COUNTY
BENT CREEK CEMETERY
(Page 13)

Inez J., Dau of J. S. &
    M. E. Rhea
Born Apr. 20, and Died Aug. 18, 1883
"Sleep on sweet babe,
And take thy rest,
God called thee home
He thought it best"
God blesses in an early death and
takes our baby unto himself.

Jennie L., Wife of
G. S. P. Wisecarver
Born July 9, 1871
Died Nov. 13, 1895
Aged 24 yrs. 4 mo. 4 da.
"Gone but not forgotten."

Father and Mother
David Rhea
Born Aug. 29, 1834
Died Oct. 31, 1896

Minerva Horner, Wife of
David Rhea
Born Jan. 4, 1840
Died June 27, 1879

In Memory of Joseph Worley
Died June 17, 1875
Age 72 yr. 3 mo.

Jane Worley, Wife of
Joseph Worley
Born Dec. 25, 1802
Died Jan. 15, 1875
Age 72 yr. 21 da.

Hugh Lawson White Kirkpatrick
Born Aug. 31, 1818
Died Aug. 30, 1853
"He was a just man, one who
feared God and eschewed evil."

In Memory of Dr. E. D. Johnson
Born Oct. 20, 1798
Died Apr. 29, 1841

Thirza, Wife of Peter Smith
Born Apr. 24, 1815
Died Mar. 14, 1879

D. W. Oakes
Born Sept. 1, 1813
Died May 3, 1892

J. W. Oakes
Born May 10, 1865
Died Sept. 9, 1891

Vanay, Consort of
J. O. A. Brown
Died Oct. 4, 1855
Age 26 yr. 6 mo. 14 da.

"Come Ye Blessed"
Nancy J. Rhea, Wife of
W. P. Climer
Born Apr. 15, 1847
Died Aug. 21, 1914

T. C. Oaks
Born Nov. 16, 1860
Died June 23, 1895
Aged 34 yrs. 7 mo. 7 da.

Howard Elsi, Son of
Claude & Dora Russell
Born Feb. 21, 1906
Died Nov. 6, 1922
"He is not dead, but sleepeth."

Welch
John T. Welch
Apr. 7, 1836
Dec. 2, 1923

His Wife
Mar. 26, 1845
Apr. 6, 1888

Elizabeth E. Yoe, Wife of
Eaton Pullen
Born Aug. 26, 1837
Died Aug. 29, 1918
"A precious one from us is taken,
A voice we loved is stilled."

Eaton Pullen
Born Aug. 2, 1824
Married Lizzie E. Yoe
Died Feb. 29, 1884
"When we leave this world of changes,
When we leave this world of care,
We shall find our missing loved ones,
In our Father's mansion fair."

Sarah Haun
Born Dec. 22, 1834
Died July 3, 1905
"God's finger touched her and she slept"

Laura C., Wife of J. M. Kirkpatrick
Born Aug. 18, 1845
Died June 13, 1903
"The Lord is my shepherd I shall not want."

Jessie O. M., Dau. of J. M. & L. C.
   Kirkpatrick
Born July 9, 1884
Died Feb. 8, 1901
"Gone but not forgotten."

Infant Dau. of J. H. & N. L. Hale
Born & Died May 22, 1904

Infant Son of J. H. & N. L. Hale
Born & Died Apr. 27, 1906

Flagg
Maj. H. G. Flagg, Son of
Dr. John M. & Elizabeth R. Flagg
Born June 20, 1828
Died April 9, 1905
Maj. Co. E. 1st Tenn. Cav. U. S. V.
War of 1861
"In God We Trust."

"In God We Trust"
Elizabeth Hughes, Wife of
Dr. John M. Flagg
Born in Maryland Jan. 31, A. D. 1800
Died at Rogersville, Tenn. Dec. 16, A. D. 1869
A Member of Methodist M. E.
"Blessed are the dead that die in the Lord"

Julia Campbell
Died April 28, 1930
Age 72 yrs.

Robert Campbell
Died Dec. 9, 1926
Age 73 yrs.

David Gough
Died June 2, 1898

Margaret Gough
Born Aug. 22, 1829
Died May 14, 1880

Margaret V. Harris
Born Apr. 4, 1882
Died Nov. 24, 1901

Emma, Wife of Perry Burton
Born June 7, 1875
Died April 7, 1897

Infant of P. & E. Burton
Born & Died May 11, 1896

Willie, Infant Son of
E. F. & L. A. Pangle
Born Aug. 28, 1900
Died Sept. 25, 1900

Patrick H., Son of
Wm. St & H. M. Pangle
Born Sept. 14, 1875
Died Apr. 6, 1880

W. D. Pangle
Born Feb. 4, 1871
Died Dec. 27, 1891
"We miss thee darling in our
home,
We cherish thy memory dear,
We trust in him whose word
subtime,
       To greet thee in A
   brighter time."

HAMBLEN COUNTY
BENT CREEK CEMETERY
(Page 15)

William N. Haun
July 31, 1841
July 1, 1924

Wife of Vany Cornelia Lane
May 22, 1842
Sept. 14, 1908

J. I. Smallwood
1844 - 1921

His Wife
Nancy A.
1850 - Jan. 29, 1921

"Our Darling"
Jodie E. Moore
Born Dec. 31, 1871
Died Oct. 22, 1888
"While we're waiting thou art
watching from thy home in Heaven
above, And we'll soon be reunited
Safe with thee in the Saviers love."

Terry Epps
Died 1870

Nannie, Dau. of W. L. & M. M. Taylor
Born Aug. 1, 1881
Died Apr. 15, 1889
"Come from this world of sorrow
The Saviours love to share
And Heaven is the brighter
That thou art waiting there."

"Gone To Rest."
Minnie E., Dau. of W. L. & M. M. Taylor
Born June 1, 1874
Died June 23, 1888
"Precious Saviour thou has done it,
And our hearts are bruised, and sore
Thou to rest for ever more."

Rual, Son of J. A. & L. M. Lane
Born Oct. 30, 1899
Died Nov. 2, 1900
"Beneath this stone in soft repose,
Is laid a mother's dearest pride."

Bithe D. Legg, Dau. of
J. W. & Francis M. Legg
Born July 8, 1851
Died Aug. 8, 1903
"Gone but not forgotten"

Cathern J., Dau. of
J. W. & Francis M. Legg
Born Oct. 28, 1849
Died Aug. 21, 1894

Francis M. Legg, Wife of
J. W. Legg
Born Jan. 20, 1831
Died Jan. 21, 1904
"A Mother from our home
is gone."

John W. Legg
Born Feb. 10, 1825
Died Sept. 13, 1889

Susannah W., Dau. of
R. S. & N. W. Taylor
Wife of William D. Drake
Born Oct. 9, 1835
Died Mar. 20, 1862

Susannah W., Dau. of
W. D. & S. W. Drake
Born Mar. 1, 1862
Died June 20, 1862

Mary M. Taylor, Wife of
Peter Smith
Born July 10, 1834
Died Dec. 29, 1899
"Mother you have been all,
a wife, and a mother could
have been, God has called
thee home, come in and take
thy rest."

Peter Smith
Born Nov. 5, 1826
Died Feb. 18, 1914

Rolandus White
Born Aug. 15, 1845
Died Oct. 1854

34

HAMBLEN COUNTY
BENT CREEK CEMETERY
(Page 16)

Rolandus White
Born Aug. 15, 1845
Died Oct. 1854

Diana Hunt
Born 1753
Died 1828

"Our Darling"
Priored, Infant son of
J. E. & L. M. Day
Born Jan. 24, 1903
Died Jan. 9, 1906

Lydie Tarter, Wife of
J. E. Day
Aug. 18, 1876
Aug. 2, 1914
"As a wife devoted. As a
mother affectionate. As a
mind ever kind and true."

Rosea D., Dau. of
S. M. & M. M. Dyer
Born Nov. 29, 1874
Died Aug. 28, 1893

Malvina, Wife of S. M. Dyer
Born 1841
Died Nov. 18, 1899

S. M. Dyer
Nov. 27, 1845
May 30, 1921
Age 75 yrs. 6 mo. 3 da.

Jennie B., Dau. of
T. M. & N. E. Shields
Born Feb. 23, 1881
Died July 25, 1899

Mollie B., Dau. of
T. & N. E. Shields
Born June 16, 1876
Died Jan. 15, 1892

W. E. Routh
Born Sept. 29, 1866
Died Mar. 15, 1879
Willie Reed in peace.

Thos. M. Shields
June 15, 1842
Mar. 9, 1918

Nannie, Wife of Thomas Shields
Born Mar. 15, 1847
Died Oct. 9, 1897
"In life beloved, In death
lamented."

Laura, Wife of Jerry Thomas
Born May 15, 1859
Died Feb. 16, 1887

Walter, Son of
J. & L. Thomas
Born Oct. 29, 1886
Died June 18, 1887

Henry Drake
Died Aug. 13, 1908
Age about 80 yrs.

Nancy C., Wife of
Mahlon White
Born June 8, 1826
Died Oct. 30, 1865
"She hath done what she could."

Mahlon White
Born Feb. 21, 1816
Died Feb. 16, 1893
"Blessed are the dead which die
in the Lord."

Mallissa J. White
Born Apr. 10, 1840
Died June 27, 1904

Thomas G. White
Born Dec. 11, 1862
Died Mar. 25, 1865

Lavana C., Wife of
Thos. Shields
Born Feb. 26, 1843
Died Feb. 4, 1874

Eliza J. Pangle, Wife of
W. A. Haun
Born June 24, 1826
Died Apr. 14, 1864
"Gone to rest."

L. M. Haun
Co. C. 8th Tenn. Cav.
Son of I. P. & Mary Haun
Born Jan. 14, 1848
Died Nov. 13, 1864
"Death leaves a shining mark"

Johny R. Roddy, Son of
E. E. & B. M. Roddy
Born June 4, 1874
Died Dec. 9, 1874

Ralph Neal, Son of
K. B. & Mable Faris
Born Sept. 28, 1906
Died July 17, 1905
"Though cast down, Were not
forsaken, Though of mirled
not alone."

Isabel Fain Roddy
Feb. 14, 1842
Mar. 29, 1912
"In loveing memories of
our mother."

Walter Thos. Roddy
Born Oct. 27, 1881
Died Aug. 16, 1904
"Blessed are the pure in heart
for they shall see God."

Oppie G. Neal
Born - 17, 1866
Died May 18, 1903
"He believed and sleeps in Jesus"

Sarah White
Born & Died Jan. 23, 1827

Mariah White
Born May 31, 1816
Died June 7, 1816

Lucy Evans
Died Mar. 20, 1926
Age 24 yrs.

John W. Horton
Born July 5, 1879
Died Apr. 18, 1916
"Respected and loved by all
who knew him."

Tives Horton
Died Apr. 4, 1931
Age 19 yrs.

Little Luther Irvin Phillips
Born Dec. 11, 1911
Died Apr. 22, 1914
"Gone but not forgotten."

James Blevins
June 15, 1915
Feb. 15, 1917
"At Rest."

Mother
Maggie Mc Kinney
May 2, 1842
Oct. 6, 1912
"Gone but not forgotten."

R. H. Chestnut

Toney Kyle Jr.
Died Jan. 14, 1937
2 yr. 15 da.

Eddie Kyle
Died Oct. 14, 1932
Age 47 yrs. 2 mo. 23 da.

Kate Irvin
Died May 24, 1929
Aged 60 yrs.

Jeanette Gaines
Died Sept. 12, 1935
Age 59 yrs.

A. B. Gaines
Died May 20, 1927
Age 57 yrs.

Sallie J., Wife of
T. J. Talley
Oct. 27, 1882
July 2, 1918
"Gone but not forgotten."

Heir of Giles & Sarah Sanders
Died Mar. 8, 1888

W. R. Harmon
Co. A. 4th Tenn. Inf.

Kate I., Wife of
W. F. Harmon
Born Feb. 5, 1855

Sam Haun
Jan. 19, 1937

Enna V., Dau. of
J. A. & L. M. Lane
Born Oct. 10, 1904
Died Nov. 20, 1914
"Gone but not forgotten"

John A. Lane
Born Dec. 9, 1876
Died May 11, 1915

His Wife
Lizzie M. Lane
Born May 24, 1878

Landon C. White
Mar. 18, 1853
Jan. 29, 1924

His Wife
June 3, 1860

Samuel S. Smith
Died Nov. 10, 1931
Age 66yr. 8 mo. 2 da.

Coffman
East Gate Lodge 680 F & A M
William L. Coffman
May 11, 1864
Sept. 17, 1924

James Henard
Age 1 yr. 1 mo.

Clifford D. Dyer Jr.
Mar. 23, 1918
Apr. 3, 1918

Dyer child of Grace Dyer

Margarette W., Dau. of
J. B. & M. D. Harmon
Mar. 26, 1917
Jan. 21, 1923
"At Rest"

Madge D., Dau. of
J. B. & M. D. Harmon
Aug. 13, 1914
Apr. 26, 1916

John P. Horner
Died Aug. 27, 1936
Age 58 yr. 11mo. 13 da.

James Horner
May 5, 1931
Age 17 yr. 4 mo. 22 da.

HAMBLEN COUNTY
BENT CREEK CEMETERY
(Page 19)

James Horner
Died Feb. 7, 1937
Age 63

Child of Ben Estess
Authority by
Mr. Urnest Lane of
Whitesburg

Oliver W. Horner
Born July 25, 1922
Died Jan. 13, 1923

Clyde Brown
Died '37

Authority by Earnest Lane

Lyde Mae Goan
Died Apr. 27, 1933
Age 55 yr. 10 mo. 27 da.

William Murphy
Co. C. S. U. S.
Vol Inf.

L. Addie, Wife of
J. B. Dyer
Mar. 24, 1864
Aug. 29, 1911
"The Lord redeemeth the Soul
of his servants."

John W. Moore
June 24, 1838
Oct. 17, 1928

His Wife
Martha A. Moore
April 12, 1842
June 11, 1916

Dick Henderson
Aug. 25, 1848
Mar. 8, 1917

Curtis A. Lane
July 13, 1879
Jan. 8, 1919

Ruby Moore Morison
Oct. 19, 1898
Nov. 23, 1924

Infant Son of,
Ruby Morison
Nov. 8, 1924

Mable V. Haun
June 29, 1891
Sept. 2, 1923
"A link that links us to
Heaven."

Ruby L. Haun
Sept. 23, 1888
Jan. 4, 1914
"Resting in hope of a
glorious resurection."

Bess Haun, Wife of
Harvey S. Miller
Sept. 25, 1881
July 30, 1911
"Darling we miss Thee."

Senter M. Haun
Feb. 8, 1849
April 10, 1934

His Wife
Ophelia K. West Haun
Born July 11, 1857

Wilkins Kirkpatrick
July 23, 1854
Mar. 13, 1926

Mary Kirkpatrick
Dec. 11, 1850
Mar. 24, 1924

Martha R. Kirkpatrick
Oct. 13, 1857
Mar. 17, 1924

Georgia L. Moore Ball,
Dau. of George & Mary Moore
1895 - 1918

HAMBLEN COUNTY
BENT CREEK CEMETERY
(Page 20)

Georgie Louise, Dau. of
Morgan and Georgie Ball
Born May 4, 1918
Died July 22, 1918

Montie Feroe Quillen
Born Sept. 6, 1891
Died Oct. 2, 1924

Pleasant Lafayette Dyer
June 17, 1857
July 19, 1925

C. J. Horner
1880 -

His Wife
Cleo Hudson
1882 - 1928

J. W. Haun
Born Apr. 9, 1844
Died Feb. 23, 1914

His Wife
Mary E. Haun
Born June 1, 1832
Died Mar. 2, 1917
"Them also which sleep in Jesus will God
will God bring with him"

James P. Smith
Jan. 18, 1859
Nov. 30, 1922

His Wife
Sarah A. Moore
July 27, 1863
Mar. 16, 1914
"Peace sweet peace the gift
of God's love."

Maymie Beatrice Cutshaw
Dec. 6, 1893
Died Aug. 16, 1925

John Hurst
1843 - 1926

His Wife
Laura J. Hurst
1856 - 1925

Loula Cobble
Oct. 7, 1884
Aug. 1, 1928

Belle Tarter, Wife of
Claude Williams
Dec. 15, 1890
Died Sept. 19, 1935

Lila Welch
Born & Died Dec. 22, 1910

Howard Welch
Born & Died June 8, 1899

Welch
James D.
1867 - 1920

His Wife
Angeline M.
1869 - 1926

Martha Henard
Died Jan. 7, 1933
Age 39 yrs. 5 mo. 27 da.

Jesse R. Henard
July 29, 1924
July 28, 1925

Manerva J., Wife of
John B. Mc New
Born June 19, 1836
Died Oct. 24, 1905

Mary Benson
Died at W. M. Murdock
Aged about 75 yrs.

HAMBLEN COUNTY
BENT CREEK CEMETERY
(Page 21)

Maude, Wife of
Cain Duff
Born May 7, 1887
Died Apr. 26, 1910

Alpha, Wife of
Andrew Tarter
Born in Wythe Co. Va.
May 1, 1808
Died June 22, 1899
"Her ways are ways of pleasantness
and all her paths were paths
of peace."

Andrew, Son of H. &
Elizabeth Tarter
Born Sept. 8, 1888
Died Apr. 12, 1897

Father & Mother
William S. Pangle
Born Oct. 15, 1839
Died June 14, 1911

Harriet W. Cockreham
Born Jan. 3, 1832
Died July 26, 1906

Mary E. A. Morgan
Born July 27, 1840
Died Aug. 20, 1903

Jacob W. Pangle
Born May 22, 1867
Died July 4, 1933

Martha G., Dau. of
W. M. & E. William
Born Jan. 19, 1855
Died Feb. 3, 1884

W. Mc Kindrie Cobble
Born Apr. 13, 1867
Died Feb. 18, 1871
Aged 3 yrs. 10 mo. 5 da.

Thos. J. Cobble
Born July 30, 1837
Died Oct. 3, 1903

Charlotte J., Wife of
Thos. J. Cobble
Born Feb. 2, 1836
Died June 9, 1911

Jun Whitaker
(No record)

Sinda Whitaker
(No record)

L. V. Brewer, Wife of
Allen Brewer
Born Nov. 29, 1855
Died Jan. 22, 1917

Sidney Witt
Born Feb. 9, 1823
Died Mar. 9, 1892

Mary Wilson
Sept. 14, 1836
May 1, 1876

Nannie May, Dau. of
Chas. M. & Emma Taylor
Died Oct. 15, 1890
Age 1 mo.

J. H. York
Co. A 1st Tenn. L. A.
(Gov. marker)

Nannie S., Wife of
J. M. Brown
Born Nov. 25, 1859
Died May 11, 1884

R. Moore

A. L. Moore

HAMBLEN COUNTY
BENT CREEK CEMETERY
(Page 22)

Nannie P., Wife of
H. G. Austin
Born Sept. 22, 1854
Died Aug. 14, 1873

Sarah A. Smith
Born Dec. 9, 1833
Died July 12, 1898

George Smith
Born Feb. 5, 1828
Died May 17, 1900

William A. Ballard
Feb. 14, 1833
Oct. 30, 1865

Francis S. Ballard
Jan. 19, 1837
Married May 11, 1855

Isaac Haun
Born Dec. 6, 1829
Died Dec. 22, 1863
Erected by his brothers &
 sisters.

Jane White
Born Aug. 23, 1830
Died June 28, 1896

Infant son of, Geo. & Mary Moore
Died Oct. 22, 1903
Age 1 mo.

Virdie, Dau. of, Geo. & Mary Moore
Died Nov. 6, 1900
Age 2 mo.

Rev. Thos. J. Lane
Born Oct. 9, 1804
Died July 3, 1888

Vany Lane, Wife of Eld. Thos. J. Lane
Born Feb. 9, 1806
Died July 8, 1883

Eliza Emeline Lane
Born Mar. 2, 1833
Died Apr. 24, 1904

Dr. T. N. Horner
Born July 17, 1820
Died July 18, 1904

Elizabeth J., Wife of
Dr. T. N. Horner
Born Nov. 6, 1822
Died June 9, 1896

Garrett Lane
Born Nov. 30, 1834
Died July 22, 1900

Sarah A., Wife of
Garrett Lane
Apr. 8, 1841
Died June 16, 1913

John S. Lane
Born Feb. 13, 1805
Died Dec. 16, 1884

Elizabeth Lane
Born Oct. 28, 181?
Died July 27, 18-

Abraham Haun
Born Dec. 13, 1804
Died July 17, 1868

Nancy Haun
Born Sept. 16, 1806
Died June 4, 1890
Aged 83 yrs. 8 mo. 18 da.

Mollie L., Dau. of
P. W. & M. M. Horner
Born Aug. 29, 1869
Died May 4, 1870

Infant Dau. of
P. & E. Horner
Born Jan. 17, 1883

HAMBLEN COUNTY
BENT CREEK CEMETERY
(Page 23)

Thomas N., Son of
P. W. & M. M. Horner
Born Apr. 24, 1871
Died Oct. 24, 1871

Pleasant W. Horner
Feb. 26, 1846
Mar. 14, 1912

His Wife
Martha M. Philips
Feb. 9, 1845
Mar. 20, 1926
"Farewell dear Father, and
Mother, sweet thy rest."

Montgomery Beard
His Wife
Eliza Beard,
Died Jan. 21, 1918
Age 75 yrs.

In Memory of Martha L. Haun,
Consort of Joseph Haun
Born May 1808
Died Oct. 1874

Lillie J., Dau. of
Joseph Haun
Born July 27, 1874
Died Jan. 29, 1887
Erected by J. W. & M. Haun

Eliza A., Dau. of
Jas. & Fannie Haun
Born ----, 1827
Died Mar. 19, 1887

Lina Cooper
Co. H, 3 rd. N. C. Inf.
Gov. marker

Patrick Nenney
Departed this life
Apr. 28, 1824
Rev. Soldier

In Memory of
James L. Nenney
Who was born Oct. 19, 1811
And died Sept. 17, 1838

Thomas Roddy
Born June 18, 1830
Died May 10, 1886

Lydia Nenney Roddy
July 30, 1801
Jan. 20, 1887

Ella J. Roddy, Wife of
J. L. Miller
Born Oct. 10, 1863
Died Sept. 4, 1895

Elizabeth Roddy
Mar. 15, 1836
July 14, 1899

Sml. White
Born ----, 1751
Died Sept. 1804

In Memory of
Hannah White
Born Feb. 28, 1887
Died Mar. 28, 1838

John Coltharp
Died 1815
Aged 66 yr.

Elizabeth Smith
Born Oct. 22, 1795
Died Feb. 8, 1873
Aged 77 yrs. 3 mo. 16 da.

Here lies the body of
Wm. Horner Sen.
Was born Oct. 30, 1748
Died Oct. 12, 1824

Elizabeth Horner
Born Aug. 17--
Died Mar. 11, 1823

Joseph Deventer, Son of
C. M. & Elizabeth Haun Walker
Mar. 31, 1872
Apr. 25, 1932

Alex----- Mc Dona-----
Born 25th, July 1768
And died 3rd Sept. 1834
"This tribute of affection was
erected to his memory by his
----- and sons."

Geo. W. Dyer
Born Sept. 26, 1827
Died Feb. 24, 1896

Sarah Jane, Wife of
Geo. W. Dyer
Born Mar. 15, 1831
Died Apr. 5, 1909

Mary Louisa, Dau. of
G. W. & S. J. Dyer
Born Aug. 21, 1855
Died Sept. 17, 1857

J. H. X
May 1741

R. C. H.
1812
Kirkpatrick
(Old lettering ,all that
was legible.)

Marion Kirkpatrick
Born Mar. 9, 1862
Died Apr. 26, 1862

Martha Kirkpatrick
Born Nov. 15, 1855
Died Oct. 17, 1856

Harriett N., Wife of
P. M. Kirkpatrick
Born Feb. 22, 1823
Died Nov. 26, 1901
"She was the sunshine of our
home."

P. M. Kirkpatrick
Born Jan. 15, 1815
Died Mar. 21, 1890
"Each of us hopes to join
you on the beautiful heavenly
shore."

Father
William P. Rippetoe
Born Dec. 27, 1830
Died Apr. 11, 1862
Aged 31 yrs. 3 mo. 14 da.
"He fought in defense of
liberty and Union."
Erected by his son J. W.
Rippetoe

Father
George W. Rippetoe
Born Mar. 14, 1834
Died Feb. 22, 1902
Aged 67 yr. 11 mo. 8 da.
"His record was an honorable
one."
Erected by his son W. I.(?)
Rippetoe.

Eliza Courtney, Wife of
G. W. Rippetoe
Born Jan. 28, 1834
Died Oct. 31, 1918
Erected by J. W. Rippetoe

Our Father
Newton Lane
Born Nov. 19, 1829
Died June 30, 1896

HAMBLEN COUNTY
BENT CREEK CEMETERY
(Page 25)

"Our Mother"
Nancy C. Coffman, Wife of
Newton Lane
Born Apr. 5, 1841
Died Mar. 4, 1900

Elder Andrew Coffman
Born Dec. 22, 1784
Died Sept. 1, 1864
Aged 79 yrs. 8 mo. 8 da.

Nancy, Wife of
Elder A. Coffman
Born Jan. 23, 1783
Died Sept. 28, 1872
Aged 83 yrs. 8 mo. 5 da.

David D. Coffman
Was born —, 1821
Died Oct. 22, 1837(?)

Eliza Coffman
Was born Mar. 20, 1843
Died Aug. 9, 1852

Eli(?) Coffman

Isaac Lane
Born Aug. 8, 1788
Died —— 21, 1866

Rebecca Lane
Was born Aug. the 4, 1790
And died Sept. 6, 1841

Etta Coffman
1858 - 1876

Wm. H. Coffman
Born Feb. 20, 1819
Married Mary Anne White
Apr. 14, 1840
Died Aug. 15, 1880 at
2 & 15 minutes A. M.
Age 61 yrs. 5 mo. 25 da.

Mary Ann, Wife of
W. E. Coffman
Born Jan. 20, 1823
Died June 10, 1882 at 9:00 P. M.
Aged 59 yrs. 4 mo. 20 da.

Mary Ann, Wife of
Wm. H. Coffman
Born Jan. 20, 1823
Died June 10, 1882 at
9:00 P. M.
Aged 59 yrs. 4 mo. 20 da.

Mollie Johnson, Wife of
W. L. Coffman
May 18, 1874
Dec. 14, 1894

Lucy Annis, Beloved wife of
Gustave Murmann
Jan. 20, 1861
Apr. 9, 1892

S. Rhea Estes
1900-1902

Sam Estes
Feb. 13, 1860
Nov. 14, 1920

Alice Estes
Oct. 27, 1859

Ordley(?) D. Estes
June 5, 1896
May 20, 1898

Jessie J. Estes
June 3, 1888
Apr. 20, 1898

Gracie Ruth, Dau. of
P. R. & F. V. Estes
Born Oct. 3, 1896
Died Feb. 19, 1900

Nora A., Wife of
J. M. Burchell
Born May 3, 1870
Died June 25, 1896

HAMBLEN COUNTY
BENT CREEK CEMETERY
(Page 26)

Catherine Estes
Born Nov. 28, 1819
Died June 22, 1883

Asa Estes
Born Apr. 10, 1817
Died Apr. 13, 1896

John T. Estes
Oct. 25, 1895
Dec. 12, 1895

Robert B. Estes
Feb. 7, 1843

    His Wife
Laurha M. Brown
Feb. 3, 1850
Oct. 10, 1917

Penelope C. Pangle, Wife of
Stephen C. Pangle
Born Apr. 30, 1828
Died June 1896

HAMBLEN COUNTY
CEDAR CREEK CEMETERY
(Page 1)

Cedar Creek Cemetery is one mile and half north of Dickerson road crossing; to the left going east of Russellville.
Copied by Rebecca Colyer, Russellville, Tennessee May 4, 1937
44 graves marked with field stones or stakes
8 unmarked graves

Katherine, Dau. of
Lewis & Mary Gibson
Born Aug. 17, 1915
Died Oct. 11, 1919
"Budded on earth to bloom
in Heaven."

George Lawson
Born Mar. 16, 1833
Died Nov. 26, 1913
"Sleep in Jesus blessed sleep
which none ever make to sleep."

Mary E. Lawson
Born Aug. 6, 1842
Died Apr. 25, 1919

Omar V. Vineyard
Born Dec. 16, 1893
Died Dec. 23, 1914

Ronald E. Vineyard
Born Jan. 2, 1900
Died Nov. 8, 1908

Jas. L. Vineyard
Born May 12, 1866
Died Aug. 7, 1909

Carson R. Vineyard
Born Feb. 7, 1904
Died May 31, 1913

Alexander Mc Carver
Born Oct. 24, 1812
Died Mar. 21, 1896

Robert E. Jones
Born May 20, 1886
Died July 8, 1900
Age 20 yr. 1 mo. 18 da.

"Gone to Meet Him"
Margaret Ann Wright
Born Dec. 26, 1826
Died Jan. 12, 1895

W. A. Wright
Born May 24, 1827

Thomas N. Robertson
Born July 10, 1860
Died Aug. 9, 1893

Chapisty Davis
Born Apr. 24, 1864
Died Nov. 11, 1866

"Father"
Ben J. Davis
Born Jan. 20, 1784
Died Mar. 31, 1860

In Memory of Sarah G., Dau. of
T. G. & D. A. Beal
Born Sept. 25, 1856
Died Dec. 27, 1856

In Memory of Louisna, Wife of
T. G. & G Beal (?)
Born Sept. 27, 1893
Died May 15, 1802

In Memory of George G.,
Son of T. G. & Delia Beal
Born Mar. 12, 1867
Died Aug. 7, 1818
"At Rest"

Sallie E., Wife of
I. R. Dyer
Born Jan. 23, 1866
Died Feb. 30, 1912

C. C. Trent
Born Jan. 18, 1878
Died Sept. 20, 1928
Killed in the field by a
    brute.
"Gone but not forgotten."

Nellie Pearl, Wife of
John M. Jenkins
Born Jan. 16, 1886
Died June 28, 1906

Ida Miter, Dau. of
H. O. & Thursa Wright
Born Sept. 28, 1877
Died Jan. 7, 1897
"We expect to meet her."

Haley Bolen
Died Dec. 13, 1844

Willis Alberta, Dau. of
W. T. & E. B. Hurst
Born Dec. 1, 1897
Died July 13, 1898
"Gone but not forgotten."

Mary Rebecca Hurst
Born Aug. 6, 1890
Died Dec. 21, 1909
"Beautiful Spirit my work is done."

William Joseph, Son of
T. A. & Kate Talley
Born Mar. 7, 1911
Died Mar. 23, 1911
"Asleep in Jesus."

W. T. Hurst
Born Mar. 16, 1850
Died Feb. 7, 1914
"He giveth his beloved sleep."

A. J. Cole
Born in 1857
Died April 9, 1922
Age 65 yrs.

    His Wife

Clemmie Potter Cole
Born Mar. 4, 1846

John Frank Cole
Born in 1880
Died April 3, 1922
Age 45 yrs.

    "Father"
Ben Potter
Born May 10, 1840
Died Nov. 10, 1927

Oninie A. Potter
Born Aug. 20, 1921
Died Aug. 26, 1930
"He was the sunshine of our
home."

"Our Darling Babe"
Annie Lee, Dau. of
J. & S. E. Blevins
Died June 18, 1894
Age 12 yr. 4 mo.

Paul L. Hugglbs, Son of
F. & Daven Potter
Born Dec. 28, 1880
Died Nov. 15, 1925

Margarette Mc Garver, Wife of
P. Grass
Born Apr. 25, 1844
Died June 15, 1910
"Gone but not forgotten."

Lampa G. Mc Garver
Born June 21, 1866
Died Sept. 25, 1867

46

HAMBLEN COUNTY
CEDAR GROVE CEMETERY
(Page1)

The church yard of Cedar Grove Baptist Church, located about one
half a mile east of Silver City, a community about five miles south
of Russellville on the road leading from Russellville to the State
Fish Hatchery, in what has long been known as the Springvale section.
There are approximately 100 unmarked graves.
Copied by Rebecca Colyer, May 21, 1937

Nancy A. Doggett
Born Jan. 26, 1846
Died July 9, 1903
Wife of
Wife of W. A. Doggett
Born June 26, 1817
Died Mar. 28, 1897

John Carson
Born Oct. 1, 1820
Died July 11, 1896

Matilda A. Carson, Wife of
J. Carson
Born April 9, 1823
Died Oct. 22, 1896

Susan C., Wife of
James N. Cunningham
Born June 3, 1820
Died Aug. 25, 1896
Age 76 yr. 2 mo. 22 da.

Elmetta Pearl Robertson
Born Nov. 15, 1894
Died June 29, 1896

Sussan J. Doggett
Born Oct. 1, 1847
Died Feb. 2, 1881

John W. Doggett
Born Mar. 29, 1852
Died June 19, 1880

Jessie E. Doggett
April 29, 1854
Feb. 26, 1879

Mother
Rosa J. Hamm
Born June 29, 1879
Died July 13, 1936

Father
W. T. Hamm
Nov. 17, 1875
June 8, 1921
"Resting in hope of a
glorious resurrection."

John W. Shippley
Born June 7, 1846
Died June 9, 1881
"Not last but gone before."

Mary Ann Robertson, Wife of
J. W. Shippley
Feb. 7, 1845
Oct. 6, 1910
"The gates of Heaven for her
shall open wide."

George E. Shippley
Born June 25, 1877
Died Sept. 4, 1915
"Gone but not forgotten."

Wade Marshall
Born April 5, 1830
Died April 7, 1901
"Sleep soldier sleep, thy
warfare is over."

Harriet E., Wife of
W. M. Marshall
Sept. 2, 1832
June 10, 1882

HAMBLEN COUNTY
CEDAR GROVE CEMETERY
(Page 2)

Thomas Isaac Marshall
Born Dec. 11, 1885
Died Mar. 11, 1904
"Resting in hope of a
glorious resurrection."

Mother
Sarah E. Estes
Aug. 27, 1871

Father
Charles H. Estes
Born Sept. 12, 1866
Died Aug. 7, 1934
"Gone but not forgotten."

James V. Estes
Born Apr. 9, 1899
Died Oct. 6, 1899
"Our Darling"

Oscar D. Estes
Born Jan. 9, 1902
Died Oct. 9, 1902
"Our Darling"

Mary Anderson, Wife of
James Estes
Born Nov. 30, 1834
Died Dec. 21, 1918
"Gone but not forgotten."

James Estes
Born Apr. 6, 1889
Died Apr. 9, 1904
"He fought in the defence
of liberty and union."

James Rhoades
Died June 30, 1887
Age 75 yrs.

Jane Vann, Wife of
James Rhoades
Died Sept. 1895
Age about 65 yrs.

Hazel, Dau. of
S. P. & M. Barding
Wife of Ike Wilson
Born Feb. 18, 1895
Died Jan. 24, 1914

S. P. Barding
Born Jan. 6, 1850
Died June 27, 1916

Martha, Wife of
S. P. Barding
Born July 3, 1851
Died June 18, 1912

Minnie, Dau. of
S. P. & Martha Barding
Born Feb. 4, 1891
Died June 18, 1912

"Our Darling"
Florence Barding
Born Jan. 1, 1892
Died May 3, 1911

Our Daughter
Dixie P. Barding
Born Oct. 7, 1883
Died Mar. 6, 1904
"At Rest"

Little W. C. Barding
Born Feb. 9, 1907
Died Apr. 27, 1911
"The Lord gave and the Lord
taketh away."

Cinda, Wife of
R. F. Barding
Born June 11, 1891
Died Feb. 3, 1930

Mother
Lula Barding, Wife of
Fred Shelton
Born Feb. 29, 187(?)
Died Mar. 18, 1926
"At Rest"

HAMBLEN COUNTY
CEDAR GROVE CEMETERY
(Page 3)

W. T. Marshall
Born Jan. 22, 1847
Died May 5, 1914

Mary J. Marshall
Born Dec. 11, 1849
Died Feb. 9, 1918

Kate Marshall
Born Nov. 28, 1871
Died Oct. 20, 1933

John B. Marshall
Born Nov. 12, 1867
Died Mar. 21, 1927

James Marshall
Born June 1, 1822
Died June 18, 1926
"The gates of Heaven for
him have opened wide."

Matilda A., Wife of
James Marshall
Born Oct. 21, 1831
Died June 28, 1902
Age 71 yrs. 8 mo. 7 da.

Temple Melton
Died Jan. 19, 1904
Age 30 yr.
"Forever with the Lord."

J. S. Melton
Died May 20, 1891
Age 65 yr.
"Not dead, but asleep"

Annie Melton
Born Nov. 10, 1869
Died Aug. 12, 1901
"Gone but not forgotten."

Lizzie Ann Burns
Born June 6, 1848
Died Feb. 16, 1917
Age 68 yr. 8 mo. 10 da.
"Thy will be done."

Rebecca Mc Pheron, Wife of
G. W. Courtney
Born June 7, 1881
Died July 28, 1900
"The gates of Heaven for her
shall open wide."

Laura A., Dau. of
G. W. & Rebecca Courtney
Born Nov. 17, 1868
Died Dec. 27, 1894
"Farewell dear sister, sweet
thy rest."

Mollie E. Courtney, Wife of
L. N. Pangle
Born Aug. 24, 1862
Died Oct. 4, 1893
"Resting in hope of a glorious
resurrection."

Sussian R., Dau. of
G. W. & Rebecca Courtney
Born Feb. 23, 1867
Died June 19, 1891
"God's finger touched her and
she slept."

William Loyd, Son of
J. M. & C. E. Fawner
Born Oct. 14, 1901
Died Aug. 7, 1903

Joseph M. Fawner
March 1, 1867

His Wife
Catherine E. Hann
Born Feb. 22, 1859
Died Feb. 8, 1929

Issac M. Fawner
Born Sept. 14, 1890
Died June 23, 1931

Issac W. Fawner
Born June 15, 1844
Died Sept. 29, 1922

HAMBLEN COUNTY
CEDAR GROVE CEMETERY
(Page 4)

His Wife
Sarah J. Fawner
Birth Sept. 21, 1849

Alexander Haun
Sept. 5, 1847
Apr. 12, 1900

Alexander Haun
Born Dec. 3, 1805
Died Nov. 9, 1885

Elizabeth, Wife of
Alexander Haun
Born Oct. 5, 1813
Died May 3, 1892
m

Emley H., Dau. of
H. & E. Thomason
Born Aug. 17, 1872
Died May 4, 1877

Enoch Marshall
Born Sept. 29, 1814
Died Dec. 11, 1881

His Wife
Sarah M. Lane
Born April 15, 1815
Died Nov. 26, 1891

HAMBLEN COUNTY
CREECH'S CHAPEL CEMETERY
(Page 1)

Creech's Chapel Methodist Church

Located one and one-half miles north of Russellville on the Whitesburg - Three Springs road.

There are about 275 graves marked with field stones or stakes, and about 50 unmarked graves.

Copied by Rebecca Colyer, Russellville, Tennessee, May 12, 1937

Maggie Pless, Dau. of
Samuel & Mary Fields
Born Sept. 9, 1877
Died Apr. 19, 1913
"Sleeping in the arms of
Jesus."

Dannie Gandler
Born Dec. 10, 1879
Died May 16, 1914
"Asleep in Jesus"

Jacob Bowman
Born May 25, 1840
Died Feb. 24, 1905
"May he rest in peace."

His Wife
Lauginda Bowman
Born July 29, 1846
Died April 12, 1923
"Her end was peace."

Carl T. Cooper
Born Feb. 28, 1898
Died Nov. 25, 1908
"Our Darling."

James Adams
Born June 22, 1845
Died Apr. 18, 1916
"Farewell my family all,
From you a father God doth call"

In loving Memory of
Fannie Victoria, Dau. of
W. H. & E. C. Johnson
Born Oct. 7, 1905
Died Aug. 18, 1906
Age 10 mo. 11 da.

J. F. Harmon
Born Jan. 31, 1845
Died Oct. 3, 1930
"In God's Care."

B. A. Harmon
Died Aug. 28, 1927
Age 79 yr. 10 mo. 7 da.
(undertakers marker)

Samuel C. Williams
Born Mar. 5, 1858
Died Dec. 7, 1894
"To angels form thy spirits,
Grown, Thy God has claimed
thee to his own."

Carrie White, Dau. of
Mr. & Mrs. Frank Gallaher
Born June 17, 1917
Died Aug. 11, 1918
"Father and Mother claimed her,
The world claimed her, But a
higher power say's she's mine."

Glenn M. Williams, Wife of
Osgar Thompson
Born June 22, 1892
Died June 20, 1927
"God's finger touched her and
she slept."

Kathern E., Wife of
W. A. Pendergrass Sr.
Born Jan. 9, 1851
Died Jan. 25, 1911

W. A. Pendergrass Sr.
Born Oct. 12, 1855
Died Mar. 24, 1936

Infant Son of
W. A. & L. D. Pendergrass
Died Aug. 13, 1920
"Christ loved him and took
him away."

Lucy Pendergrass
Born Dec. 12, 1875
Died Feb. 7, 1935

Ruth M., Dau. of
C. H. & O. L. C. Shipley
Born Nov. 6, 1910
Died Mar. 14, 1913
"Sleep on dear Ruth, and
take thy rest, God called you
He knows best."

Father
James H. Creech
Born Nov. 23, 1846
Died Aug. 17, 1913

Mother
Mollie E., Wife of
J. H. Creech
Born June 8, 1850
Died Jan. 16, 1910
"Gone but not forgotten."
(Double rock)

Evelyn, Dau. of
J. M. & E. J. Young
Born May 19, 1904
Died Mar. 12, 1905

Audley J., Son of
J. H. & M. E. Creech
Born Mar. 24, 1883
Died July 2, 1906

Frank E., Son of
J. H. & M. E. Creech
Born Oct. 10, 1888
Died Jan. 31, 1907
"The gates of Heaven for them
have opened wi de."

L. E. Couch
Born Jan. 19, 1877
Died Nov. 1, 1923

H. W. Couch
Born Feb. 9, 1857
"Blessed are the dead which
die in the Lord."
(Double rock)

Frank, Son of
Samuel & Mary Fields
Born Oct. 12, 1893
Died July 19, 1915
"Gone but not forgotten."

Rosa Lee, Wife of
G. A. Bettis
Born Aug. 31, 1889
Died May 17, 1912
"At Rest"
"The gates of Heaven for her
opened wide."

Minnie G. Fields
Died Aug. 17, 1910
Age 19 yr. 8 mo. 14 da.
"Gone Home."

Samuel Fields
Born July 1, 1855
Died June 29, 1923
"Gone but not forgotten."

Mary J., Wife of
Samuel Fields
Born Apr. 5, 1848
Died May 16, 1910
"Gone but not forgotten."

Violet Hann
Died Jan. 17, 1909
Age 22 yr. 7 mo. 13 da.
"At Rest"
Put up by Samuel Fields.

HAMBLEN COUNTY
CREECH'S CHAPEL CEMETERY
(Page 3)

R. L. Livesay
Born Apr. 9, 1873
Died May 21, 1896
"We will meet thee again."

Infant of
Mr. & Mrs. E. A. Fields
Born May 3, 1916
Died May 8, 1916

Peter Epps
Died Apr. 11, 1904
Age 74 yrs.
"Gone but not forgotten"

Sarah, Wife of Peter Epps
Died Sept. 17, 1915
Age 75 yrs.
"At Rest"

     Mother
Fannie Horner
1873 - 1919
(Erected by Ross Horner)

Mary E., Dau. of
R. M. & K. D. Shipley
Born July 30, 1912
Died July 8, 1913
"A precious one from us
has gone."

Mrs. Nellie Kesterson
Died Mar. 3, 1931
Age 51 yr. 9 mo. 14 da.
(undertakers marker)

O. K. Kesterson
Died Feb. 14, 1934
Age 55 yrs.
(undertakers marker)

Millie B., Son of
O. R. & G. A. Walker
Born July 14, 1914
Died Aug. 14, 1915
"Suffer little children to
come unto me."

Paul F. Epperson
Born Jan. 26, 1906
Died Oct. 26, 1922
"May he rest in peace."

"Come Ye Blessed"
Willie H. Epperson
Born June 30, 1887
Died July 24, 1920
"Gone but not forgotten."

Edd Horner
Born July 10, 1893
Died May 14, 1922
"In God's Care."

Roy G. Yount
Born Jan. 7, 1928
Died Jan. 10, 1928
"Asleep in Jesus."

Ruby F., Wife of
Evard Yount
Born Oct. 22, 1905
Died June 9, 1930
"She is not dead but sleepeth"

Charlsie Janet Creech (?)
Died Dec. 1, 1936
(undertakers marker)

George W. Stubblefield
Born 1868
(Dead but not date given)

     His Wife
Neva Stubblefield
Born 1869
Died 1919
"Gone but not forgotten."

Rhoda, Wife of J. M. White
Born Feb. 24, 1845
Died June 2, 1898
     "Our Mother"

HAMBLEN COUNTY
CREECH'S CHAPEL CEMETERY
(Page 4)

John Willard Long
Died May 25, 1936
Age 5 yr. 5 da.
(undertakers marker)

Cecil Long
Died Dec. 29, 1935
Age 29 yr. 3 mo. 12 da.
(undertakers marker)

Lucy Heck
Born May 8, 1871
Died Dec. 24, 1909

Sarah Jane Heck
Born Feb. 5, 1847
Died April 13, 1921
"Asleep in Jesus."

Nathaniel R. Heck
Born June 2, 1843
Died Jan. 19, 1927
"Asleep in Jesus."

Son of G. W. & C. L. Long
Born Dec. 6, 1898
Died Feb. 14, 1901
"Asleep in Jesus."

Wilbur Talley
Born July 21, 1928
Died Jan. 5, 1929
"Asleep in Jesus."

Bertha Talley
Born Mar. 1, 1891
Died Mar. 16, 1923

Ronald Gene Ballard
Died Mar. 21, 1931
Age 1 mo. 12 da.
(undertakers marker)

M. G., Dau. of
J. H. & B. N. Harris
Born Dec. 1, 1899
Died Sept. 20, 1902

M. M., Dau. of
J. H. & B. N. Harris
Born Jan. 3, 1902
Died Dec. 20, 1902

Murl White
Born Jan. 29, 1897
Died June 10, 1923

Gurtrude White
Born Sept. 12, 1893
Died Mar. 30, 1913

Karl White
Born Jan. 29, 1897
Died Jan. 30, 1897

Infant Son of
E. C. & Luda Y. White
Born Mar. 2, 1901
Died Mar. 8, 1901
"Budded on earth to bloom
in Heaven."

Mary R., Wife of
J. H. Dodson
Born Dec. 25, 1858
Died Sept. 28, 1889
"The gates of Heaven have
opened wide for her."

Frankie, Son of
G. C. & S. E. Beckner
Born Sept. 27, 1888
Died Mar. 29, 1889

Mattie B., Wife of
R. Y. Williams
Born Oct. 18, 1888
Died Jan. 9, 1911
"Farewell, dear wife sweet
thy rest."

Loyd H., Son of
R. Y. & H. B. Williams
Born & Died Jan. 3, 1911

Catherine, Wife of
Robert Williams
Born Apr. 4, 1836
Died June 3, 1908
"The gates of heaven for her
have opened wide."

Hannah M., Dau. of
J. H. & M. Williams
Born Oct. 19, 1884
Died May 12, 1887

Joseph S. Ballard
Born Sept. 30, 1836
Died Jan. 9, 1915

Martha M. Ballard
Born Jan. 12, 1849
Died June 12, 1917
"Earth has no sorrow that
Heaven cannot heal."
(Double rock)

B. A. Creech
Born 1817 -

G. N. Creech
Born Feb. 6, 1854
Died Mar. 4, 1904
"God's finger touched him
and he slept."

Mollie E. Walker, Wife of
G. N. Creech
Born Aug. 25, 1858
Died May 30, 1909
"Thy trials ended thy rest won."

Mattie L. Creech
Born July 14, 1875
Died Oct. 31, 1916
"Safe in the arms of Jesus."

Landon M. Cooper
Born Jan. 6, 1860
Died July 26, 1899

Lucy E. Cooper
Born July 7, 1861
Died July 11, 1922
(Double rock)

Carl D. Cooper
Born Apr. 1, 1892
Died July 27, 1899

Elizabeth Woods
Died Aug. 1886

George R. Cooper
Born Feb. 15, 1885
Died Mar. 15, 1885

Elmira A. Parvin
Born Mar. 28, 1848
Died Feb. 24, 1893
"Sweet be thy slumber."

Henry C. Marshall
Born Oct. 19, 1893
Died May 10, 1897

Effie Mae, Dau. of
F. M. & J. S. Read
Born Oct. 4, 1888
Died June 5, 1893

Arthur T. Read
Born Dec. 25, 1889
Died Sept. 25, 1895
"Safe in the arms of Jesus."

F. M. Read
Born May 9, 1844
Died Jan. 1, 1921
"He that ever cometh shall
inherit all things."

Infant of
Mr. & Mrs. H. L. Read
Died Sept. 28, 1925
(undertakers marker)

HAMBLEN COUNTY
CREECH'S CHAPEL CEMETERY
(Page 6)

Jessie Kirkpatrick Read
Died Sept. 22, 1928
Age 24 yrs. 6 mo. 29 da.
(undertakers marker)

Hugh B. Marshall
Born Feb. 13, 1903
Died Feb. 18, 1903

Aleda A. Marshall
Born May 2, 1907
Died Feb. 5, 1919

Earnest E. Marshall
Born June 23, 1916
Died Feb. 5, 1919

Alford V. Marshall
Born Aug. 25, 1904
Died Mar. 4, 1919

Wilford A. Marshall
Born Dec. 19, 1900
Died July 2, 1926

Nannie Fawbush
Born Jan. 10, 1915
Died April 17, 1935
"In God's Care."

Susan E. Knight
Born July 24, 1834
Died Nov. 28, 1912
"Gone but not forgotten."

Rutledge Marshall
Born July 19, 1834
Died Apr. 3, 1908

C. B. Moore
Died July 14, 1934
Age 43 yr. 6 mo. 23 da.
(undertakers marker)

Anderson Long
Born Apr. 18, 1827
Died Feb. 15, 1923

Fannie Long
Born Nov. 13, 1844
Died Apr. 14, 1916
"Resting in hope of a glorious
resurrection."
(Double rock)

Wm. Price
Co. H. 3 Tenn. Inf.
Born Sept. 27, 1828
Died Mar. 18, 1900

Hurbert W. Creech
Born July 21, 1892
Died April 11, 1930

B. A. Creech
Born Aug. 9, 1870
Died Mar. 11, 1921

Myrtle Creech
Born Feb. 10, 1875

W. L. Messick
Born Mar. 9, 1869
Died July 22, 1906

Josephine, Wife of
W. L. Messick
Born May 29, 1867
Died Oct. 20, 1929
"At Rest"

Ida Louise Lee
Born Aug. 15, 1922
Died July 11, 1924

Billie Woods
Born May 31, 1927
Died Oct. 18, 1927
"Budded on earth to bloom
in Heaven."

Oscar D. Dellias
Born Mar. 13, 1901
Died Dec. 15, 1928

Domenic Dellias
1862 - 1935
(Double rock)

Polly A. Dellias
1866 -
(still living)

Margarette E., Wife of
Garret L. Read
Born Aug. 29, 1843

Garret L. Read
Born Aug. 26, 1820
Died Jan. 19, 1897
"He sleepeth nearer my God
to Thee." "Resting in hope
of a glorious resurection."
(Double stone.)

John W. Woods
Died Dec. 21, 1880
Age 2 yr. 21 da.

In Memory of C. A. Woods
Born Jan. 17, 1811
Died 26th of Jan. 1811

D. Woods
Died July 5, 1882

J. C. Woods
Died July 6, 1885

W. A. Woods
Died Aug. 10, 1886

Francis Marion Acuff
Born Nov. 8, 1846

Liza J., Wife of Wm. White
Born May 23, 1851
Died May 12, 1885

B. A. Taylor

W. M. Taylor

Wm. G. Bentley
Born Aug. 14, 1816
Died Jan. 31, 1897

J. W. Knight
Born Dec. 29, 1876
Died May 14, 1912

D. E. Campbell
Born Dec. 4, 1840
Died May 8, 1885
"Blessed are the dead which
die in the Lord."

Infant child of
R. E. & D. E. Campbell

Joe W. Long
Born Oct. 30, 1858
Died May 1, 1930

Rebecca White
Born Feb. 26, 1812
Departed this life July 18, 1898

William A. Dickerson
Died Jan. 26, 1934
Age 65 yrs.
(undertakers marker)

W. J. Whitaker
Died June 13, 1877

Elizabeth, Wife of
John Whitaker
Born June 30, 1836
Died June 21, 1877

Maggie, Wife of
L. C. White
Born June 19, 1857
Died Feb. 1, 1887

Hattie, Dau. of
L. C. & M. R. White
Born Apr. 9, 1880
Died May 26, 1880

HAMBLEN COUNTY
CREECH'S CHAPEL CEMETERY
(Page 8)

Birdie, Dau. of
L. C. & M. R. White
Born Aug. 29, 1881
Died May 18, 1893

Alice L. Garry
Born June 21, 1872
Died Sept. 25, 1887
"Like the dove to the ark
Thou hast flown to thy Rest."

Mollie R., Wife of
L. C. White
Born Feb. 15, 1857
Died Mar. 17, 1883

HAMBLEN COUNTY
DODSON CEMETERY
(Page 1)

Located one-half mile east of Bright's Mill on the road leading
to Russellville.

There are 18 graves marked with field stone or stakes, and 2 unmarked graves.

Copied by Rebecca Colyer, Russellville, Tennessee, May 4, 1937

Horse Lee, Son of
S. L. & J. D. McCarver
Born Aug. 4, 1903
Died Mar. 3, 1904
"Our Loved One."

Louis Howery
Born Feb. 22, 1811
Died June 29, 1887

Albert M., Son of
A. T. & C. E. Howery
Born Sept. 7, 1877
Died Sept. 28, 1877

Adellia, Dau. of
A. T. & C. E. Howery
Born Dec. 25, 1867
Died Feb. 20, 1879

J. Will, Son of
A. T. & C. E. Howery
Born May 8, 1879
Died Oct. 25, 1900
"At Rest"

Allen T. Howery
Born May 13, 1839
Died Mar. 3, 1901
"At Rest"

Elizabeth Howery
Born July 4, 1845
Died Apr. 12, 1927
"At Rest"

Luda M., Wife of
T. E. Amis
Born Nov. 29, 1866
Died July 26, 1904

Roy D., Son of
J. S. & A. L. Currier
Born Nov. 24, 1922
Died Aug. 9, 1907
"Budded on earth to bloom
in Heaven."

Allen T. Currier
Born July 10, 1892
Died July 28, 1915
Rev. 21:4

In Memory of Julia P., Wife of
Bubell T. Foster
Born Apr. 22, 1857
Died Nov. 18, 1878
Age 21 yr. 6 mo. 26 da.
"Gone home to rest."

Elisha Dodson
Born Nov. 1, 1801
Died June 17, 1874
Age 73 yr. 5 mo. 16 da.

James Dodson
Born Jan. 10, 1824
Died Mar. 4, 1885
Erected by N. A. Dodson

His Wife
Narcissus A. Dodson
Born Jan. 28, 1831
Died Mar. 14, 1914
"Gone home to rest ."

Lenah E. Dodson
Born July 25, 1886
Died July 19, 1888

Mary P. McCarver
Born Nov. 1855
Died May 1863

S. J. Mc Carver
Born May 1830
Died May 10, 1864
(Double slab)

Obediah Robertson
Born June 2, 1840
Died Apr. 4, 1877

Nancy J. Robertson
Born June 28, 1840
Died Aug. 23, 1887

Lillan M. Cozart
Born Mar. 4, 1874
Died Nov. 3, 1879

Charlie Cozart
Born May 2, 1879
Died Oct. 2, 1880

James H. Cozart
Born Nov. 3, 1852
Died Apr. 11, 1886

Lamina Mc Carver Jr.
Died Aug. 30, 1837
Age 3 yr. 11 mo. 5 da.

William Robertson
Born Mar. 12, 1801
Died Feb. 22, 1879
"He is at rest with his Savior."

Mary Robertson
Born Aug. 23, 1808
Died Sept. 29, 1880
"She was a pure good woman."

Derbby A., Wife of J. D. Robertson
Born Feb. 7, 1855
Died June 30, 1888

John D. Robertson
Born Oct. 9, 1850
Died June 23, 1888

Mary E., Dau. of
J. D. & D. A. Robertson
Born May 10, 1877
Died July 4, 1887

J. C., Infant Son of
J. D. & D. A. Robertson
Born Jan. 15, 1882
Died July 20, 1887

James D. Robertson
Born Mar. 7, 1827
Died Sept. 7, 1908
"The gates of Heaven for him shall open wide."

Rev. William E. D. Jones
Born Mar. 12, 1829
Died July 30, 1908
"He is at rest with his Savior." "Peace be to his dust till we meet again."

"At Rest"
Marian G. Robertson, Wife of
Rev. W. D. Johns
Born Apr. 7, 1834
Died Mar. 3, 1911
"The gates of Heaven to her have opened wide."
"Our Mother"

"At Rest"
Joseph E. Johns
Born Mar. 22, 1862
Died Apr. 12, 1882
"He died as he lived trusting in the Lord."

HAMBLEN COUNTY
DOVER CEMETERY
(Page 1)

The church yard of Dover Prebyterian Church, located six miles
southeast of Morristown. Turn to the right off the Morristown to
Russellville pike at Barton Springs, and go east two miles. Part of
the ground was donated by Rev. William Sample, and part was bought from
Mr. Morgan by four men belonging to the church, it now all belongs to
the church.There are about 67 graves marked with field stones or stakes
and about 23 unmarked graves.
Copied by Rebecca Colyer, Russellville, Tenn. April 24, 1937

S. D. Jones
Born June 3, 1858
Died July 28, 1883
He founded the church
Dec. 5, 1883, and remained
till death.

Rev. William Sample
Born Sept. 30, 1803
Died Aug. 28, 1880

His Wife
Sarah E. Silvers
Born Nov. 27, 1845 —
"Truth was their motto, in
God their trust."
(Double rock)

Lara C. Hull
Born July 16, 1871
Died June 13, 1918

W. A. Hull
Born July 23, 1827
Died Feb. 6, 1906

Jane Mc Donald, Wife of
W. A. Hull
Born Oct. 27, 1828
Father - Mother
(Double rock)

Alice Cornelia, Dau. of
W. A. Hull
Died Nov. 10, 1876
Age 8 yr. 4 mo. 10 da.

Margarette, Dau. of
W. A. & J. Hull
Died July 3, 1875
Age 3 yr. 11 mo. 17 da.

In Memory of John Mc Hull
Died Nov. 7, 1874
Age 25 yr. 4 mo. 22 da.

Mary J., Wife of
M. J. Purkey
Born Oct. 30, 1850
Died June 25, 1881
"Seperation is our lot,
Meeting is our hope."

Crofford Hull
Born Feb. 22, 1857
Died Oct. 5, 1887
"At Rest"

James Hull
Born Jan. 9, 1863
Died Jan. 19, 1889

Nellie J. Purkey
Born Nov. 11, 1875
Died June 15, 1897
"Gone to Rest"

Elizabeth, Wife of
William Ingle
Born Mar. 18, 1837
Died May 12, 1887
"The gates of Heaven to her
shall open wide."

Milburn C. Dickerson
Born Oct. 28, 1859
Died Apr. 29, 1887

Mary J. Dickerson
Born Apr. 7, 1844
Died Aug. 30, 1917
"Faithful to her trust even
unto death."

Charles C. Dickerson
Born Jan. 23, 1834
Died June 18, 1876
"Gone but not forgotten."

Abraham Silvers
Born Mar. 31, 1799
Died Nov. 18, 1888
"Safe in the arms of Jesus."

Dellilah, Wife of
Abraham Silvers
Born Oct. 1806
Died Feb. 24, 1891
"Farewell dear Mother, sweet
thy rest."

Son of C. M. & H. A. Trobough
Born Dec. 5, 1880
Died Aug. 13, 1883
"A little flower of love that
blossomed but to die, Trans-
planted now above, To bloom
with God of Love."

Martha J., Wife of
John Y. Staples
Born Apr. 28, 1838
Died Dec. 31, 1884
"Gone but not forgotten."

Jesse Hubert, Son of
H. A. & S. C. Stewart
Born Sept. 11, 1890
Died Oct. 8, 1890

Rogers
H. F. Rogers
Born Sept. 6, 1868
Died Nov. 23, 1932

William Brittion
Born Feb. 2, 1850
Died May 28, 1930

His Wife
Liddie Brittion
Born Oct. 11, 1855
Died Apr. 29, 1925

Infant Son of
J. E. & N. E. Anderson
Born & Died Jan. 17, 1915
"Gone to be an angel."

Price
Stekely W. Price
Born Dec. 5, 1849
Died Jan. 27, 1933

Millard F. Mace
Born Dec. 7, 1857
Died Mar. 9, 1924

His Wife
Catherine M. Hull
Born June 28, 1852
Died June 30, 1928

Little Florence, Dau. of
H. T. & L. A. Mace
Born Oct. 17, 1904
Died July 10, 1906

Father and Mother, we miss you,
we miss you in our homes."
Elizabeth Mace
Born 1834
Died June 26, 1902

James M. Mace
Born July 26, 1831
Died Mar. 3, 1905

HAMBLEN COUNTY
DOVER CEMETERY
(Page 3)

W. L. Gentry
Co. L. 13 Tenn. Co.
Born Dec. 20, 1883
Died Nov. 19, 1905

Mary L. Shipley
Born Nov. 6, 1844
Died Dec. 4, 1923

Infant Son of
J. W. & M. L. Shaw
Born & Died Apr. 3, 1818

Clvey Mildred, Dau. of
T. H. & M. E. Smith
Born Dec. 29, 1900
Died Nov. 10, 1909
"Again we hope to meet thee,
When the day of life is led
And in Heaven with joy to greet
thee, Where no farewell tears
are shed."

James Ellis Erwin
Born June 29, 1910
Died July 31, 1919
"A little bud of love,
To bloom with God above."

Ella May Quinn
Died Nov. 13, 1931
Age 53 yrs. 4 mo. 23 da.
(undertaker's marker)

Ora Lucile, Dau. of
D. C. & Ida Cantwell
Born June 11, 1918
Died Mar. 9, 1922
"Another little angle."

J. O. Quinn
Born Mar. 3, 1889

His Wife
Della Mae Russell
Born Dec. 6, 1907
Died Sept. 6, 1926
"We will meet again."

T. H. Arwood
Born Aug. 24, 1864

M. C. Lane, Wife of
T. H. Arwood
Born July 3, 1864
Died Jan. 27, 1935

Lillie Mace Cox
Born Jan. 14, 1872
Died July 21, 1932
"Asleep in Jesus."

Florence Thompson Lane
Born Dec. 9, 1881
Married to H. A. Lane
Oct. 28, 1908
Died Jan. 23, 1911
"The gates of Heaven for her
have opened wide."

In my Father's house are many
Mansions"
Mary M., Wife of J. W. Hale
Born June 4, 1878
Died Mar. 29, 1900

Alice Vivain, Dau. of
Mr. & Mrs. J. L. Green
Died June 2, 1929

Kenneth Jr., Son of
Mr. & Mrs. A. K. Green
Died Nov. 2, 1932

Luther B. Green
Born June 2, 1876
Died June 7, 1923
"To him we trust a place is
given among Christ Saints up
in Heaven."

Gladys, Dau. of
J.L. & M. A. Haun
Born Mar. 20, 1908
Died Dec. 16, 1908
"Mother's little dau. baby
is shadowed in the grave."

HAMBLEN COUNTY
DOVER CEMETERY
(Page 4)

John L. Cooper
Born Mar. 11, 1842
Died Feb. 3, 1916

Mary A. Cooper
Born Sept. 29, 1843
Died Apr. 8, 1906
(Double rock)

George Leslie, A twin Son of
Joseph & Harriett Susong
Born Nov. 27, 1888
Died Oct. 20, 1918
"Watch therefore, for ye know
not what hour your Lord doth
come."

Margaret Jean, Dau. of
R. L. & F. I. Ewing
Born Sept. 22, 1917
Died Oct. 24, 1918

Hazel, Dau. of
C. B. & Hylda Thompson
Born Feb. 4, 1904
Died Mar. 9, 1904
"Budded on Earth to bloom
in Heaven."

Emily, Wife of
J. W. Thompson
Born 1839
Died Mar. 15, 1907

J. W. Thompson
Born Nov. 9, 1834
Died Aug. 4, 1896

Mel, Son of
J. W. & Emily Thompson
Born Mar. 25, 1874
Died May 22, 1906

Fannie Susong
Born Jan. 24, 1867
Died July 19, 1928

W. M. Susong
Born Jan. 24, 1866
Died Apr. 2, 1920

Father
Charlie Lee Self
Born July 12, 1895
Died May 9, 1929
"Gone but not forgotten."

Dyer
Ruth Hale Dyer
Born 1894
Died 1935

Hale
Laura Mc Ghee, Wife of
T. N. Hale
Born May 25, 1870
Died May 28, 1916

Lukes Thomson
Born Mar. 11, 1823
Died Mar. 20, 1901

Joanah Thomson
Born Mar. 28, 1830
Died Feb. 22, 1897

Mary Ruth, Twin Dau. of
J. C. & A. Green
Born Dec. 18, 1901
Died July 15, 1902
"Meet me in Heaven."

R. A. Thompson
Born Aug. 5, 1861
Died Aug. 27, 1932

Haun
Walter E. Haun
Born Feb. 7, 1873
Died Apr. 22, 1936

Ella B. Hale, Wife of
W. E. Haun
Born Oct. 1, 1874
Died Apr. 2, 1919

HAMBLEN COUNTY
DOVER CEMETERY
(Page 5)

Jr. O. U. A. M.
James E. Hann
Born Dec. 31, 1882
Died July 21, 1922

Mollie Green
Born Apr. 23, 1878
Died Nov. 20, 1936
"At Rest"

Green
James R. Green
Born Apr. 17, 1867
Died Apr. 9, 1936
"Farewell to thee dear son,
Your earthly cares are o'er
God has sent to you a summons
  to dwell with him for ever more."

Andrew J. Green
Born May 28, 1844
Died Aug. 1931

His Wife
Mary Reece Green
Born April 30, 1847
Died July 17, 1936
"How desolate our home,
Bereaft of Thee."

Edwards
Martha Thompson, Wife of
J. N. Edwards
Born Mar. 24, 1864
Died Feb. 10, 1934

Mrs. S. C. Coates

"Our Brother"
Adolphus Susong
Born May 13, 1885
Died Dec. 8, 1923

Rebecca Ann Lynn
Born June 16, 1842
Died May. 6, 1931

E. L. Mc Ghee
Born May 2, 1856
Died May 23, 1894
Age 38 yr. 21 da.
"His life was worth living,
We miss thee from our home
dear,
We miss thee from thy place,
A shadow o'er our life is cast,
We miss the sunshine of thy face,
We miss thy and willing hand,
Thy fond and earnest care, our
home is dark with out thee,
We miss thee everywhere."

Mary, Wife of
R. H. Mc Ghee
Born Oct. 5, 1827
Died Feb. 16, 1902
"Faithful to her trust, even
unto death." "As a wife devoted
as a mother, affectionate, as a
friend, ever kind and true."

Ms. J. Robert H. Mc Ghee
Born Nov. 9, 1822
Died Mar. 16, 1907

Nina Lee, Dau. of
Dr. O. E. & Lizzie Fuller
Born Nov. 3, 1885
Died July 6, 1889
"Safe in the arms of Jesus."

Mary Junior, Dau. of
Mr. & Mrs. Dewey White
Born Mar. 14, 1920
Died Mar. 14, 1932

Little Tot, Son of
J. R. & R. D. Inman
Born Mar. 4, 1905
Died Feb. 18, 1907
"Meet me in Heaven."

HAMBLEN COUNTY
DOVER CEMETERY
(Page 6)

Charles D. Rhoades
Born Aug. 4, 1859

His Wife
Louise Hann
Born Aug. 11, 1861
Died June 2, 1936

Ethel Almeda Rhoades
Born Sept. 22, 1891

Dortha Irene Rhoades
Born Apr. 8, 1899
Died Mar. 19, 1935

William C. L. Bryan
Born Jan. 3, 1854
Died July 13, 1928

His Wife
Emma A. Bryan
Born Jan. 1, 1859
Died ——
(Double rock)

Mary Edith Spurgeon
Born Mar. 10, 1923
Died Oct. 24, 1924

Dyer
S. E. Dyer
Born Dec. 13, 1888
Died Mar. 10, 1926

His Wife
Carrie B. Dyer
Born Aug. 21, 1889
(Double rock)

Mother and Father
Mary E. Marstin
Born Dec. 2, 1836
Died Nov. 28, 1918

Richard S. Marstin
Born Aug. 19, 1830
Died Dec. 11, 1919

Tinna Carson
Age 22 yrs.

Alley M. Hickey, Wife of
William M. Goan
Born Dec. 10, 1842
Died Sept. 8, 1893
"Gone but not forgotten."

"Our Loved One"
Ada Ruth Goan, Wife of
Vernon White
Born May 20, 1908
Died Nov. 3, 1929
"Is it well with the child
And she answered, It is well."

In Memory of Helen Kate,
Dau. of B. R. & S. K. Sutton
Born May 26, 1885
Died Oct. 22, 1904
Age 19 yr. 4 mo. 24 da.
"Sleep on in thy Beauty, Thou
sweetened child, By sorrow
unblighted, By sin undefiled,
like the dove to the ark, That
has flown to thy rest, from the
wild sea of strif, To the house
of the blessed."

"Lead Kindly Light"
Mother
Mary E., Wife of
E. W. Susong
Born Mar. 31, 1869
Died Sept. 6, 1905

William E. Susong
Born Apr. 23, 1853
Died Sept. 8, 1906

Eva Susong
Born Nov. 15, 1869
Died June 21, 1903
(Double rock)

HAMBLEN COUNTY
DOVER CEMETERY
(PAGE 7)

Charles E., Son of
Will & Eunice Susong
Born Mar. 30, 1917
Died Jan. 21, 1923

Infant Dau. of
W. E. & Eva Susong
Born Feb. 17, 1903
Died May 7, 1903
"Our Baby"

George Deny, Son of
W. E. & Eva Susong
Born Nov. 19, 1898
Died Sept. 7, 1899
"Gone So Soon."

Zachariah Haun
Born Mar. 6, 1835
Died Mar. 21, 1894

Henrietta Elizabeth Haun
Born June 18, 1854
Died Jan. 17, 1921
(Double rock)

Mother
Susan Stokes, Wife of
G. W. Arwood
Born May 10, 1829
Died Mar. 18, 1915
"Asleep in Jesus."

Thomason
John J. Thomason
Born Feb. 19, 1863

His Wife
Catharine E. Thomason
Born Aug. 30, 1859
Died Jan. 22, 1916
"Sinners saved by Grace."

Wealthly M. Morgan, Wife of
Albert M. Heath
Born May 11, 1885
Died July 25, 1919
"Gone but not forgotten."

Ida Rader

J. C. Rader

Charlie T. Stewart
Born July 5, 1881
Died Nov. 19, 1920

His Wife
Mollie Mae Stewart
Born Feb. 10, 1883
(still living)

Stewart
Henry A. Stewart
Born Feb. 1, 1865
Died Dec. 6, 1919

His Wife
Sussie Stewart
Born Nov. 26, 1863

Williams
Emma M. Stewart, Wife of
I. L. Williams
Born Apr. 15, 1888
Died Mar. 21, 1915
"Thou wert fair as the beam of
the morn, Though lost to sight
to memory dear."

Elizabeth Lane, Wife of
W. H. Stewart
Born Jan. 1, 1843
Died June 27, 1909
"Dearest Mother, thou hast
left us here, thy loss we dearly
feel."

John Wesley, Son of
John Morgan
Born May 20, 1859
Died Aug. 28, 1917
Age 58 yr. 3 mo. 8 da.
"Asleep in Jesus."

HAMBLEN COUNTY
DOVER CEMETERY
(Page 8)

Mother
Hannah E., Wife of
John Morgan
Born in 1849
Died Apr. 5, 1918
"Gone but not forgotten."

Thomas Stransberry
Died June 22, 1912
Age about 65 yrs.
"Thy will be done."

Cecil P., Son of
J. E. & L. M. Rightsell
Born Mar. 13, 1901
Died Nov. 7, 1908
"Gone Home to be with Jesus."

Ida Nice, Infant

Eva Nice

Ella, Dau. of
John & Hannah E. Morgan
Born Nov. 21, 1883
Died Aug. 20, 1903
"The gates of Heaven for her
are opened wide."

John Morgan
Died Feb. 19, 1899
Age about 72 yrs.
"At Rest"
"Sleep on Dear Father
Take thy rest, God hath
called Thee, He knows best."

Peter H. Poston
Born May 20, 1831
Died Oct. 5, 1902

William Hawington
1869 - 1920

J. M. Hawington
1879 - 1919

Martha A. Hawington
Born Apr. 1, 1848
Died Feb. 2, 1927
"Gone but not forgotten."

Richard L., Son of
Rufus & Harriet Lane
Born Oct. 29, 1890
Died Mar. 24, 1894

Infant Dau. of
Rufus & Harriet E. Lane
Born Oct. 13, 1896
Died Oct. 19, 1896

James Rufus Lane
Born May 28, 1851
Died June 28, 1915
Age 57 yr. 1 mo.

Lane
Joseph Furman Lane
Born June 17, 1886
Died June 14, 1919

Margaret Bell
Born May 4, 1826
Died Aug. 4, 1912

Lynch
William D. Lynch
Born Apr. 12, 1856
Died Mar. 29, 1922

Carver
Louise Carver
Born Oct. 29, 1840
Died May 2, 1901
"Sleep on dear Mother, take thy
rest, God has called thee, He
knows best."

Paul Edward, Son of
W. S. & C. V. Minx
Born July 19, 1909
Died Aug. 10, 1912
"Gone to be with Jesus."

HAMBLEN COUNTY
DOVER CEMETERY
(Page 9)

Father
C. T. Stalcup
Born Apr. 28, 1836
Died Jan. 9, 1919

Elbert S. Horner
Born July 10, 1873
Died Sept. 24, 1904
"Oh God how strange and
mysterious are thy ways, to
take him from us in the best
of his days."

HAMBLEN COUNTY

TOMB STONE RECORDS

ECONOMY CEMETERY

ECONOMY METHODIST CHURCH, SOUTH

Located at Economy Methodist Church about 2 miles west of
Morristown, a short distance to the right of, and easily
seen from the Andrew Johnson Highway. Copied by Williard
Nee- November 1936.

PRICE'S HISTORY OF METHODISM, Vol. II, page 283 says:

"James Landrum was a local Methodist preacher and lived
near the mouth of Lick Creek at the time the Camp Ground
(Sulphur Springs) was built. He afterwards settled two
miles west of Morristown and aided in building the first
Methodist Church in that neighborhood. It was built at
a point so easy of access from every direction that Rev.
David Fleming gave it the name of Economy. Brother Landrum was among the first to find a grave in the graveyard at Economy.
(James Landrum was a Revolutionary soldier and his grave
is so marked.)

In Memory of Magnolia E.
Simmons
Born Sept. 6, 1852
Died June 9, 1928
"Asleep in Jesus"

J. P. Collins
Born June 25, 1845
Died Jan. 15, 1902

Horace Collins
Born Nov. 21, 1870
Died Apr., 12, 1908

Annie Lou, Dau. of
Geo. and Sarah Clontch
Died Jan. 26, 1902
Age 18 years

Kissie Simmons
Died Apr. 22, 1919
Age 65 years

S. C. Simmons
Born Mar. 10, 1845
Died May 8, 1920

Martha E. Spoon
Wife of S. C. Simmons
Born Dec. 23, 1849
Died Mar. 7, 1911

Mary B. Simmons
Born Dec. 7, 1880
Died Feb. 1, 1911

Maggie Simmons   (Pg.2)
  Wife of Marion Noe
Born Sept. 18, 1875
Died Oct. 13, 1905

Wade H. Hunter
Born Dec. 1, 1876
Died May 6, 1905

Mary E. Hixson
Born Jan. 22, 1849
Died Sept. 29, 1904

Julia A. Hixson
Born Jan. 19, 1830
Died May 18, 1902

Sarah C.
  Dau. of S. P. & J. Lynn Hixson
Born Sept. 23, 1851
Died Apr. 12, 1897

F. A. Lilly
Born Dec. 31, 1865
Died May 19, 1897
  "At Rest"

Hardy Lilly
Born May 5, 1839
Died Sept. 23, 1913

Donald E. Cardwell
Born May 23, 1897
Died Nov. 25, 1918

Sarah L. Michell
  Wife of Fernando Clarkson
Born Feb. 3, 1846
Died Nov. 14, 1904

Fernando Clarkson
Died Dec. 26, 1899
Age about 58,years

W. B. Anderson
Born Sept. 25, 1876
Departed this life
  Nov. 22, 1914

Geo. B. Anderson
Mar. 7, 1845
May 30, 1887

    His Wife

Sallie Anderson
Mar. 6, 1843

J. W. Turner
Born Apr. 15, 1831
Died July 16, 1905

Betsey Ann
  Wife of J. W. Turner
Born July 30, 1826
Died May 30, 1904

Joseph M. Ivy
Died Apr. 9, 1905
"Gone but not forgotten."

Martha A. Ivy
Born Nov. 28, 1824
Died Jan. 2, 1907
"She was the sunshine of
        our home."

Manson Ivy
Born Feb. 28, 1825
Died May 11, 1916

Jonnie H. Smith
Born Apr. 30, 1879
Died Dec. 26, 1905

Pricilla E., Wife of
  Pleasant Smith
Born Feb. 12, 1842
Died May 24, 1907

Pleasant Smith
Born Feb. 14, 1834
Died May 7, 1910

James M. Cowan
Died Jan. 4, 1933
Age 67 yrs. 3 mo. 17 da.

Thomas Hodge
Born Nov. 6, 1872
Died July 27, 1931
"At Rest"

John L. Simmons
Born Feb. 5, 1847
Died Dec. 20, 1919
"Gone but not forgotten".

Lucinda J. Loyd, Wife of
  William Austin
Born Apr. 29, 1842
Died July 27, 1919

William Austin
Born Jan. 10, 1830
Died May 20, 1903
Co. G. 61 Reg. Tenn. Vol.
    C. S. A.

Mary Mc Bride
Born Aug. 21, 1819
Died Apr. 27, 1904

Anna Mae, Dau. of Mr. & Mrs.
    J. C. Austin
Born Oct. 9, 1912
Died Aug. 23, 1913

W. F. Cutshaw
Born May 12, 1863
Died Dec. 23, 1914
"Resting in hope of a glorious
    resurrusection.

P. W. Wright
Born Jan. 1, 1861
Died Apr. 6, 1923

Laura M. Austin, Wife of
    P. W. Wright
Nov. 11, 1866

Susan Joe Ella, Dau. of
    C. & Isabella Ridey
Born June 5, 1889
Died Aug. 24, 1907

Cornelius Ridley
Born Oct. 25, 1850
Died Mar. 16, 1920

        His Wife

Isabel Ridley
Born Dec. 19, 1853

Minnie I. Hazelwood, Wife of
J. W. Smith
Born Oct. 2, 1876
Died Aug. 25, 1910

Joseph R. Hazelwood
Born Feb. 1, 1851
Died June 9, 1913

C. H. Stephens
Born July 17, 1853
Died June 10, 1928
"Gone but not forgotten."

J. C. Stephens, Son of
    Rev. J. H. & Mollie Stephens
Born Dec. 28, 1904
Died Jan. 2, 1905

Sallie E., Dau. of
    Dr. F. & Sarah L. Clarkson
Born Mar. 19, 1881
Died Dec. 23, 1900

Robert Smith
Died Jan. 29, 1936
Age 72 yrs. 3 mo.

Charlie E. Smith
Born Sept. 30, 1894
Jan. 16, 1919

Sarah F. Woods
Born Aug. 6, 1835
Died May 10, 1913

Inis Brady
Born May 22, 1879
Died Jan. 29, 1913

Mary J. Williams
Born Oct. 16, 1842
Died Dec. 22, 1902

Victoria Brady
Born Apr. 1, 1840
Died July 23, 1913

Lillie E. Lee
Born Mar. 30, 1897
Died Oct. 3, 1911
"Asleep in Jesus."

Benjamin Jackson
Born in 1846
Died Sept. 14, 1920
Age about 74 yrs.
Co. B. First Tenn. Cavalry
    Volunteers

Carl Britton Lee
Died Feb. 10, 1934
Age about 75 yr. 9 mo. 10 da.

Dallas Olivia Harvey
Born Nov. 7, 1908
Died Apr. 25, 1930

Ira, dau. of B. & Lucy B. Aulton.
Born July 4, 1899
Died July 4, 1899

Mollie, Wife of J. K. Cockrum
Born Aug. 6, 1868
Died Nov. 8, 1919

Mary E., Wife of M. R. Jollay
Born Oct. 11, 1884
Died June 15, 1918

Anna May Inman
Born Aug. 30, 1928
Died Dec 2, 1928

Bettie Louise Cox
Died Aug. 5, 1935
Age 4 mo. 10 days.

William H. Austin
Born Dec. 21, 1869
Died Apr. 2, 1923
"Gone but not forgotten."

Mary Cowan
Died May 4, 1933
Age 57 yrs. 3 mo. 1 da.

Emma Biggs, dau. of
W. M. Biggs
Born Oct 30, 1883
Died Sept. 17, 1909

In loving remembrance of my
dear husband C. H. Read
Died Aug. 12, 1906
Age 47 yrs.

Mary E. Elswick
Born Dec. 5, 1851
Died June 17, 1917
She has gone to her home in Heaven
and all her afflictions are o'er.

James Hancock
Born Mar. 4, 1874
Died Apr. 5, 1929
"I love you."

Little Ruth, dau. of
J. T. & E. M. Gray
Born Mar. 1919
Died July 7, 1922
"Gone to be an angel."

Joe Gregg
Died Dec. 1930
Age 60 yrs.

John A. Williams
Born Apr. 30, 1853
Died Jan. 29, 1915

John W. Harvey
Born Dec. 14, 1879
Died Jan. 16, 1823
"Gone but not forgotten."

Nellie A. Luttrell
Wife of Rev. T. F. Marsh
Born Sept. 14, 1885
Died June 6, 1926
Our loss is Heavens gain.

Infant son of B. M. &
Maxie Bell
Born Aug. 16, 1905

Solomon Spangle
Born 1836-Died 1907

His Wife

Mary E. Spangle
Born 1839-Died 1915

Sarah Ann Spangle
Born Aug. 1, 1870
Died Oct. 19, 1903

Mary E. Belven, Wife of
Louis Morgan
Died Apr. 22, 1902

W. H. M., Son of
M. M. & A. E. Wine
Born Mar. 8, 1901
Died Oct. 18, 1903

Florabel, Dau. of
J. W. & Mary A. Cardwell
Born Oct. 31, 1905
Died June 2, 1907

Mary A. Harrison, Wife of
J. W. Cardwell
Born Nov. 7, 1872
Died Nov. 8, 1911
"Mother is gone but not forgotten."

Ella E. A. McCaleb, Dau. of
Rev. J. L. Cardwell
Born Oct. 23, 1859
Died July 19, 1918

Frank Horner
Born Oct. 29, 1852
Died Dec. 24, 1826

Clara E., Dau. of
H. & L. M. Horner
Born Dec. 30, 1885
Died June 10, 1904

Hamp Horner
Born Feb. 1, 1851
Died Oct. 13, 1913

Syntha E., Dau. of
E. F. R. & M. A. Stephens
Born Aug. 6, 1882
Died Aug. 22, 1896

Martha Marsh, Wife of
E. F. R. Stephens
Born Mar. 29, 1858
Died Aug. 27, 1899

E. F. R. Stephens
Born Mar. 18, 1852
Died Mar. 18, 1907

John W. Long
Born Feb. 21, 1837
Died Apr. 24, 1907

Infant of L. B. & M. L. Hodge
Born Nov. 27, 1905
"Budded on earth to bloom in
Heaven."

Doahia, Dau. of J. W.
& Emmeline Long
Born Aug. 21, 1881
Died July 21, 1899
"Gone but not Forgotten."

Mary A., Wife of
M. W. Hodges
Born Jan. 1, 1870
Died June 21, 1908
"Gone but not Forgotten."

M. E. Presley
Born Nov. 27, 1871
Died Feb. 10, 1911

Walker Skeen
Born Nov. 14, 1877
Died Sept. 27, 1904

Henderson Skeen
Born Dec. 7, 1848
Died Sept. 11, 1922

Rachel C. Skeen
Born Mar. 1, 1850
Died Dec. 14, 1895

S. W. Sunderland
Born Dec. 25, 1821
Died Apr. 11, 1898
"Children, meet me in
Heaven."

Jennie C. Hazlewood
Wife of J. W. Inman
Born Oct. 24, 1869
Died June 16, 1895
"Gone but not Forgotten."

Mary Katharine, Wife of
John R. Hazlewood
Born Aug. 1, 1845
Died Aug. 31, 1922

Sallie E. Dodson
1862-1898

Dewie Dodson
1898-1899

Emma O., Wife of
  Thomas Hodge
Born Jan. 5, 1877
Died Mar. 16, 1903

Josephine, Wife of
  D. W. Hazelwood
Born Mar. 20, 1864
Died July 27, 1930
  "At Rest."

Ida B., Wife of
  Jos. W. Long
Born June 20, 1875
Died Nov. 12, 1897

Gracie Lee, Dau. of
  J. W. & M. C. Long
Born Feb. 28, 1907
Died Mar. 22, 1907
"Gone to be an angel."

Joseph W. Long
Born Sept. 18, 1866
Died Apr. 12, 1925
"Gone but not forgotten."

A. H. Long
Born Dec. 27, 1846
Died May 1, 1912

  His Wife

Susan E. Long
Born Oct. 20, 1845
Died June 5, 1917

Nicholas Long
Born July 15, 1811
Died June 26, 1896

  His Wife

Jane Long
Born Sept. 4, 1814
Died Nov. 6, 1900

Sarah A. L., Wife of
  G. W. Mc Kinney
Born Dec. 9, 1840
Married Aug. 19, 1866
Died Mar. 16, 1899
"Well will meet again."

John Quinton
Born Feb. 14, 1842
Died Feb. 25, 1922
Co. M. 9 Reg. Tenn. Cal.

  His Wife

Laura Quinton
Dec. 22, 1864-
"Gone but not Forgotten."

Ulisses Sherman, Son of
  W. P. & Harriet Turner
Born Jan. 12, 1893
Died Sept. 11, 1899

William Moore
Born Aug. 30, 1815
Died Aug. 2, 1897

Martha Moore
Died June 24, 1903
Aged about 82 years.
"Mother at rest."

John Thurman Inman
Born June 27, 1890
Died Mar. 16, 1923

Saletha Howell, Wife of
  W. A. Howell
Born May 28, 1837
Died Mar. 21, 1923
  "At Rest."

Wm. A. Howell
Born Oct. 27, 1830
Died Apr. 2, 1902
  "At Rest."

J. L. Howell M. D.
Born Sept. 7, 1854
Died July 28, 1900

Nannie Lou Quarels
Born Mar. 22, 1874
Died July 16, 1895

(PG. 7)

Julia A. Curl, Wife of
David Bowman
Born Mar. 5, 1869
Died Aug. 1, 1890

Frank W., Son of
D. W. C. & Rebecca Smith
Born Feb. 15, 1876
Died July 1, 1893

Rebecca, Wife of
D. W. C. Smith
Born Oct. 29, 1852
Died Jan. 3, 1914

D. W. C. Smith
Born Dec. 29, 1854
Died Aug. 13, 1920
Go and dwel'th with him
above. Happy in the
Saviors love.

Lou, Wife of B. T. Smith
Born Jan. 22, 1872
Died Apr. 25, 1895

Florence E., Wife of B. T. Smith
Born June 15, 1863
Died Aug. 24, 1887

Richard W. Brown
Born Nov. 30, 1837
Died July 2, 1909

Mary A. Brown
Born May 31, 1839
Died Sept. 3, 1922
A tender mother and a
faithful friend.

Maggie Lee Brown, Wife of
W. H. Manley
Born Aug. 8, 1870
Died May 19, 1924

Mary A., Wife of
Hardy Lilly
Born Apr. 8, 1834
Died Sept. 18, 1889

George E. Hale
Born Feb. 9, 1896
Died Apr. 24, 1928
At Rest

Eliza Jane Long Hanks
Born Jan. 6, 1850
Died May 14, 1934

Henry Hanks
Aged 82 years

Sallie J., Wife of
L. L. Adams
Born Aug. 16, 1858
Died Mar. 15, 1882

Katie E. Parker
Wife of D. T. Morris
Born Mar. 3, 1852
Died Nov. 4, 1896

Pauline Graves
Born Sept. 24, 1899
Died Sept. 13, 1924

Mattie A. Maine
Born Mar. 1, 1845
Died Dec. 11, 1898

Dudley B. Ivy
Born Mar. 4, 1855
Died Sept. 17, 1919

His Wife

Mary E. Ivy
Born July 27, 1855
Died May 16, 1926
"Gone but not Forgotten."

Eli Thacker
Born 1830
Died Oct. 20, 1912
Age about 82 yrs.

Elizabeth Mc Kinney
Wife of Eli Thacker
Died Mar. 15, 1899
Age about 59 years

Cornelia K., Dau. of
Elizabeth & Eli Thacker
Born Mar. 7, 1865
Died Nov. 3, 1888

(Pg.8)

Luther, adopted son of
T. B. & A. E. Lilly
Born Mar. 14, 1877
Died Aug. 26, 1890

Thomas B. Lilly
Born Jan. 15, 1848
Died June 7, 1912

Cassie Hunt
Died July 19, 1884
Age 52 yrs.

Rachel M., Wife of
L. L. Baber —— ?
Born Jan. 5, 1848
Died Nov. 14, 1899

William Mastin Moore
Born June 9, 1848
Died Aug. 9, 1888
"Farewell dear Father
sweet thy Rest."

Belle E. Stephens
Wife of A. W. Carmichael
Born Nov. 17, 1860
Died Nov. 13, 1897

Joseph M. Sunderland
Born Aug. 29, 1856
Died Apr. 26, 1924

T. J. Carmicheal
Born Aug. 1, 1830
Died Mar. 13, 1906

Rebecca, Wife of T. J.
Carmicheal
Born July 25, 1833
Died Oct. 10, 1888

P. J. Carmicheal
Born Mar. 14, 1865
Died Aug. 1, 1886
Age 21 yrs. 5 mo. 24da.

Ema N., Dau. of W. H. &
M. W. Milligan
Born Feb. 27, 1895
Died 1899

Susan N. Akers
Born July 10, 1869
Died Jan. 4, 1878

Julia A., Wife of G. T.
Bettis
Born Aug. 21, 1870
Died Sept. 22, 1902
"Gone but not forgotten."

Ruby E., Dau. of G. T. &
A. E. Bettis
Born Feb. 15, 1897
Died Mar. 1, 1903
Thy will be done.

Sarah E., Wife of Jacob
Akers
Born Feb. 15, 1853
Died Dec. 15, 1906
"Asleep in Jesus."

Frances I. Akers
Born Nov. 9, 1917
Died Nov. 10, 1917

James E. Akers
Born Nov. 9, 1917
Died Nov. 10, 1917

Kate L., Wife of
J. C. Carr
Born May 14, 1830
Died Jan. 6, 1890
Member of the M. E.
Church South.

Lucurgus S. Jones
Born June 10, 1848
Died Apr. 13, 1899

His Wife

Miranda Ivy Jones
Born Oct. 3, 1857
Died July 25, 1899

J. M. Presley
Born Aug. 19, 1848
Died Feb. 13, 1919

Emma A., Wife of J. M.
Presley
Born May 11, 1851
Died Mar. 18, 1929

Edd M., Son of
M. M. & I. R. Presley
Born May 29, 1902
Died Mar. 9, 1920
Age 17 yrs. 9 mo. 9 da.

P. A. Spoon
Born Jan. 22, 1839
Died Feb. 21, 1912

R. B. Smith
Died Nov. 15, 1902
Age 65 years

William A. Marsh
Born Aug. 17, 1816
Died Apr. 13, 1893

His Wife

Rebecca Smith
Died Apr. 7, 1914
Age 74 years

Annie, Wife of
William A. Marsh
Born Aug. 17, 1827
Died Feb. 24, 1907

Mary E, Wife of E. Baird
Born June 7, 1853
Died July 25, 1870

H. Rosco Mc Bride
Born Sept. 29, 1888
Died Apr. 5, 1889

W. H. C., Son of M. E. &
E. Baird
Born Sept. 17, 1869
Died July 19, 1870

Sarah A. Graham
Born Nov. 9, 1840
Died Mar. 12, 1885

Gale Smyth
Born July 30, 1886
Died Dec. 17, 1918

Sarah, Wife of
Robert Smith
Born Oct. 22, 1825
Died June 9, 1890

Nancy, Wife of E. Black
Born Aug. 20, 1861
Died Apr. 14, 1890

B. C. Sunderland
Died July 30, 1930
Age 46 years

Rachel A. Johnson, Wife of
W. C. Looney
Born Mar. 15, 1821
Died Jan 18, 1899

Charlie Quinton
Died June 2, 1909
Age about 55 years

William C. Looney
Born June 9, 1822
Died Sept. 11, 1893

Florence, Wife of
Charlie Quinton
Born Mar. 31, 1865

John H. Long
Born Sept. 18, 1866
Died Mar. 11, 1931

L. M. Sunderland
Wife of John Mckeehan
Died June 4, 1907
Age about 68 years

His Wife

Lucy J. Long
Born Mar.20, 1871
Died

M. E. Witt
Born Oct. 3, 1820

Delila E. Spoon
Born Dec. 1, 1842
Died Oct. 17, 1911

Taylor Witt
Died Aug. 11, 1911

Age 79 years

Emily Witt
Born Aug. 12, 1805
Died Nov. 9, 1886

J. Snow Witt
Born Dec. 11, 1865

Lee Witt
Died Sept. 20, 1862

Lou U. Fletcher
 Wife of John C. Stephens
Born Nov. 2, 1876
Died Apr. 28, 1912

Armanda, Wife of J. H. Ivy
Born Apr. 15, 1852
Died Dec. 13, 1856

Infant Dau. of I. D. &
H. L. Walker
Born & Died Feb. 15, 1895

Annie Baker, Wife of
Alexander M. Wood
Born Sept. 27, 1829
Died Mar. 2, 1907

Alexander M. Wood
Born May 28, 1831
Died July 6, 1887

James E. Hill
Born Jan. 24, 1892
Died Aug. 10, 1911

Walter O. Hill
Born Mar. 1884
Died Feb. 26, 1919

Horace M. Smith
Born Apr. 29, 1857
Died Apr. 23, 1923

Angie M. Smith
Born May 1. 1856
Died Mar. 18, 1928
"Gone but not forgotten."

Susan E. Smith
Born Mar. 29, 1834
Died May 12, 1893

B. F. Smith
Born Aug. 20, 1830

Died Feb. 1, 1913
"Gone but not forgotten."

Mother Fannie Hubbard
Wife of C. H. Stephens
Born July 4, 1856
Died Nov. 19, 1886

D. W. Hazlewood
Born Apr. 18, 1853
Died May 29, 1915

Jane, Wife of
 M. Spoon
Born July 17, 1823
Died Mar. 5, 1890

Henry Baxter Ivy
Born Mar. 9, 1879
Jan. 11, 1881

Benjamin F. Ivy
Born Aug. 20, 1844
Died July 30, 1868

Rev. Barnett Smith
Founder of Economy Church
                1835
Born Oct. 11, 1790
Died Mar. 5, 1879

Aunt Betsie
Consort of Barnett Smith
Born Jan. 27, 1797
Died Apr. 18, 1873

Everett B. Smith
Died Dec. 29, 1851
Age 1 mo. 21 da.

O. F. Smith
Born Mar. 11, 1836
Died Oct. 27, 1840

J. B. Smith
Born June 30, 1839
Died Nov. 27, 1841

William T. Hazlewood
Born June 16, 1838
Died June 9, 1859

Nancy C., Wife of
Nathan B. Morelock
Born 1834
Died 1851

Hannah J. Hazlewood
Died Feb. 17, 1804
Age 34 years

Joshua Hazlewood
Born Mar. 31, 1808
Died May 15, 1862

Blany Hazlewood Born 1765
Died Oct. 25, 1862
Age 97 years

Lhiu Bettis
Born Apr. 27, 1850
Died Nov. 20, 1866

J. R. C. Quarrells
Born Apr. 22, 1872
Died Apr. 26, 1873

Inis P. Howell
Born & Died
Feb. 8, 1871

Elnor C., Wife of J. S. Howell
Born June 13, 1842
Died July 26, 1881

Lovel Walker
Born May 10, 1823
Died Nov. 29, 1879

Armanda J. Walker
Born Apr. 4, 1826
Died Aug. 20, 1912

Nathan W. Quarrels
Born June 27, 1838
Died Nov. 20, 1881

Mollie E., Wife of
J. T. John
Died Sept. 20, 1883
Age 23 yrs. 5 mo. 18 da.

Elenor S. Quarrels
Born Aug. 30, 1834
Died Mar. 13, 1884

John W., Son of
P. C. & C. W. Bettis
Born Mar. 15, 1886
Died June 24, 1887

Paul C., Son of
E. J. & J. R. Bettis
Born Mar. 4, 1880
Died Sept. 22, 1887

H. M., Wife of A. P. C.
Bettis
Born July 25, 1821
Died Sept. 7, 1890

Jessie Williams
Born July 21, A. D. 1808
Died Jan. 9, A. D. 1886

L. M. Ivy
Born June 19, 1849
Died Apr. 8, 1909

W. N. Ivy
Born Aug. 27, 1847
Died Apr. 17, 1889

W. I. Ivy
Born June 10, 1855
Died Dec. 29, 1885

L. W. Ivy
Born Mar. 10, 1823
Died Jan. 30, 1901

Delila, Wife of L. W. Ivy
Born Mar. 9, 1824
Died July 27, 1884

J. S. Howell
Born May 6, 1840
Died Jan. 10, 1922

Rowena O. Lyle, Wife of
J. S. Howell
Born Feb. 9, 1848
Died Jan. 29, 1889

In Memory Of
Rev. Nathan Hobbs
Born Oct. 2, 1797
Died Sept. 1, 1863

Emma J. Carriger
Born Oct. 26, 1858
Died Sept. 14, 1874

Mary J., Wife of
J. F. Graves
Born Nov. 11, 1849
Died June 23, 1876

Hiram C. King
Born July 1, 1843
Died Dec. 1, 1926

His Wife

Margaret J. Carriger
Born Dec. 5, 1843
Died Aug. 8, 1917

Isabella M., Wife of
W. H. B. **Graves**
Born July 26, 1857
Died Dec. 27, 1879

W. H. B. Graves
May 2, 1851
Apr. 4, 1917

Grace, Dau. of
E. L. & M. B. Miller
Born Feb. 19, 1900
Died July 15, 1900

Alice C. Ritchie
Born Sept. 17, 1851
Died July 11, 1883

Martha A. Larkin
Born Jan. 10, 1846
Died Apr. 6, 1893

S. P. Livingston
Born Apr. 17, 1812
Died Sept. 3, 1895

John B. R., Son of
S. N. & J. M. Catron
Born Oct. 22, 1913
Died July 11, 1915

William Hubert, Son of
J. W. & S. M. Woods
Born Mar. 14, 1889
Died Nov. 27, 1891

M. Lou Graves
Born Oct. 1, 1841
Died May 29, 1907

Rev. W. H. Harrison
Born May 12, 1831
Died Mar. 30, 1886

His Wife

Armanda A. Perryman
Born Apr. 17, 1841
Died Dec. 16, 1922

Sterling G. Perryman
Born Nov. 24, 1812
Died Feb. 10, 1885

Malinda M. Perryman
Born 1800
Died May 25, 1885

Sabella M. Graves
Wife of J. H. Havely
Born Aug. 20, 1849
Died Mar. 11, 1900

Maggie Lou, Dau. of
J. H. & S. M. Havely
Born Nov. 16, 1879
Died June 17, 1887

Mary A. T., Dau. of W. C. &
M. W. Graves
Died Aug. 24, 1866
Age 23 years

C. E. Carriger
Born Jan. 23, 1815
Died May 25, 1885

Isabella P. Carriger
Consort of C. E. Carriger
Born Feb. 18, 1820
Died July 26, 1859

Rev. William C. Graves
Born Aug. 13, 1815
Died Jan. 29, 1896

Jemina, Consort of
S. W. Sunderland
Died Mar. 30, 1856
Age 32 years

Eleanor Howell
Born Mar. 27, 1800
Died Mar. 25, 1865

Jessee Howell
Born Feb. 22, 1799
Died Feb. 24, 1871

Ester E. Jones
Born Oct. 28, 1825
Died Apr. 26, 1889

P. J. Jones
Born Aug. 4, 1833
Died Aug. 25, 1871

Mary E. Jones
Born Dec. 30, 1850
Died Sept. 1, 1867

B. Jane, Wife of H. W.
Williams
Born Jan. 14, 1833
Died Feb. 25, 1863

Mary A. D., Wife of
H. W. Williams
Born 1826
Died 1881

Laura M., Wife of
H. Williams
Born Mar. 5, 1840
Died Feb. 12, 1905

H. Williams
Born June 1, 1830
Died July 26, 1915

Maj. Wm. Williams
2 PA. Regt. Rev. War.

Silas B. Stevens
Born Mar. 15, 1801
Died Dec. 30, 1876

Luvicy Mathes, Wife of
Silas B. Stevens
Born Aug. 23, 1804
Died Sept. 7, 1882

James A. Stephens
Born July 21, 1847
Died Sept. 18, 1874

T. A. Horner
Born Mar. 18, 1824
Died 13, 1865

J. H. Horner
Born May 29, 1846
Died Oct. 8, 1864

Jas. Landrum, Va. Mil
Rev. War
Sarah Malimda, Wife
of Jas. Landrum
1775

Robert Potter
Born Jan. 25, 1808
Died June 31, 1884
Robert Potter & Family
sleeps heare

Sallie Smalley
1847- 1882

Smith H. Hunt
Born Dec. 27, 1821
Died Feb. 2, 1882

Patrick Birdwell Ivy
Born Dec. 21, 1849
Died Feb. 27, 1921

Minnie Jane Ivy
Born Feb. 11, 1884
Died Mar. 21, 1926

Mahala L. Breeden
Born Aug. 19, 1856
Died Sept. 19, 1932

Norma Afton Noe
Born Aug. 4, 1919
Died Dec. 13, 1919

Unicy Stubblefield
Born Mar. 12, 1814
Died Sept. 1, 1872

D. R. Miller
Born June 18, 1842
Died June 16, 1905

N. E. Miller, Wife of
D. R. Miller
Born Dec. 11, 1847
Died Mar. 10, 1910

Mary B., Wife of
J. Y. R. Harrison
Born Oct. 25, 1843
Died May 12, 1893

**Jemima, Consort of
S. W. Sunderland
Died Mar. 30, 1856
Aged 32 y, 7 m, 15 d**

TOMBSTONE RECORDS

HAMBLEN COUNTY

EMMA JARNAGIN CEMETERY

Commonly called "JARNAGIN CEMETERY".

Located just beyond the city limits of Morristown, to the left of the Valley Home Road.

It was dedicated in 1906 by W. Porter Jarnagin, "In memory of his Mother".

Many graves and markers have been moved to this cemetery from the old City cemetery and from cemeterys in the county. Most of the graves are marked, those not recorded have undertakers markers which the weather has effaced.

Copying completed. October 6, 1937.

By Willard Noe.

Morristown, Tennessee.

"JARNAGIN LOT".

Enclosed with a stone wall and iron fence.
A large monument bears the following inscription:

Pleasant J. Jarnagin.   Emma R. Jarnagin.
Jan 1, 1809,   Feb 22, 1822,
Feb. 24, 1882.   Dec. 30, 1896.

IN WHOSE MEMORY THIS CEMETERY WAS DEDICATED.

HAMBLEN COUNTY

JARNAGIN CEMETERY CONT.

(Pg. 2)

(Jarnagin Lot Continued)

W. Porter Jarnagin.
Feb 21, 1841,
Dec. 26, 1909.

Hampton L. Jarnagin.
July 2, 1843,
June 25, 1846.

John H. Jarnagin,
Jan. 24, 1854,
Feb. 27, 1854.

Lewis Riggs.
June 30, 1793,
Oct. 6, 1854.

Wm. Hightower.

Nancy E. Riggs.
Sept 27, 1797,
May 8, 1889.

Lewis B. Jarnagin.
June 5, 1836,
Oct. 7, 1857.

Pleasant E. Jarnagin.
March 2, 1848,
April 14, 1889.

John H. Jarnagin.
Aug. 5, 1849,
March 28, 1867.

Nelson Jarnagin.
(Our old family servant).
His last request was:
"I want to be buried
near my Master's children.

HAMBLEN COUNTY

JARNAGIN CEMETERY CONT.

(Pg. 3)

William Donaldson.
(Rev Soldie)
1738 - 1819.

Mary Sweeney Donaldson
(His Wife)
1741 - 1840.

Robert Sevier Leeper.
Sept 15, 1905,
Oct. 9, 1918.

Sam E. Leeper.
June 20, 1875,
Sept 10, 1898.

B. Jarnagin Leeper.
Mar 4, 1835,
Dec. 10, 1901.

Charles B. Graves,
Jan 1, 1884,
Jan 8, 1937.

Walter B. Graves.
Oct 18, 1879,
Mar. 6, 1914.

(One Stone)
Jason P. Graves.
Dec. 11, 1846,
Sept 30, 1937.

Margaret V. Graves.
(His Wife)
May 5, 1848,
Sept 29, 1912.

(One Stone)
William Henry Dick.
Mar 5, 1831,
April 14, 1914.

Martha Anne Dick.
Feb 6, 1833,
March 26, 1911.

Edward Jarnagin Dick.
Dec. 10, 1915,
Feb 3, 1920.

Harold Kenneth Willing,
May 17, 1908,
July 31, 1910.

(One Large Monument
with the following
Inscriptions.)

MORRIS
James T. Morris.
1853 - 1880.

Mollie E. Morris
1857 - 1878.

George Morris.
1860 - 1861.

Sue D. Morris.
1872 - 1878.

Daniel G. Morris.
1849 - 1855.

Jehu Morris.
1852 - 1896.

HAMBLEN COUNTY

JARNAGIN CEMETERY CONT.

(Pg. 4)

(Morris Cont.)

Drury Morris.
1823 – 1876

Susan E. Morris.
1830 – 1874.

Marie Morris Henderson.
Sept 26, 1895,
Mar 28, 1921.

(One large stone
with the following
Inscriptions)

Elizabeth McCrary Badham Branson.
1902 – 1916.
1905 – 1928.

David William Badham.
1868 – 1905.

Horace Milford Branson.
1856 – 19—

Elizabeth McCrary Branson.
1878 – 1928.

(One large stone
with the following
Inscriptions)

George B. McCrary.	.1836 – 1911.
Hannah J. McCrary.	1846 – 1891.
Annie May McCrary.	1881 – 1883.
Ralph S. McCrary.	1891 – 1893.
Rev. W.H. Harrison.	1805 – 1874.
Elizabeth J. Harrison.	1816 – 1879.
David Pence.	1829 – 1893.
Mary A. Pence.	1841 – 1911.
Mary Sherwood.	1856 – (Still Living)
John McCrary.	1811 – 1885.
Sabrina McCrary.	1811 – 1890.
Hugh H. McCrary.	1876 – (Died since 1931)

In Memory of 16 unknown
Confederate Soldiers
Erected in 1910
By Sam Davis Chapter U. D. C.

We know not from what
homes they came
We can but guess their
dreams of fame
But lamps for them did
vainly burn
And mothers waited their
return.

HAMBLEN COUNTY

JARNAGIN CEMETERY CONT.

(Pg. 5)

(McCrary Cont)

Frank McCrary. 1886 - (Died since 1931)
Helen McCrary Garcia . 1888 - (Living)
Joseph M. Garcia 1917. (Living)

Nancy Aurelia Jarnagin.
June 26, 1851.
July 1, 1934.

Spencer Clark Jarnagin.
March 2, 1843,
Feb. 24, 1928.

His Wife
Sara Jane Nelson McPherson.
Nov. 30, 1851,
Feb. 4, 1930.

Geo. A. Carmichael
Sept 9, 1844,
Oct. 30, 1913.

Darthula Caldwell,
Wife of
John M.L. Allen.
April 7, 1841,
July 3, 1909.
"Thy Kingdom come,
Thy will be done in
earth as it is in Heaven".

John Jarnagin,
Son of T.R. and A.K. James.
Mar 10, 1913,
Aug. 30, 1913.

Lucy Catherine Hannah,
Wife of
William Calvin Jarnagin.
Sept. 24, 1838,
Oct. 22, 1916.

(One Stone)
Henry Temple Jarnagin.
1847 - 1928.
Mary Carmichael Jarnagin.
1851 - 1932.

Katherine Rebecca ,
daughter of
M.P. and Effie J.T. Reeve.
1904 - 1923.

Lucy Lanier Tomlinson Jarnagin.
1867 - (Still Living)

John Robert Jarnagin.
1867 - (Still Living)

Thomas Chesley Jarnagin.
1875 - 1931.

Dorthea Effinia Jarnagin.
Jan 23, 1908,
June 15, 1908.

Daisy Pierce Jarnagin.
March 11, 1920,
July 6, 1921.

Thomas Phillips Jarnagin.
Jan 17, 1913,
May 4, 1926.

(One Stone)
James C. Inman.
(Co. D. 8th, Tenn. Inf.)
Aug. 19, 1837,
Oct. 25, 1899.
His Wife
Martha N. Moore.
May 12, 1853,
July 14, 1936.

HAMBLEN COUNTY

JARNAGIN CEMETERY CONT.

(Pg. 6)

Joseph B. Stubblefield
(Father)
May 29, 1857,
July 16, 1920.

James B. Stubblefield.
Oct. 7, 1901,
Aug. 8, 1923.

Mollie M. Eckel,
May 13, 1852,
Aug. 26, 1929.

Jennie E. Eckel.
Aug. 3, 1855,
Oct. 14, 1924.

Jno. G. Mathes.
Dec. 13, 1850,
Sept. 15, 1917.

Ella P. Mathes.
May 8, 1853.
(Still Living)

Daniel C. Morris.
Jan 19, 1855,
Jan 28, 1930.

Dan C. Morris, Jr.
May 3, 1899,
June 17, 1901.

Sarah Etta Doak Morris,
May 25, 1868,
June 30, 1934.

Mary Doak,
June 10, 1845,
Mar. 31, 1920.

W.C. Doak.
July 20, 1844,
Nov. 25, 1917.

Nettie B. Sanders.
Born May 18, 1841,
Died April 18, 1905.

Myrle V. - Son of
W.H. & Lora Branton.
Born Jan 19, 1906,
Died June 6, 1906.

Lora Mathes Branton.
Died April 4, 1930,
Aged 65 yrs - 24 days.

Louisa R. - Wife of
J.W. Donaldson.
Jan 31, 1850,
Dec. 18, 1919.

Infant son of
Clinton D and Ollie Kate Mater,
Born Sept 7, 1905.

Mary McKinney Grigsby.
Feb 3, 1901,
Mar. 7, 1915.

Milton A. Goodson,
Dec. 29, 1846,
June 7, 1912.

His Wife
Matilda J. Goodson,
Sept 15, 1845,
July 9, 1927.

Nora Goodson Drinnon,
Aug 19, 1876,
June 24, 1939.

John A. Rhea,
1848 - 1913.

Lora I. Rhea,
1860 - 1929.

HAMBLEN COUNTY

JARNAGIN CEMETERY CONT.

(Pg. 7)

(Rhea Cont.)

Mary Hasson Rhea,
1903 - 1904.

Wm. A. Rhea,
1882 - 1904.

John L. Rhea,
1893 - 1929.

G.B. Cope,
July 15, 1851,
May 27, 1934.

His Wife,
Rebecca Cope,
Feb 17, 1852,
Dec. 1, 1915.

Lucy Lee, Wife of
Syd Hively,
Born June 15, 1886,
Died April 18, 1913.

Rosa Myers Hardy,
Oct. 4, 1860,
Dec. 17, 1916.

Earnest G. Holley,
April 29, 1889,
Jan 5, 1919.

George R. Donaldson, Jr.
1896 - 1918.

George R. Donaldson,
1868 - 1936.

Pete P. Deka,
Born at Kavaia, Albania,
June 29, 1886,
Died at Harriman, Tenn..,
Oct. 26, 1918.

Lewis T. Johnson,
May 1, 1882,
April 8, 1919.

Henry, Son of
Charles and Dora McKinney,
Jan 15, 1903,
June 5, 1919.

Jane E. Evans,
1915 - 1919.

Jessie Grant George,
1890 - 1919.

Margaret Virginia,
Wife of J.I. Holley,
July 12, 1862,
July 4, 1917.
"In Gods Care".

Juanita B. Lints,
Daughter of
Mrs. D.B. Wise.
Aug. 2, 1913,
Feb. 28, 1922.

Mother.
Armanda M. Holley,
June 1, 1854,
Nov. 9, 1933.

Dr. J.E. Robertson,
Nov. 15, 1825,
Sept 24, 1896.

Nancy G. Robertson,
May 19, 1837,
Jan 18, 1876.

Children.
Robert M. Robinson,
Oct. 2, 1863,
Oct. 3, 1863.

HAMBLEN COUNTY

JARNAGIN CEMETERY CONT.

(Pg. 8)

Robertson Cont)

Lizzie T. Robertson,
May 14, 1857,
Sept 7, 1866.

Dashea S. Robertson,
April 25, 1853,
May 9, 1871.

Hampton C. Robertson,
April 4, 1861,
Oct 11, 1881.

Curtis R. Robertson,
Oct 2, 1964,
Jan 1, 1884.

Guyan L. Henderson,
Jan 39, 1843,
Dec. 10, 1920.

        His Wife,
Rosannah Tarter,
Nov. 8, 1844,
June 8, 1930.

Son and Daughter.
Gaines Cooper,
Feb 8, 1875,
July 20, 1903.

Minnie Lou Hedricks,
Aug 31, 1882,
Aug. 23, 1906

G.W. Belt,
Feb. 23, 1861,
Dec. 19, 1913.

Kate Lear Belt,
Mar 7, 1868,
Oct. 4, 1934.
"Gone but not forgotten".

Iulus J. Hodges,
Born and Died
Feb. 39, 1893.

Henry,
Born June 23, 1895,
Died Oct. 32, 1895.
(Infants of
J.I. and Ida L. Hodges.)

Katherine Caldwell,
Died Mar. 25, 1930,
Age. 89 Years.

Edward Caldwell,
Mar 4, 1845,
July 18, 1910.
U.C.V.

William M. Fitzgerald.
July 11, 1850,
Sept 4, 1909.

Alta,- Daughter of
J.F. and Jeshia M. Mathes.
Born Feb 12, 1895,
Died Oct. 27, 1897.

W.H. Mullins.
Dec. 3, 1859,
Dec. 23, 1936.

P.H. Manley.
Born Aug. 3, 1874,
Died Mar. 28, 1909.

Stanley B. Mullins.
Feb. 27, 1890,
Oct. 23, 1918.

James L. Anderson.
Jan 1, 1860,
Mar 6, 1932.

Eliza Ann Anderson,
July 22, 1868,
May 25, 1935.

Susan Ida Vaught,
Wife of T.B. Moody. Jr.
Sept 30, 1875,
July 6, 1911.

Maggie Seagle Robinson,
Dec. 25, 1875,
Sept 8, 1933.

Arthur W. Collins,
Aug 15, 1879,
July 1, 1921.

Margaret E. Collins,
Sept 23, 1961,

Conley Collins,
Oct. 1, 1859.

Sarah V. Nutter,
May 16, 1890,
April 17, 1916.

Edward R. Myers,
Sept 26, 1886,
Jan 12, 1935.

Billie Marie Shorter,
Died Aug. 17, 1933.
Age. 9. Mo. 27 days.

T.S. Myers,
1867 - 1935.

William Robert Shelton,
Died July 20, 1937,
Age 66 yrs, 5 Mo. & 8 days.

James A. Taylor,
Dec. 7, 1837,
Dec. 23, 1901.

Caroline Taylor,
Dec. 12, 1840.
--

Rev. James Chester Rockwell.
Born Jan. 21, 1868,
Died Sept. 14, 1883.

Lieut. Kiffin Yates Rockwell.
Sept. 20, 1892,
Sept 23, 1916.
Aviator. Killed in action
over Thann, Aslace,.
Burried at Luxevil, France.

James W. Easley,
Feb. 19, 1840,
Feb. 4, 1893.

Nancy Lyles Moore,
Wife of
Lafayette Moore.
May 3, 1839,
Jan 1, 1939.

Margaret E. Moore,
Died Oct. 26, 1934,
Age 63 Yrs. 10 Mo. & 30 Days.

French McThomas Bushong,
Aug. 8, 1863,
Oct. 7, 1912.
"Gods finger touched him
and he slept".

Mary E. Taylor,
Mar 14, 1841,
Mar 21, 1913.

Jessie Day Rippetoe,
Apr 21, 1885,
July 20, 1921.

Clarence H. Rippetoe,
Dec. 7, 1881,
Dec. 24, 1928.

HAMBLEN COUNTY

JARNAGIN CEMETERY CONT.

(Pg. 10)

J. Lafayette Craig.
July 5, 1843,
Jan 26, 1917.

Porter D. Moore,
Aug. 21, 1872,
Aug. 4, 1936.

Lena Breyles Harris,
Died June 4, 1937,
Age. 54 years.

Samuel A. Smith.
Nov. 12, 1860,
Feb. 28, 1929.

Nellie Murphey,
Wife of R.O. Gallaher,
1875 - 1919.

Mrs Rosa Fortrum Mills.
June 21, 1870,
April 9, 1910.

Nell F. Jarnagin.
1885 - 1923.

H.E. Jarnagin.
1847 - 1907.

Susan Katherine Dice,
Beloved Wife of
John Braselton Fillmore Dice. Jr.
Lieut. U.S. Army.
Born Mar. 1, 1913,
Mountain City, Tennessee.,
Died Feb. 13, 1936.
Fort Monroe, Va.

John Braselton Fillmore Dice.
Son of Geo. W. & Elizabeth Dice,
Born July 3, 1856,
New Market, Tennessee.,
Married Flora B. Neal,
March 3, 1881,
Married Alice C. Murphy,
June 10, 1907,
Died Dec. 13, 1914.
Morristown, Tennessee.

Aurelia C. Jarnagin.
1846 - 1920.

Lucy L. Jarnagin.
1885 - 1930.

Mary Jane Baucher.
Oct 5, 1860,
Jan 7, 1931.

Syd. C. Johnson.
Jan. 30, 1867,
July 23, 1926.

Roy H. Helton.
Jan 20, 1891,
March. 27, 1932.

Charles F. McPheren.
Aug. 3, 1880,
Oct. 20, 1936.

Mary Donna Kinskie.
Dec. 15, 1894,
Dec. 8, 1918.

HAMBLEN COUNTY

JARNAGIN CEMETERY CONT.

(Pg. 11.)

J.S. Cassell.
Dec. 31, 1870,
Mar 3, 1914.

Lucinda C. Portrum Hale.
Jan 12, 1837,
Feb. 12, 1918.

Samuel S. Portrum,
July 3, 1877,
Nov. 13, 1910.

Orlena Miller,
Nov. 11, 1849,
May 30, 1916.

John Samuel Miller,
Jan 11, 1850,
Nov. 8, 1910.

Mary Francis Walker,
Wife of
W.T. McCorkle.
1870 - 1932.

J.X. Corpening,
Feb. 10, 1866,
May 2, 1913.

Florence Pryde Howell,
Aug. 20, 1854,
Nov. 11, 1933.

Mary B. Rich.
July 31, 1896,
June 5, 1918.

Flora K. Williams,
Jan 2, 1875,
June 6, 1927.

Lydia Fisher,
Wife of
H.M. Sherwood,
Oct. 13, 1850,
Aug. 25, 1906.

David M. Butt.
Dec. 1867,
June 1924.

Paul E. Butt,
Oct. 1897,
Mar. 1913.

Mildred L. Butt.
Oct. 1909,
Jan. 1911.

Franklin Walter Taylor,
Son of
Franklin Wm. Taylor,
Oct. 9, 1854,
Jan. 1, 1919.

Otella Southern.
Sept 14, 1895,
Mar. 37, 1912

Robert L. Southern,
Aug. 19, 1870,
Oct. 29, 1919.

William D. Rich,
Feb. 16, 1862,
Jan 18, 1926.

William G. Smith,
May 13, 1857,
June 31, 1913.

Mollie E. Mooney,
Nov. 30, 1861,
May 23, 1932.

Geo. S. Mooney,
June 15, 1860,
July 9, 1926.

William Yance Farnsworth,
Mar 21, 1862,
Sept. 12, 1933.

Margaret. - Wife of
W.C. Massengill,
July 31, 1896,
Jan. 31, 1925.

Sam C. Harrell,
Sept. 7, 1868,
Aug. 28, 1919.

Samuel L. Williams,
June 30, 1873,
Nov. 3, 1929.

James Emory Baird,
Aug. 18, 1871,
July 4, 1931.

Jane Harrison Baird,
Oct. 6, 1833,
June 30, 1930.

Israel Charles Baird,
April 9, 1847,
July 13, 1917.

Minnie Daily Garrell
1873 - 1929.

Mary Louise Johnson Kirkpatrick,
April 12, 1857,
Jan. 18, 1925.

Granville Kirkpatrick,
Dec. 29, 1846,
April 12, 1917.

Emma J. Gobble,
Jan 9, 1866,
Oct. 22, 1919.

Jessie Utsman Black
Sept 21, 1891,
Mar 32, 1935.

Geo. W. DeVerger,
Dec. 10, 1863,
May 8, 1920.

James Patton Tyler,
Sept 22, 1886,
Oct 2, 1927.

Eula. - Wife of
J.P. Tyler,
1886 - 1920.

Clyde Park Greene,
Sept 22, 1880,
Dec. 1, 1917.

John E. Mitchell,
May 14, 1868,
Jan. 23, 1917.

Luke M. Mitchell,
Nov. 10, 1893,
Oct. 2, 1933.

Frank Hodges,
Sept 3, 1884,
Aug. 17, 1916.

Thomas J. Hale,
1874 - 1912.

His Wife,
Kate Yoe Hale,
1870 - 1929.

Woodlie F. Noe,
Wife of
Samuel L. Hoffmeister,
Jan 24, 1859,
April 13, 1933.

HAMBLEN COUNTY

JARNAGIN CEMETERY CONT.

(Pg. 13.)

J. Dan Noe,
June 1, 1853,
July 24, 1908.

Cornelia A. Noe,
April 16, 1859,
May 6, 1917.

Charles F. Davis,
Born Sept. 16, 1837,
Died July 27, 1899.

Harriet Jennings Davis,
Born Jan 5, 1836,
Died Jan. 16, 1908.

Elizabeth Jennings Wilkinson.
Nov. 30, 1843,
Aug. 18, 1938.

Joe Morgan Peoples,
Died Oct. 1, 1937.
Age 3 years, 1 month
and 6 days.

Henry M. Sherwood
Born July 5, 1847
Died March 8, 1924

HAMBLEN COUNTY
JARNAGIN CEMETERY
(Page 14)

Jennie Dean Hazzelwood
Born Jan. 19, 1856
Died Dec. 21, 1929

J. B. Hill
1857 - 1927

George W. Mc Kinney
Born Jan. 1, 1844
Died May 17, 1927

Williams
Uncle Joe

Laura Williams
Born May 21, 1863
Died Aug. 23, 1863

Robert B. Lee Williams
Born July 28, 1864
Died Aug. 12, 1865

Daisy Lee Williams
Born Aug. 29, 1866
Died July 27, 1869

Hattie M. Williams
Born Aug. 21, 1868
Died June 22, 1869

Newton A. Williams
Born July 28, 1850
Died Dec. 27, 1872

Mollie J. Williams, Wife of
Rev. James F. Hale
Born Mar. 31, 1857
Died June 2, 1877

Martha A. Williams
Born Mar. 9, 1884
Died Oct. 15, 1900

John M. Williams
Born Aug. 4, 1852
Died Jan. 11, 1934

Bessie Williams, Wife of
Vernon Clarkson
Born Aug. 2, 1881
Died Dec. 11, 1910

Gilbert, Son of
L. S. & D. B. Blair
Born July 11, 1910
Died Jan. 11, 1911

Clyde Lee
Died June 23, 1935
Age 46 yr.

Margaret Miller
Born May 9, 1857
Died Jan. 13, 1929

John B. Wagner
Born Nov. 17, 1867
Died Aug. 27, 1918

Jennie E. Wagner
Born Mar. 31, 1873
Died Apr. 28, 1920

Minnie L., Wife of
J. J. Goan
Born Sept. 18, 1891
Died Dec. 18, 1919

F. M. D. Clark
Born Oct. 13, 1861
Died Apr. 17, 1920

Kate Moore
Born Apr. 30, 1878
Died Oct. 22, 1926

H. W. Morley
1889 - 1925

Charles P. Mills
1856 - 1927

Mary Mills
1858 - 1929

Mary A. Johnson, Wife of
W. M. Johnson
Born 26, 1875
Died Oct. 24, 1927

Gaswell T. Hammond
Born Mar. 4, 1840
Died Dec. 1915

His Dau.

Maggie Ray
Born Apr. 12, 1883
Died Jan. 15, 1919

Howard Lee Isenberg
Born Nov. 28, 1907
Died Oct. 15, 1926

Lillie A. Lee, Wife of
S. M. Isenberg
Born Dec. 6, 1877
Died Dec. 31, 1915

Ella Virginia Litz
1871 - 1927

David Harold Litz
1866 - 1921

James Harold Litz
1920 - 1920

Isaac C. Crawford
Born Oct. 16, 1828
Died Mar. 10, 1910

Elizabeth, Wife of
I. C. Crawford
Died Apr. 16, 1903
Age 72 yr.

James H. Armstrong
Born Sept. 28, 1843
Died May 15, 1917

Rhoda B. Armstrong
Born Feb. 22, 1828
Died Jan. 21, 1919

Lawrence P. Speck
Born Oct. 28, 1841
Died Nov. 19, 1898

Elizabeth J. Speck
Born Aug. 9, 1842
Died Dec. 28, 1901

Ruth O. Armstrong
Born Nov. 22, 1906
Died Mar. 7, 1912

Elmer K. Armstrong
Born June 23, 1898
Died June 11, 1898

James M. Hill
1831 - 1904

Mary M. Hill
1835 - 1911

Ionia Hill
1864 - 1906

Mrs. Nettie Louisa Sanders
Died May 29, 1935
Age 46 yr. 8 mo. 5 da.

Cora B. Hunt, Wife of
E. W. Taylor
Born Nov. 12, 1875
Died Aug. 28, 1903

Arthur A. Moore
Born Nov. 21, 1873
Died Feb. 14, 1900

R. L. Speck
1884 - 1937

Mary Ellen Speck
Born June 7, 1915
Died May 28, 1919

George E. Speck
Born Jan. 16, 1845
Died Oct. 23, 1897

HAMBLEN COUNTY
JARNAGIN CEMETERY

(Page 16)

M. Ellen Speak
Born July 31, 1849
Died Jan. 8, 1914

Margaret Olean Mc Cord, Wife of
Harry S. Speak
Born June 19, 1874
Died Feb. 10, 1898

Laura Belle, Wife of
A. J. Robertson
Born June 30, 1870
Died Apr. 23, 1933

Laura E. Harris
Born July 3, 1857
Died Nov. 4, 1935

James Amos Dalton
Born Feb. 17, 1881
Died June 12, 1911

Dayton M. Atwood
Born Nov. 29, 1883
Died Jan. 15, 1931

Sarah E. Page Bayless
Born Aug. 30, 1840
Died Nov. 27, 1906

R. Moore Bayless
Born Feb. 19, 1823
Died July 19, 1896

Cairo S. Moore, Wife of
H. N. Witt
Born May 10, 1861
Died Dec. 27, 1932

Henry N. Witt
Died Aug. 7, 1936
Age 76 yr. 11 da.

Nancy M. Page Witt
Born July 19, 1845
Died May 21, 1906

Nannie, Dau. of
G. H. & N. M. Witt
Born Dec. 3, 1834
Died Dec. 10, 1834

Harry B., Son of
H. N. & C. S. Witt
Born June 25, 1888
Died Nov. 14, 1891

Roy W., Son of
H. N. & C. S. Witt
Born May 18, 1887
Died July 10, 1888

Everett B. Smith
Born Aug. 11, 1862
Died Feb. 11, 1933

Azzie Lee Taylor, Wife of
Everett B. Smith
Born Nov. 1, 1865
Died May 26, 1932

J. D. Smith
Born Apr. 22, 1830
Died Apr. 24, 1905

His Wife

Addie Smith
Born Jan. 16, 1844
Died Jan. 26, 1919

Dorman Gerald Pearson
Died Aug. 17, 1935
Age 4 da.

Edna Smith
Born Dec. 23, 1904
Died May 21, 1928

William L. Long
Born Sept. 19, 1840
Died June 15, 1920

Tabitha Long
Born Dec. 15, 1847
Died July 16, 1916

Mary Mc Farland Hunt
Born Feb. 12, 1846
Died July 30, 1909
"The Lord is my Shepherd."

Lillie, Wife of
G. L. Gastile
Born Jan. 20, 1882
Died July 19, 1915

Clem Tomlinson
Born Dec. 17, 1863
(still living)

Lizzie M. Murphey, Wife of
Clem Tomlinson
Born Mar. 3, 1869
Died Oct. 4, 1915

Anna Belle Murphey, Wife of
Hugh M. Kirkpatrick
Born Oct. 7, 1879
Died Sept. 11, 1911

Infant son of
W. G. & E. L. Ruble
Born Mar. 11, 1914
Died Mar. 11, 1914

John Murphey
Born Nov. 23, 1839
Died Apr. 23, 1908

Susan P. Murphey
Born Dec. 4, 1845
Died Oct. 4, 1926

W. A. Beckler
Died Apr. 29, 1937
Age 54 yrs.

John S. Capps
Born July 17, 1847
Died Jan. 31, 1913

Elizabeth Strode Capps
Died Dec. 26, 1906

Mary M. Strode
Died Jan. 17, 1910
Eliza Reed Strode
Died Apr. 5, 1925

Eula Hale, Dau. of
W. V. & Ida Brimson
Born Feb. 12, 1903
Died Apr. 17, 1906

Effie May Hartman
Born May 15, 1883
Died Sept. 17, 1899

Looney M. Dotey
Born Nov. 11, 1903
Died Oct. 9, 1933

Ada Pearl Haun, Wife of
Looney R. Dotey
Born Aug. 4, 1908
Died June 7, 1931

Robert Glenmore Wood
1874 - 1932

Eula Farmer Wood

Nannie Gibbs
Died Aug. 29, 1933
Age 48 yr. 11 mo. 22 da.

Rev. W. W. Overholt
Born Feb. 25, 1883
Died Apr. 3, 1934

James S. Mc Cravey
1871 - 1924

HAMBLEN COUNTY
JARNAGIN CEMETERY
(Page 18)

Hazel D. West
Born Nov. 9, 1894
Died Sept. 17, 1896

James A. West
Born Sept. 9, 1846
Died Feb. 20, 1929

James M. West
Born Oct. 18, 1892
Died Oct. 3, 1918

A. Frank Cutts
Born June 4, 1886
Died Feb. 10, 1924

Anliza Manis, Wife of
Rev. D. L. Manis
Born Dec. 17, 1848
Died June 30, 1933

Rev. L. D. Manis
Born Aug. 2, 1845
Died Aug. 18, 1926

W. C. Manis, Son of
D. L. & Annie L. Manis
Born Aug. 24, 1885
Died June 16, 1924

Miller Johnson Easley
Died Dec. 8, 1935
Age 56 yr. 9 mo. 20 da.

D. W. Long
Born Apr. 1, 1845
Died Feb. 3, 1928

Sallie C. Long
Born May 23, 1848
Died Mar. 19, 1925

Brant C. Housley
Born June 25, 1870
Died Dec. 18, 1925

Mary J. Corpening
Born Mar. 22, 1856
Died Aug. 16, 1929

John N. Corpening
Born Sept. 16, 1852
Died Apr. 8, 1931

Robert M. White
Born Mar. 12, 1867
Died Nov. 29, 1925

Mary V. Sullenbarger
1851 - 1934

Joseph M. Wood
Born Sept. 12, 1843
Died Mar. 29, 1920

His Wife

Arlene Virginia
Born Mar. 23, 1853
Died Jan. 9, 1934

Alexander Ross
Born Sept. 17, 1843
Died June 16, 1924

His Wife

Harriet A. Maxey
Born June 18, 1861
Died Apr. 24, 1923

Margaret Darnell
1851 - 1930

Mayme Darnell
Born May 7, 1884
Died July 7, 1923

William F. Cutts
Born June 9, 1855
Died June 3, 1905

HAMBLEN COUNTY
JARNAGIN CEMETERY
(Page 19)

Dr. Charles G. Gass
Born Nov. 15, 1859
Died Aug. 20, 1912

Sadie S. Gass
Born Dec. 2, 1860

John R. Gass
Born July 7, 1886
Died Jan. 7, 1906

Coy S. Gass
Born July 1, 1878
Died Nov. 15, 1923

Mary Alma Corpening, Wife of
E. F. Harrell
Born Nov. 20, 1896
Died Mar. 9, 1931

Byrl F. Manis
Born Feb. 18, 1883
Died Dec. 9, 1932

John W. Catron
Born June 16, 1848
Died Apr. 17, 1923

Fannie W. Catron
Born Feb. 20, 1857
Died Apr. 20, 1925

Patsy Teamster Anderson
Died Dec. 28, 1932
Age 55 yr. 10 & 20 da.

Charles L. Anderson
Died Jan. 30, 1929
Age - -

Jennie Anderson
Born Oct. 3, 1840
Died Feb. 2, 1909

Charles S. Anderson
Born June 15, 1836
Died Dec. 7, 1920

Mary J. Hodge
Born May 18, 1842
Died Jan. 14, 1903

M. W. Hodge
Born Jan. 18, 1855

L. M. Allen
Born Feb. 11, 1845

Frances R. Allen
Born Jan. 28, 1872

Sophia Moss French
1861 - 1925

Rev. George D. French
1843 - 1923

Dora F. Barrow
1878 - 1930

Robert W. Barrow
1868 - 1917

Catherine Rader, Wife of
V. V. Vanhuss
Born Sept. 1, 1850
Died Sept. 19, 1924

Roy Cox Angel Jr.
Born Oct. 19, 1914
Died July 6, 1927

G. Caswell Wigington
Born Dec. 3, 1866
Died Nov. 23, 1930

Bessie Marsh
Born Mar. 6, 1914
Died Mar. 7, 1914

Nellie Marsh
Born Mar. 22, 1911
Died Nov. 12, 1913

Rev. Geo. S. Porter
Born Nov. 27, 1852
Died Jan. 25, 1925

HAMBLEN COUNTY
JARNAGIN CEMETERY
(Page 20)

Otis W. Harvel
Born July 29, 1916
Died Jan. 28, 1928

Arthur Harvel
Born Apr. 6, 1883
Died Feb. 16, 1925

Billie Fortune
Born Nov. 7, 1914
Died July 1, 1920

Kenneth Gray Ferguson
Born Feb. 4, 1879
Died Dec. 6, 1920

Sue Virginia Ferguson
Born July 1, 1915
Died Nov. 19, 1931

Julia Lyons Charles
Born Dec. 21, 1872
Died Sept. 4, 1934

Joseph S. Charles
Born June 28, 1861
Died Feb. 4, 1932

Leon Garland Perrow
Born Oct. 9, 1890
Died Jan. 18, 1928

Charles H. Perrow
Born Feb. 23, 1841
Died Feb. 3, 1925

Sue Graham Perrow
Born May 19, 1851
Died Mar. 13, 1936

R. H. Turley
Born Feb. 8, 1859
Died Sept. 16, 1909

John W. Lackey
Born Nov. 10, 1872
Died Sept. 21, 1929

Samuel A. Coile
Born Jan. 18, 1857
Died May 9, 1923

Ethel B. Jones, Wife of
Raymond E. Mills
1908 - 1934

T. J. Cantwell
Born Apr. 7, 1857
Died June 18, 1923

Mollie J. Cantwell
Born Dec. 24, 1860
Died Mar. 21, 1916

Nina Chestnut
Died July 22, 1932
Age 66yrs.

Lena Leonard Hughes
Born Nov. 4, 1896
Died Mar. 12, 1922

John H. Parrott
Born July 2, 1844
Died Apr. 6, 1924

Lou J. Parrott
Born May 13, 1856
Died Mar. 31, 1924

Alice M. Rippetoe
Born Sept. 6, 1861
Died Nov. 11, 1902

W. T. Rippetoe
Born Oct. 22, 1849
Died Oct. 25, 1920

Mary L. Rippetoe
Born May 1, 1854
Died July 22, 1879

Le Roy Ryder
Died Nov. 29, 1932
Age 38 yr.

HAMBLEN COUNTY
JARNAGIN CEMETERY
(Page 21)

Joseph F. Rippetoe
Born Oct. 18, 1876
Died Jan. 19, 1899

Martha F. Rippetoe
Born Aug. 15, 1872
Died Oct. 21, 1880

Grant Allen
1869 - 1920

Barbaba K. Zirkle Bell
Born Nov. 6, 1853
Died Dec. 1, 1920

Robert Climer
1870 - 1920

Catharine King Watkins
Born Apr. 22, 1857
Died Jan. 28, 1923

Tillie Elizabeth Massengill,
Wife of Willard Bales
Born June 30, 1903
Died Jan. 18, 1928

Mary Miller Massengill,
Wife of W. S. Murrell
Born May 29, 1898
Died Feb. 21, 1924

Edna Florence Cross, Wife of
W. D. Massengill
Born July 29, 1865
Died Nov. 29, 1923

W. D. Massengill
Born Mar. 8, 1863

Nancy Sloan Willing
Age 68 yr.

George W. Willing
Age 75 yr.

Sarah E. Willing
Born May 23, 1839
Died Apr. 14, 1877

David Willing
Born May 12, 1835
Died Jan. 23, 1915

Laura Garrison Willing
Age 64 yr.

Malissa Angeline Willing
Born Feb. 29, 1868
Died June 26, 1873

Etta De Vault Sullenberger
Born Feb. 11, 1890
Died Jan. 31, 1937

Jennie E. Noe
Born Aug. 26, 1887
Died July 15, 1930

J. H. De Vault
Born Apr. 11, 1862
Died Nov. 16, 1925

Agusta J. Holston
Born Oct. 9, 1858
Died Nov. 21, 1929

Samuel H. Holston
Born Dec. 21, 1852
Died Oct. 11, 1920

James Calvin Farmer
Born May 4, 1845
Died Sept. 13, 1932
Mary E. Farmer
Born Oct. 7, 1860
Died June 11, 1921

John H. Helms
Born Nov. 2, 1840
Died Aug. 7, 1922
Enlisted July 10, 1861
Co. E. 61 Reg.
Served 4 yr. in Inf.

Mary Frank Rader
Born & Died
Oct. 20, 1924

HAMBLEN COUNTY
JARNAGIN CEMETERY
(Page 22)

William P. Rippetoe
Born Oct. 17, 1870
Died June 9, 1899

Hattie Mae Rippetoe
Born Dec. 28, 1890
Died Feb. 9, 1919

Rhoda Inman Hale
1884 - 1916

Verna Wilmeth Hale
1886 - 1917

C. A. Shockley
1855 - 1926

Pauline Shockley
1924 - 1924

James J. Moody
Died Jan. 8, 1936
Age 58 yr.

Ruth J. Mc Corkle
Born Feb. 3, 1873
Died May 29, 1935

M. Elizabeth Morelock
1858 - 1923

Sallie N. Mefford
1898 - 1904

James N. Mefford
Born Oct. 9, 1847
Died Feb. 17, 1920

His Wife

Sarah N. Mefford
Born Jan. 17, 1852
Died Aug. 20, 1927

W. D. Trammell
1836 - 1896

Mrs. J. P. Davis
Born Dec. 7, 1873
Died Mar. 17, 1935

Dr. J. P. Davis
Born Sept. 8, 1870
Died Mar. 3, 1933

C. Frank Davis Jr.
Born Feb. 11, 1933
Died Feb. 13, 1933

Margaret T. Spillman
1848 - 1920

M. C. Booth
1861 - 1931

Mary Alice Booth
1871 - 1923

Will H. Burke
1890 - 1904

Kathryn A. Trobaugh
Born Sept. 6, 1903
Died June 18, 1907

William P. Trobaugh
Born July 1, 1852
Died July 20, 1909

Dorcas Rowe Trobaugh Franklin
1870 - 1925

N. N. Franklin
Born Feb. 23, 1841
Died Nov. 1, 1906

Mary T. Franklin
Born Apr. 6, 1844
Died Apr. 12, 1919

Lexie Franklin Williams,
Wife of
Joseph R. Williams
Born Nov. 28, 1876
Died Sept. 21, 1935

HAMBLEN COUNTY
JARNAGIN CEMETERY
(Page 23)

Mary Anna Hale
Born Nov. 24, 1876
Died Feb. 27, 1923

Sarah Ann Hale
1850 - 1934

Richard Spencer Hale
1850 - 1927

Rosa Ellen Hale
Born Mar. 1, 1873
Died Nov. 14, 1874

William Carl Pettigrew
Born Sept. 28, 1908
Died May 8, 1926

Edwin French Taylor
Born Mar. 23, 1912
Died Sept. 24, 1912

Mary V. Taylor
1846 - 1926

Rufus F. Taylor
1846 - 1923

Ada B. Taylor
Born Apr. 7, 1875
Died June 27, 1895

Glen G. Alexander
Born Sept. 13, 1903
Died May 30, 1928

Virginia N. Andre
Born Aug. 22, 1900
Died Sept. 7, 1924

Charles Andre Jr.
Born Mar. 5, 1897
Died Dec. 27, 1900

Evelyn Andre
Born Feb. 9, 1904
Died Nov. 17, 1907

James G. Rose   3
Born Sept. 1, 1845
Died June 5, 1904

Virginia J. Rose
Born May 31, 1845
Died May 4, 1922

John Rector
1841 - 1921

Malinda Rector
1830 - 1884

Frank D. Tate
Born Nov. 29, 1877
Died Oct. 17, 1930

John Henry Tate
Born Aug. 20, 1840
Died Nov. 19, 1925

Mrs. Belle Dickerson Tate
1859 - 1912

Robert Mc M. Jones
1847 - 1923

George G. Duncan
1863 - 1931

George M. Trobaugh
Born Sept. 15, 1840
Died Oct. 17, 1907

Hester Anna Trobaugh
Born Oct. 31, 1852
Died Aug. 6, 1922
"They being dead yet speaketh."

Clarence Bales
Jan. 16, 1916

Claud Bales
Nov. 30, 1920

HAMBLEN COUNTY
JARNAGIN CEMETERY
(Page 24)

Lula Josephine Havely
Born Sept. 30, 1870
Died Feb. 7, 1930

Mary Elizabeth Havely
Born Mar. 7, 1841
Died Mar. 7, 1922

Charles Benton Havely
Born Nov. 10, 1840
Died Aug. 17, 1922

Tillman H. O'Dell
Born Aug. 3, 1847
Died June 3, 1925

Nolan G. O'Dell
Born Apr. 5, 1897
Died Feb. 14, 1922

Glenn Bales
Born Feb. 13, 1908
Died Sept. 27, 1915

Edith Muriel Bales
Born Nov. 18, 1912
Died Feb. 17, 1933

John J. Wilkinson
Powhatan, Va.
Born Jan. 19, 1856
Died Feb. 24, 1931

Robert M. Rogers
Born Nov. 13, 1856
Died Aug. 26, 1933

William Edward Jones
Died Sept. 26, 1936
Age 46 yr. 5 da.

Lena B. Bartley
Jan. 25, 1936
Age 63 yr. 4 mo.

Frank E. Bartley
Born May 9, 1879
Died Dec. 31, 1932

George Washington Ivy
Died June 19, 1937
Age 70 yr.

Clarence Turley Murphey
Born Oct. 20, 1898
Died Nov. 9, 1924

Martha Turley Murphey
Died Mar. 6, 1934
Age 67 yr.

Leonard Charles Murphey
Born Feb. 24, 1924
Died May 21, 1929

Willard V. Bales
Died July 26, 1937
Age 37 yr. 10 mo. 29 da.

Henry Lee Bales
Born Aug. 17, 1888
Died Aug. 21, 1932

R. F. Bales
Born May 10, 1859
Died Nov. 16, 1936

Robert Clinton Bales
Died July 27, 1937
Age 82 yr. 3 mo. 8 da.

Lula Chase Portrum
Born Aug. 23, 1888
Died Oct. 7, 1890

Susan Kirkpatrick, Wife of
T. W. Portrum
Born June 21, 1847
Died Jan. 10, 1909

Thomas W. Portrum
Born Nov. 15, 1837
Died Sept. 25, 1892

I. Ernest Broyles
Born Dec. 3, 1884
Died Apr. 4, 1920

HAMBLEN COUNTY
JARNAGIN CEMETERY

(Page 25)

Emily Louise Mc Corkle
1912 - 1927

Mollie Cain Mc Corkle
1864 - 1934

Francis Pickens Mc Corkle
1861 - 1929

Joseph O. Atkins
Born Oct. 1, 1862
Died Oct. 8, 1929

Minnie B. Arnott, Dau. of
Sarah & A. H. Arnott
Died Apr. 14, 1898

Sarah J. Arnott
Died Sept. 23, 1895

A. H. Arnott
Died Aug. 1, 1897

Jack Graham
Died Mar. 26, 1937
Age 27 yr.

Rachael F. Jaynes
Died Jan. 4, 1936
Age 14 yr. 8 mo. 11 da.

James H. Loving Jr.
Born Sept. 24, 1926
Died July 5, 1935

William C. Barron
Born Oct. 3, 1842
Died Oct. 6, 1906

Eva L. Barron
Born June 17, 1853
Died May 20, 1935

Herbert W. Barron
Born Dec. 17, 1879
Died Aug. 28, 1908

Jarvis L. Williams
Born July 6, 1913
Died May 2, 1929

Mary Ruth Moore
Died May 7, 1933
Age 2 yr. 9 mo. 5 da.

Jennie Copenhaver, Wife of
A. W. Edwards
Born Dec. 17, 1862
Died June 14, 1935
"Be ye also ready; Saved by
Grace."

Hiram P. Daily
Born Mar. 12, 1835
Died July 19, 1877

William E. Daily
Born Mar. 6, 1871
Died Nov. 2, 1926

Earl D. Hill
1888
Age 2 mo.

Edna W. Hill
1888
Age 3 mo.

Elaine Yard Hill
Born Jan. 29, 1910
Died Apr. 22, 1910

Edward Yard Hill
Born Sept. 1, 1882
Died Nov. 8, 1926

Anna Hill Portrum
Born Sept. 23, 1880
Died Nov. 3, 1927

Dr. Judson S. Hill
Born June 3, 1854
Died Sept. 14, 1931

HAMBLEN COUNTY
JARNAGIN CEMETERY
(Page 26)

Maher Yard Hill
Born June 17, 1894
Died July 5, 1934

John S. Carriger
Born Mar. 24, 1863
Died Dec. 21, 1931

Dr. Charles Thomas Carroll Jr.
Born Feb. 22, 1873
Died July 26, 1933

Minnie Hale Carter
Died May 13, 1937
Age 65 yr.

John Rowan Carter
Died June 5, 1936
Age 66 yr. 8 mo. 4 da.

Harriet Susong
Died May 2, 1937
Age 76 yr. 3 mo. 20 da.

Sim Shockley
Born Feb. 9, 1884
Died Aug. 15, 1933

James Susong Gentry
Died Apr. 12, 1937
Age 18 yr. 11 mo.

Fain Anderson, Son of
Mr. & Mrs. J. L. Kanode
Jan. 24, 1929

Sallie V. Reinhardt
Born March 6, 1901
Died Dec. 19, 1926

William Decater Bushong
Died Oct. 3, 1937
Aged 72 yrs. 10 mo. 2 da.

HAMBLEN COUNTY
JARNAGIN CEMETERY

(Page 27)

Rev. J. G. Graichen
1852 - 1929

Born Jan. 14, 1855
J. Seward Chapman
Died Sept. 6, 1935

Robert A. Lyle
Born Nov. 8, 1872
Died Mar. 12, 1931

Matilda F. Murrell
Born Apr. 23, 1861
Died Dec. 29, 1932

Melville M. Murrell
Born Nov. 9, 1855
Died Feb. 20, 1933
(One stone)

George L. Hefner
Born Apr. 2, 1903
Died Sept. 22, 1935

James G. Templin
Born May 23, 1868
Died Feb. 23, 1930

Mable P. Isely

D. A. Isely
Born Aug. 10, 1878
Died July 21, 1929

Ella Grattan Payne, Dau. of
David Bryce & Helen James Payne
Wife of Dr. George Kempton Turner
Born in Lynchburg Va.
Dec. 14, 1842
Died in Morristown, Tenn.
July 27, 1894

Dr. George Kempton Turner, Son of
George W. & Rebecca Murrell Turner
Born in Lynchburg Va., Apr. 22, 1840
Died in Morristown, Tenn., Mar. 26, 1898

G. A. Russell
Born Feb. 16, 1858
Died Feb. 26, 1931

Robert D. Russell
Born Mar. 31, 1862
Died Nov. 24, 1936

Murphy M. Purkey
Died Apr. 14, 1931
Age 46 yr.

Ben M. Toney
Born Apr. 20, 1873
Died Apr. 23, 1931

Paul Eugene Toney
Born Apr. 5, 1902
Died Oct. 27, 1907

Josh M. Toney
Born Jan. 6, 1892
Died Nov. 21, 1913

Nancy J. Toney
Born Apr. 23, 1856
Died Apr. 24, 1933

Robert R. Andrews Jr.
Born Apr. 27, 1920
Died May 10, 1920

William Lee Baird
Died Apr. 1, 1936
Age 37 yr. 1 mo. 8 da.

John Alexander Baird
Died Mar. 4, 1918
Age 51 yr.

Hagan Conkin
Died June 9, 1937
Age 70 yr. 8 mo. 8 da.

Mack Clyde Johnson
Born July 26, 1909
Died Oct. 27, 1936

HAMBLEN COUNTY
JARNAGIN CEMETERY

(Page 28)

Grace Johnson Blount
Died Jan. 24, 1937
Age 23 yr. 10 mo. 20 da.

Robert Thomas Cain
Died Sept. 29, 1935
Age 30 yr. 1 mo. 8 da.

Mrs. H. N. Cain
Died Apr. 14, 1935
Age 56 yr.

James O. Christmas
Born Nov. 11, 1869
Died Oct. 31, 1933

Abraham Lincoln Smith
Born Apr. 15, 1865
Died Aug. 4, 1932

George W. Chilton
Born Jan. 16, 1886
Died June 17, 1888

John L. Chilton
Born May 26, 1894
Died Nov. 14, 1896

Robert Harle Miller
Died May 11, 1935
Age 58 yr. 7 mo. 7 da.

John Woodfin, Son of
A. B. & B. F. Waggoner
Jan. 14, 1924

J. N. Fisher
Born Dec. 12, 1859
Died May 29, 1932

Florence M. Fisher
Born Jan. 8, 1867
(still living)

Maxwell T. Smith
Born June 27, 1888
Died July 9, 1931

Dr. W. G. Ruble
Born Mar. 17, 1874
Died Apr. 27, 1926

Emma Legg Harle
Born Aug. 5, 1861
Died June 17, 1924

Baldwin Harle
Born Mar. 30, 1858
Died Dec. 18, 1934

Ross, Son of
Jas. F. & Ida Mathes
1910 - 1912

Robert Toney
Born Oct. 4, 1896
Died Mar. 20, 1931

Guy Toney
Born Mar. 29, 1900
Died Apr. 12, 1900

Nancy M. Toney
Born Dec. 24, 1870
Died Apr. 29, 1919

John H. Dickenson
1895 - 1926

Helen Bible
Born Sept. 2, 1910
Died Apr. 19, 1927

Bernice House Hawk
Born Aug. 8, 1892
Died Nov. 23, 1929

Infant Son of
Mr. & Mrs. J. B. Hawk

Joseph Scruggs Harmon
1914 - 1924

Sarah Catharine Hawkins
Died June 24, 1936
Age 76 yr. 7 da.

HAMBLEN COUNTY
JARNAGIN CEMETERY
(Pg.29)

Thomas Harrell Gill
Born Feb. 22, 1905
Died Dec. 8, 1924

Annie Carriger Gill
Born Jan. 18, 1867
Died Jan. 1, 1933

James Shields Gill
Born Oct. 12, 1857
Died Sept. 26, 1927

Frank C. Jarnagin
Born July 30, 1876
Died Sept. 21, 1929

Frank Taylor Nance
Born Feb. 21, 1863
Died Mar. 1, 1927

Flora Augusta Hobson
Born Sept. 28, 1861
Died Sept. 10, 1930

Mary Nula Shields
Born July 4, 1864
Died Jan. 27, 1928

John L. Chilton
Born Sept. 17, 1856
Died Mar. 16, 1924

Horace B. Chilton
Born Nov. 27, 1895
Died Jan. 27, 1896

Harris Whiteside Helms
Born Feb. 27, 1893
Died Jan. 30, 1926

H. T. Senter, Wife of
Gov. D. W. C. Senter
Born Jan. 22, 1841
Died Feb. 13, 1916

Ex. Gov. De Witt Clinton Senter
Born Mar. 26, 1830
Died June 14, 1898
Member of Tenn. House of
Representatives from 1852 to
1861, of the Senate from 1867
to 1869
Gov. of Tenn. two terms.
"After Life's fitful fever he
sleeps well."

Lucy J., Dau. of
D. W. & Lizzie Sullenberger
Born Apr. 11, 1879
Died Dec. 18, 1898

Owen
Elizabeth Jane Sullenberger
Born Apr. 20, 1852
Died May 16, 1928

D. W. Sullenberger
Born Dec. 25, 1851
Died July 21, 1925

Robert Mc Farland
Born Nov. 27, 1863
Died Nov. 20, 1902

Jessie Trent Mc Farland
Born July 4, 1869
Died Feb. 12, 1899

A. R. Epps
Born Jan. 10, 1920
Died July 4, 1921

H. C. Epps
Born Oct. 8, 1924
Died Oct. 8, 1924

Hubert C. Coffey
1900 - 1928

Katie S. Coffey
1902 -

HAMBLEN COUNTY
JARNAGIN CEMETERY
(Pg.30)

Jennie Whiteside, Wife of
H. L. Douglass
Born Oct. 31, 1869
Died Dec. 21, 1903

Harry Lockwood Douglass
Born July 6, 1864
Died Dec. 13, 1927

Dr. William Fox
1863 - 1929

Mary Elizabeth Peters
Born Mar. 6, 1921
Died Aug. 7, 1924

W. B. Hodges
Born Jan. 7, 1870
Died Jan. 22, 1925

Adolphus White
Born Dec. 20, 1866
Died Dec. 30, 1924

Denver C. Cary
Born Nov. 27, 1899
Died Jan. 5, 1926

Ray S. Cary
Born Aug. 18, 1899
Died Jan. 7, 1925

Dorothy Edith Cary
Born Feb. 16, 1934
Died Dec. 22, 1934

Mary A., Bogar, Wife of
Dr. J. E. Miller
Born Jan. 9, 1861
Died May 18, 1924

Dr. Jacob Eastman Miller
Born June 26, 1854
Died Sept. 30, 1929

Robert L. Holmes
1882 - 1923

Thomas T. Mc Whirter
1854 - 1932

Dr. D. Samuel Bruner
Born Dec. 11, 1868
Died May 28, 1924

Fannie Morgan Hickey
Died Nov. 28, 1934
Age 56 yr. 10 mo. 15 da.

Katherine Rebecca Rutledge,
Wife of Oliver C. King
Born Mar. 6, 1843
Died Sept. 13, 1925

Oliver Caswell King,
Eldest Son of
L. M. & Penelope L. King
Born Aug. 4, 1841
Died May 24, 1893

Penelope Louisa Massengill,
Wife of L. M. King
Born Feb. 15, 1818
Died July 1, 1905

Leander Montgomery King
Born July 29, 1818
Died Dec. 12, 1884

Louisa M. Walker
1856 - 1930

Rufus Morgan Hickey
Born Aug. 4, 1880
Died July 8, 1926

Robert E. Sharp
Born Mar. 2, 1896
Died Feb. 4, 1927

HAMBLEN COUNTY
JARNAGIN CEMETERY
(Page 31)

Ida Easley
Died Dec. 31, 1908

James Carlyle Easley
Died Apr. 15, 1933
Age 49 yr. 4 mo. 29 da.

Mary Lydia Easley
Died 1933
Age 54 yrs. 7 mo.

William Mc Farland
Born Sept. 15, 1821
Died Apr. 12, 1900

Nancy A. Turley Mc Farland
Born Aug. 25, 1829
Died Feb. 25, 1863

Children
Pauline   — William
Walter   — Thomas
John   — Mary

Ida Trent Mc Farland
Born Jan. 13, 1871
Died Feb. 12, 1928

Henry P. Waugh
Born May 6, 1874
Died Nov. 12, 1924

Mary A. Waugh
Born Dec. 16, 1833
Died Oct. 14, 1924

Rev. H. P. Waugh
Born 1825
Died July 10, 1898

Jay Crowell Brown
Born Nov. 1, 185-
Died Jan. 28, 1917

Allie Proctor Brown
Born July 15, 1854
Died Nov. 9, 1930

Alex Nelson Stuart
Born Oct. 2, 1878
Died Sept. 11, 1912

A. G. Stuart
"Uncle Am"
Born Aug. 24, 1853
Died Mar. 17, 1926

Sallie Nelson Stuart
Born May 25, 1855
Died Dec. 19, 1892

George Elliott Stuart
Born July 14, 1892
Died Nov. 3, 1892

Grace De Armond, Wife of
Gaines Stuart
Died Oct. 13, 1928

Dr. Oscar R. Tomlinson
Born Mar. 7, 1870
Died Aug. 27, 1930

Howard A. Robertson
Born Nov. 20, 1895
Died Aug. 15, 1930

James Allison Carriger
Born Nov. 30, 1845
Died May 23, 1930

Julia Lenoir Carriger
Born Jan. 12, 1850
Died Aug. 11, 1892

Julia Lenoir Carriger
Born Aug. 10, 1892
Died Sept. 14, 1892

Nathaniel L. Mc Canless
Born Oct. 31, 1831
Died May 23, 1897

Margaret C. Mc Canless
Born Nov. 27, 1847
Died Jan. 24, 1910

Michael Carriger Mc Clanless
   Born May 6, 1874
   Died Sept. 20, 1927

George W. Folsom
1824 - 1898

Sarah Ellen Folsom
1848 - 1920

Infant Dau. of
H. A. & J. F. Peck 1901

Wiley Housley
Died Jan. 14, 1927
Age 65 yr. 5 mo. 14 da.

Mrs. J. G. Macferrin
1844 - 1932

Joseph D., Son of
Rev. J. G. & L. S. Mc Ferrin
Born Dec. 18, 1885
Feb. 10, 1891

Rev. J. G. Mc Ferrin
1846 - 1917

Ida M. Daily
Born May 1, 1869
Died July 21, 1935

Sarah N. Daily
Born Mar. 20, 1845
Died June 23, 1934

Billie Pierce Beets
Born Feb. 14, 1927
Died Oct. 28, 1928

Will F. Beets
Born Sept. 3, 1885
Died Dec. 28, 1926

Brooks Manly Beets
Born July 22, 1894
Died Sept. 14, 1928

Betty Jo Boatman
Born Oct. 26, 1930
Died Sept. 22, 1936

James William Atchley
Born Oct. 15, 1878
Died Sept. 19, 1932

Rowe

James F.
Age 3 yr.

Edward N.
Age 1 yr.

Geo. A.
Age 3 da.

G. A. Rowe
Born Dec. 25, 1834
Died June 13, 1910

Susan C., Wife of
G. A. Rowe
Born Feb. 24, 1831
Died July 13, 1899

Jas. S. Beal
Born June 19, 1848
Died Nov. 27, 1925

Argyra G. Beal
Born Dec. 8, 1848
Died Mar. 28, 1925

Wilmer K. Price
Born Feb. 8, 1904
Died Oct. 16, 1928

Frank Warren Donaldson
Born May 19, 1878
Died June 3, 1931

Joseph Eckel Donaldson
Born Sept. 25, 1854
Died Jan. 13, 1904

Wayne Franklin Taylor
Died Nov. 21, 1931
Age 27 days

HAMBLEN COUNTY
JARNAGIN CEMETERY

(Page 33)

Jennie Fulkerson, Wife of
Chas. E. Baylor
1855 - 1929

Bessie L. Willis
Born Jan. 5, 1889
Died Oct. 8, 1902

Cora E. Willis
Born Mar. 22, 1892
Died July 23, 1896

Cecil K. Willis
Born Feb. 24, 1900
Died Oct. 3, 1906

Lilly E. Willis
Born July 25, 1902
Died Dec. 17, 1921

Willie Gertrude Purkey
Died Dec. 24, 1928
Age 25 yr. 5 mo. 24 da.

Mother

Ivy Belle Foard
1886 - 1932

Geraldine Earl Curtis
1927

Lexie Mae Champ
Died Mar. 26, 1936
Age 35 yr.

Lula White
Born May 3, 1873
Died Oct. 25, 1911

Landon C. White
Born July 10, 1844
Died July 25, 1912

Hannah E. White
Born June 30, 1846
Died Apr. 19, 1936

J. Alvin Cox
Born Dec. 21, 1848
Died May 5, 1936

Mary C. Helm
Born Mar. 29, 1818
Died May 17, 1900

Dr. W. M. F. Helm
Born June 8, 1818
Died Nov. 7, 1883

Sue C. Maine
Born Apr. 12, 1849
Died Oct. 27, 1877

Mamie Kate Helm
Born Jan. 11, 1868
Died Nov. 19, 1893

Willie Helm
Born Aug. 18, 1871
Died Jan. 20, 1888

Sallie Eckel Helm
Born Sept. 5, 1844
Died Jan. 7, 1888

Henry C. Helm
Born July 3, 1844
Died July 13, 1879

Jennie S. Hurst
Born Sept. 23, 1848
Died Apr. 18, 1925

John Edward Conkin
Died Feb. 5, 1928
Age 59 yr. 11 mo. 11 da.

Guy Carter
Died Nov. 7, 1936
Age 30 yr. 6 mo. 15 da.

May Crider
Died May 2, 1935
Age 35 yrs.

HAMBLEN COUNTY
JARNAGIN CEMETERY

(Pg. 34)

William H. Lowry Sr.
Born Mar. 24, 1869
Died Sept. 7, 1936

William H. Lowery Jr.
Born Oct. 18, 1907
Died Mar. 29, 1930

Betty Swan Lowry
Died Sept. 9, 1932
Age 8 mo. 23 da.

Clifford E. Lowry
Died March 6, 1937
Age 37 yr. 5 mo. 1 da.

Stewart Mc Crary
Died July 4, 1934
Age 55 yr. 8 mo. 5 da.

Minnie Lee Hill Bierley
Died Jan. 10, 1934
Age 32 yr. 7 mo. 21 da.

Jennie Marie Inman
Died Dec. 2, 1935
Age 27 yr.

A. J. Cole
Born Oct. 10, 1885
Died June 30, 1929

Nancy J. Cole
Born Oct. 12, 1859
Died Nov. 19, 1929

Lola Taylor
Died Apr. 22, 1930
Age 30 yr. 1 da.

Marvin Stublefield
Died Jan. 3, 1936
Age 1 yr. 5 mo. 13 da.

Frank A. Speek
Born July 18, 1859
Died Apr. 28, 1915

Martha E. Armstrong
Born Dec. 4, 1859
Died Apr. 6, 1933

Charles M. Armstrong
Born Oct. 14, 1857
Died Mar. 1, 1934

Josie M., Dau. of
Mr. & Mrs. Pete Elmore
Born July 20, 1932
Died May 28, 1935

Mother
Mary J. Riley

Father
Thomas W. Riley

Son
Willis L. Riley

William M. Brogan
Died Aug. 28, 1936
Age 81 yr. 14 da.

America M. Trent
Born Dec. 25, 1860
Died June 1, 1932

Rosa L. Teno
Died Aug. 18, 1934
Age 52 yr. 8 mo.

Our Darling
"She was the sunshine of our
Home."

Ruby Jean Brady
Born Jan. 10, 1933
Died Dec. 19, 1935

Darling
Kenneth Roy, Son of
Mr. & Mrs. Crosby Haun
Born Aug. 7, 1935
Died Nov. 16, 1935

HAMBLEN COUNTY
JARNAGIN CEMETERY
(Pg. 35)

John N. Shipley
Died July 2, 1934
Age 70 yr. 17 da.

W. K. Williams
1854 - 1929

Robert L. Black
Born Mar. 12, 1870
Died Sept. 26, 1929

Mary E. Black
Born Oct. 10, 1867
Died Oct. 24, 1929

Elijah Richardson
Born Sept. 16, 1844
Died May 29, 1911

Martha Richardson
Born Apr. 2, 1853
Died Jan. 7, 1923

John H. Franklin
Born Feb. 15, 1856
Died Oct. 25, 1924

Charley B. Holley
Born Dec. 21, 1845
Died Apr. 13, 1919

Addie Holley
Born Feb. 16, 1868
Died June 24, 1915

Earnest O. Franklin
Born Aug. 6, 1894
Died Feb. 6, 1908

Authur D. Patchen
Born Aug. 15, 1870
Died June 30, 1923

Chas I. Oldham
Born Feb. 1, 1878
Died Nov. 24, 1914

Selma L. Oldham
Born Oct. 5, 1885
Died July 13, 1935

Homer L. Williams
1889 - 1927

Dr. R. B. Owens
Born June 22, 1838
Died Sept. 26, 1889

Joseph B. Wice
Born Jan. 2, 1853
Died June 30, 1915

His Wife

Eliza T. Wice
Born Jan. 27, 1857

W. F. Johnson
Born Apr. 24, 1880
Died May 4, 1927

Ada Johnson
Born Apr. 18, 1882

Mary Moore, Late Wife of
Amos Moore
Born Apr. 10, 1904
Died May 17, 1936

Sadie Moore, Wife of
Amos Moore
Born June 10, 1893
Died Aug. 18, 1928

Hattie Carrie Walker
Died May 26, 1937
Age 62 yr.

Sue Bell Mc Rae
Died July 4, 1906
Age 43 yr.

HAMBLEN COUNTY
JARNAGIN CEMETERY
(Page 36)

John D. Riley Jr.
Born Oct. 5, 1893
Died Dec. 14, 1931

Edna L. Gamble
Born Oct. 31, 1894
Died Oct. 21, 1907
"Of such is the kingdom
of heaven."

Nannie King, Wife of
Samuel W. Gill
1847 - 1892

Gill, Son of
J. M. & M. A. Wooten
Born Dec. 1, 1888
Died May 5, 1900

William R. Wheeler
Born Sept. 10, 1872
Died Apr. 20, 1931

Ruby Pauline Anderson
Died May 14, 1937
Age 24 yr. 15 da.

Nannie Hypsher
Born July 24, 1873
Died Sept. 4, 1936

Bettie Lee Hypsher
Born May 23, 1920
Died July 5, 1934

J. W. Duncan
Died May 24, 1925
Age 53 yr. 7 mo. 8 da.

Millard Glenn Shannon
Died Aug. 18, 1936
Age 30 yr. 5 mo. 3 da.

Alcesta L. Crozier
1855 - 1915

William Clyde Franklin
Born Feb. 26, 1896
Died Oct. 2, 1935
World War Veteran

Anne Lewis Hasson Russell
Born Sept. 7, 1891
Died Jan. 2, 1932

Louise Susong, Wife of
Horace N. Quinton
Born Aug. 7, 1901
Died Nov. 14, 1932

Carrie Lowry, Wife of
Earl R. Mc Gimpsey
Born Mar. 22, 1896
Died June 25, 1934

Mary Bob Russell
Born Sept. 14, 1861
Died May 5, 1935

Ella Hodge Travis
Born Apr. 7, 1894
Died Sept. 2, 1935

W. T. Travis
Born May 15, 1886

Joseph H. Horner
Died July 6, 1935
Age 26 yr. 25 da.

Alice Bassett Cooper
Born Apr. 19, 1906
Died July 29, 1935

Amos Watson Lotspeich
Died Nov. 7, 1936
Age 79 yr. 6 mo. 19 da.

M. J. Roberts
Born Jan. 19, 1855
Died June 5, 1907

NO PAGE 120

Located one mile west of Whitesburg on old pike to Russellville.
It was orginally on the farm of Rev. R. J. Hyatt, who started it as a
family burying ground, the first interment was of his little daughter
Georgia Mc Emily Hyatt who died March 13, 1877. It gradually become
a public burying ground, and when Rev. Hyatt sold his farm, he set
the graveyard aside as public property.

This information was given by Frank Hyatt of Russellville, a son
of Rev. Hyatt.

There are 13 graves marked with field stones, and about 17 unmarked
graves.

Copied by Rebecca Colyer, Russellville, Tennessee, May 11, 1937

J. R. Rhea
Born Sept. 6, 1874
Died Sept. 24, 1904
"How desolate our home
bereft of thee."

Emma Kilgore
Born Feb. 25, 1839
Died July 28, 1912
"In my Father's house are
many mansions."

Mollie Kilgore
Born Aug. 23, 1872
Died Oct. 15, 1897
"Blessed are the dead which
die in the Lord."

Beulah Kilgore
Born May 10, 1870
Died Sept. 24, 1887
"Budded on earth to bloom
in Heaven."

Sarah, Wife of Robert Sanders
Born June 12, 1837
Died Feb. 27, 1882
Age 44 yr. 8 mo.

Annie Frye
Born 1830
Died 1880
Age 50 yrs.
"Gone ye blessed."

Charley B., Son of
A. & M. Stubblefield
Born Nov. 15, 1893
Died May 8, 1919
"Gone to be an angle."

Ray, Son of
W. H. & J. B. Lowery
Born July 5, 1903
Died Jan. 7, 1905
"Budded on earth to bloom in
Heaven."

Johnie L. Beckner
Born Aug. 12, 1888
Died Aug. 13, 1901

Ida E. Beckner
Born Mar. 20, 1883
Died Sept. 9, 1898

P. N. Roddy
Born Mar. 20, 1838
Died Sept. 9, 1898

His Wife
Mary Ellen Stacks
Born Aug. 23, 1844
Died July 9, 1882

Johnie W. Beckner
Born May 30, 1848
Died April 12, 1898

Robert Menard
Born April 15, 1853
Died May 4, 1907
"Gone but not forgotten."

Emma Kloiss, Dau. of
Charles & Fannie M. Ott
Born Aug. 15, 1894
Died Feb. 23, 1899
"Darling we miss thee."

Mattie J. Bird
Born April 21, 1860
Died Feb. 22, 1890
"Rest in Hope."

G. Victoria Bird
Born Dec. 2, 1837
Died May 1, 1878
"In peace she rests."

Georgia Mc Nulty Hyatt
Born Feb. 29, 1876
Died March 13, 1877

Cecil G. A. Hyatt
Born March 19, 1884
Died Dec. 11, 1884

Rev. E. J. Hyatt
Born Dec. 25, 1843
Died Jan. 31, 1889
"Asleep in Jesus."

Elizabeth, Wife of
Rev. E. J. Hyatt
Born Dec. 8, 1846
Died June 24, 1895
"She hath done what she could."

Ephriam Hyatt
Died July 10, 1935
Age 67 yrs.

Anabell, Infant Dau. of
W. A. & M. H. Eader
Born & Died Aug. 13, 1890

Elsa Kerber
Born Sept. 1, 1887
Died May 19, 1888

Sacred to the Memory of
Hannah Marie Kellerd
Born Brooklyn, N. Y.
April 5, 1868
Died in Whitesburg
June 21, 1891
"Rests in Peace."

Carrie Lizzie, Dau. of
Thomas & Malinda Wilson
Born May 23, 1883
Died July 29, 1922
"We Miss Thee."

Joseph L. White
Born Mar. 14, 1868
Died Oct. 19, 1917
"At Rest"
Woodman marker.)

J. H. L. White
Born May 28, 1858
Died June 17, 1919
"Gone but not forgotten."

George W., Son of
W. H. & M. Stewart
Born May 22, 1876
Died Aug. 17, 1885
"We shall meet thee up there,
in our home in Heaven."

W. K. Stewart
Born Dec. 21, 1821
Died Mar. 1, 1883
"Resting in hope of a glorious
Resurrection."

Dau. of R. & Sarah Hurst
Born Aug. 17, 1873
Died Mar. 8, 1903
Maggie Allen
"At Rest"

Mother
Sarah, Wife of R. Hurst
Born May 7, 1848
Died Mar. 7, 1915

Violet Morton
Born in Scott County Va.
Jan. 2, 1884
Died Jan. 28, 1895
"Come Ye Blessed."

Bobbie L., Wife of
A. M. Weathers
Born Mar. 25, 1877
Died Nov. 30, 1901
"Gone but not forgotten."

Willie Hardin, Son of
G. D. & A. Hopper
Born Feb. 11, 1886
Died July 10, 1886

In Memory of Wansy, Son of
W. S. & M. E. Bird
Born May 25, 1878
Died Jan. 23, 1879

HAMBLEN COUNTY
KIDWELLS RIDGE CEMETERY
(Page 1)

Kidwell's Ridge Cemetery is located approximately seven miles northwest of Morristown in Hamblen County. This cemetery may be reached by highway from Morristown over the Andrew Johnson highway in a westward direction about three miles to Pratt's store, thence northwardly over Ivy Hollow pike about four miles to Kidwell's Ridge Baptist church. The cemetery is just at the back and east of the church.

There are approximately 25 unmarked graves in this cemetery.
Copied by Willard Noe, June 15, 1937

Margaret V. Jones
Jan. 1, 1848
Nov. 6, 1927
"Meet me in Heaven."

C. H. Mayes
Died Oct. 11, 1918
Aged about 70 yrs.

Annie Kate Mayes
Born Aug. 12, 1925
Died Dec. 12, 1927

James Mayes
Came from Shelby, N. C. 1830
Served in the war of 1812
Died 1858

Millard Harerlls(?)
Mar. 19, 1935
Age 16 yr.

Claude Huston Pettigew
Died June 11, 1936
Age 43 yr. 1 mo. 8 da.

Myrtle D., Wife of
C. H. Pettigew
July 5, 1900
Dec. 7, 1923

Julia, Wife of
J. W. Pettigrew
Mar. 14, 1863
Jan. 10, 1921
"At Rest"

C. B. Mayes
Born Aug. 11, 1810
Died May 10, 1887

Jane, Wife of
W. Ramsey
Died Feb. 10, 1880

J. R. Branton
Born Apr. 15, 1839
Died Sept. 14, 1900

S. M. Branton
Born Feb. 15, 1844
Died Feb. 1, 1911

Nay Dandy Stubefield
Died Aug. 2, 1936
Age 18 yr. 4 mo. 9 da.

Lula Mitchell
Died Aug. 12, 1930
Age 33 yr. 1 mo. 16 da.

W. M. Mayes
Oct. 4, 1868
Apr. 8, 1923

His Wife
Olevia Thacker
Apr. 13, 1882
Oct. 20, 1924

Nannie C. Jackson
Born June 9, 1883
Died Mar. 7, 1906

Mahala, Wife of
R. F. Jackson
Born Oct. 26, 1860
Died Nov. 10, 1923

Annabell C. Jackson
Born Nov. 28, 1898
Died Jan. 16, 1900

R. F. Jackson
Born July 19, 1860
Died Oct. 26, 1913

J. H. Mathes
Born Feb. 11, 1937
Died Mar. 27, 1890

Luther, Son of
J. P. Mayes
June 7, 1881
Sept. 29, 1913

James P. Mayes
Co. M. & H. 1st Reg.
Tenn. Cav.
Aug. 14, 1844
Dec. 20, 1928

Louisa Mayes, Wife of
George Irish
Apr. 1, 1894
Dec. 29, 1934

James B. Morell
Dec. 19, 1857
Mar. 14, 1928

His Wife
Mollie Cain
Apr. 3, 1857

William S. Underwood
Born Dec. 30, 1844
Died

Nancy L. Long, Wife of
W. S. Underwood
Born July 18, 1843
Died June 30, 1908

Sallie Lee
Born Dec. 5, 1878
Died Oct. 10, 1920
"Gone but not forgotten."

John A. Mayes
Born May 23, 1885
Died June 13, 1911

Erastus L. Mayes
Jan. 22, 1880
Oct. 16, 1918

Andrew J. Mayes
Dec. 11, 1856
Nov. 15, 1929

His Wife
Maranda Mathes
Aug. 1, 1862
Apr. 18, 1932

Mrs. A. J. Mayes
Died Apr. 18, 1932
Age 69 yr.

Sarah E. Hill
Died Jan. 12, 1934
Age 80 yr.

Allie Hill, Wife of
Henry Klepper
Died June 28, 1922
Age 23 yr.

HAMBLEN COUNTY
KIDWELL'S RIDGE CEMETERY
(Page 3)

Rev. William B. Kirk
Died Feb. 24, 1932
Age 62 yr. 9 mo. 11da.

R. C. Long
Born Oct. 6, 1850
Died Jan. 7, 1925

Cassie A., Wife of
Andrew Mayes
July 8, 1876
May 16, 1918

HAMBLEN COUNTY

TOMB STONE RECORDS

LIBERTY HILL CEMETERY
LIBERTY HILL M. E. CHURCH, SOUTH

An historical sketch given by Mr. Sam Anderson, Superintendent
of the Sunday School of Liberty Hill Church in 1936.

In 1844 and 1845 services were held in the log house near More-

lock Cemetery and organized into the Liberty Hill Church.

Ground was donated by Thomas Fulton in 1846 and in this same year

Milton Shields, who operated a paper mill nearby, closed his mill

and used one hundred and twenty laborers with Thomas Garrison as

Foreman, to build the church. D. E. Shields, son of Milton Shields;

one of the first new members, is now a doctor of medicine in Morris-

town and has through the years kept in contact with this church.

The completion of the structure was in 1847, and Mrs. Eliza Estes

was the first member to be buried from it. The oldest living mem-

ber is Miss Nannie Long, who resides at her ancestral home, (River-

side) in Grainger County.

Frank and John Stubblefield, charter members, together with Sam

Holston moved their membership from Liberty Hill to Morristown in

1880.

Five former pastors sleep in the little cemetery adjoining the

church.

HAMBLEN COUNTY

TOMB STONE RECORDS

LIBERTY HILL CEMETERY

LIBERTY HILL M.E. CHURCH SOUTH

Leaving Morristown on Andrew Johnson Highway turn to left about a mile east of town at Liberty Hill Road and follow same to church and cemetery.

The cemetery is fenced in and is kept in very good condition by the members of the church.
Copied by Willard Noe, Oct. 1936

Catharine, Wife of Wm. Estes
Born May 25, 1807
Died Oct. 8, 1846

William Estes
Born Oct. 2, 1803
Died June 11, 1886

Elizabeth, Wife of Wm. Estes
Born Jan. 20, 1820
Died Mar. 3, 1887

Wm. M. Estes
Born Apr. 7, 1839
Died June 15, 1864

Mrs. Addie E. Portrum
Died Sept. 12, 1871
Age 34 yrs.

Samuel Milton, Son of
  Rev. Charles T. & Lizzie
  E. Carroll

Eliza J. Black, Wife of
  Samuel Long
Born June 10, 1851
Died Feb. 27, 1915

Emma C., Wife of E. Love
Born Dec. 1832
Died May 3, 1863

Adaline, Wife of
  Geo. Williams
Born May 14, 1827
Died Sept. 2, 1865

George Williams
Born Jan. 4, 1838
Died May 27, 1863

Ezekiel Williams
Born Jan. 4, 1838
Died Nov. 8, 1905

George B. Williams
Born Mar. 27, 1868
Died Jan. 21, 1890

Henry Counts
Died May 20, 1878
Age 84 yr. 7 mo.

Mary Stubblefield Counts
Born Apr. 19, 1806
Died Aug. 26, 1888

Mary Ann, Wife of
  John Pryde
Born Sept. 14, 1814
Died Aug. 13, 1885

George A. Russell
Born July 8, 1828
Died June 26, 1863

William G. Sehorn
Born Apr. 15, 1807
Died Aug. 26, 1873
Age 66 yrs. 4 mo. 11 da.

J. R. Sullenbarger
Born Sept. 9, 1832
Died Jan. 26, 1888

James F. Sullenbarger
Born Sept. 13, 1864
Died Sept. 14, 1864
Age 1 day

Isaac L. Sullenbarger
Son of A. & M. R.
Sullenbarger
Died July 17, 1862
Age 18 yr. 6 mo. 19 da.

Willie Frank, Son of
C. N. & Ollie Epps
Born Nov. 30, 1908
Died Nov. 11, 1918

Ernest Epps
Born Sept. 22, 1916
Died June 17, 1919

Sarah Hearn, Wife of
James Thompson
Born Mar. 24, 1811
Died May 10, 1898
"At Rest."

Lillian, Dau. of
J. L. & E. L. Wall
Born May 6, 1898
Died July 24, 1898

Eva Lee Wall
1871- 1930

Gid Noe
Born Mar. 24, 1846
Died July 23, 1901
May he rest in peace.
Weep not he is at rest.

Margaret, Wife of
J. B. Petty
Born Mar. 22, 1850
Died Mar. 30, 1913

Sallie Hays, Wife of
A. J. Smith
Born Jan. 29, 1867
Died Apr. 9, 1918

Matilda E., Wife of
J. B. Petty
Born Apr. 9, 1857
Died Mar. 10, 1907

Bessie Moore, Wife of
R. R. Davis
Born Dec. 4, 1866

Haul G., Son of
R. R. Davis
Born Sept. 21, 1907
Died June 5, 1908

Rachel Jane Turner
Died Jan. 6, 1933
Age 1 yr. 4 mo. 29 da.

19
Jack Keyes
Confederate Soldier
U. D. C.

Nellie Easley, Wife of
L. M. Goan
Born Mar. 7, 1881
Died July 21, 1923
She was a kind affectionate
wife, a fond mother, a
friend to all.

Morris L. Goan
Died Mar. 8, 1936
Age 24 yrs. 5 mo. 22 da.

James D. Jenkins
Born June 18, 1879
Died Aug. 17, 1933

Maggie Jenkins
Born Aug. 29, 1905
Died Nov. 18, 1908

Earnest Jenkins
Born Oct. 29, 1916
Died Aug. 6, 1917

Charles H. Jenkins
Born Sept. 18, 1919
Died Mar. 22, 1921

June Duncan
Nov. 25, 1919
Aug. 7, 1920
"At Rest."

Allice Carson, Wife of
Chas. Hartman
Born Oct. 29, 1892
Died Feb. 22, 1927

Charlie C. Medlin
Born Feb. 15, 1897
Died July 12, 1897

Phebe, Wife of
J. W. Medlin
Born Nov. 21, 1849
Died Mar. 14, 1912

J. W. Medlin
Born Apr. 3, 1849

T. J. Payne
Born Oct. 28, 1858
Died Dec. 8, 1919

John G. Easley
Born Aug. 31, 1848
Died Mar. 31, 1928

Maggie Easley
Born Nov. 1, 1859
Died Jan. 6, 1931

Iva B. Easley
Born June 6, 1887
Died Mar. 14, 1936

117- Inf.
App Smalley
1889- 1928

Wilson Carpenter
1840- 1927

Jane Carpenter
1871-

Mollie, Wife of
W. M. Johnson
Born July 12, 1889
Died July 2, 1926
"Gone but not
forgotten."

Sparrel Foster
Born Jan. 24, 1845
Died June 22; 1893

Emma G., Dau. of
Jos. & Eliza Robertson
Born Oct. 6, 1884
Died Nov. 3, 1884

Rev. John N. Hobbs
Born Jan. 14, 1854
Died Sept. 23, 1922

His Wife

Maggie C. Hobbs
Born Nov. 18, 1854
Died Nov. 28, 1922
There is no death; the stars
go down to rise upon some
other shore. And bright in
Heavens jewelled crown they
shine forever more.

Infant child of J. M. &
M. C. Hobbs
Jan. 28, 1861

In Memory of Marvin A. Range
Son of W. A. & D. P. Range
Born Oct. 10, 1908
Died Nov. 10, 1910

Ellen Augusta, Dau. of
Joseph & Jane Gray
Born Nov. 16, 1856
Died July 12, 1886

E. J. Gray
Born July 2, 1823
Died June 19, 1891

Wylie P. Noe
Born July 26, 1849
Died Mar. 8, 1912

His Wife

Fannie Noe
Born Oct. 8, 1852
Died Sept. 10, 1929

Betty Ann Counts
Born June 6, 1821
Died Mar. 9, 1914

S. L. Huffmaster
Born Apr. 12, 1812
Died July 19, 1882

Maggie L. Swatts
Born Apr. 27, 1855
Died June 30, 1878

Rev. D. B. Carter
Born Aug. 25, 1803
Died June 30, 1878

Mary W. Aston, Wife of
Rev. D. B. Carter
Born Jan. 29, 1820
Died Aug. 12, 1893

Clinton K. Thompson
Born Sept. 5, 1860
Died Jan. 19, 1876

James N. Thompson
Born Oct. 17, 1837
Died Oct. 4, 1871

H. E. Thompson
Born July 24, 1866
Died Sept. 20, 1885

John H. Thompson
Born June 5, 1830
Died May 5, 1909

Katherine D. Thompson
Wife of John H. Thompson
Born Mar. 2, 1839
Died Feb. 6, 1924

James K. S., Son of
John & A. E. Portrum
Born Feb. 29, 1856
Died June 28, 1858
Of such is the Kingdom of Heaven.

Dr. C. D. Riggs
Born June 9, 1832
Died July 30, 1899

Samuel E. Pettigrew
Born Apr. 7, 1843
Died Apr. 17, 1897
Age 54 yrs. 10 da.

Nannie C. Hutson, Wife of
Samuel E. Pettigrew
Born Feb. 14, 1850
Died Feb. 17, 1887
Age 37 yr. 3 days

Mary Thompson, Wife of
Wm. M. Thompson
Born Nov. 1823
Died Mar. 1867

John R., Son of
Wm. & Mary Thompson
Born Aug. 1, 1862
Died July 17, 1880

Anne, Dau. of Wm. & M.
Thompson
Died Nov. 1861
Age 1yr. 1 mo.

Lizzie, Wife of J. W.
Midkiff
Dau. of T. & S. A. Holley
Born July 7, 1850
Died Aug. 16, 1883
We will never forget thee.

Agusta Ann, Dau. of J. W.
& E. Midkiff
Born June 20, 1878
Died June 27, 1880

Margaret A. Holley, Wife of
P. F. Whiting
May 12, 1880
Age 27 yr. 4 mo. 6 da.

Our Babe

Born Jan. 1, 1880 Died Jan. 3, 1880

Della, Wife of John
Humphreys
Born Sept. 2, 1811
Died Oct. 31, 1887
Heaven is my home.

(Pg. 56)

James W. Range
Born Jan. 3, 1854
Died Mar. 23, 1919

Mary A. Humphreys
Born July 9, 1857
Died Nov. 12, 1903

John T. Landrum, Son of
W. N. & M. S. Landrum
Born Nov. 18, 1878
Died Feb. 28, 1886

Bessie Lee, Dau. of W. N. & N.S.
Landrum
Born Apr. 26, 1807
Died Oct. 11, 1890

Jacob S. Grubb
Born Oct. 29, 1887
Died Mar. 19, 1909

Orlena Jane, Wife of
J. S. Grubb
Born Feb. 1, 1841
Died May 24, 1907

Phoebe Dyer, Wife of
Joseph Dyer
Born July 1, 1842
Died Apr. 13, 1899

Addie Dyer
Born July 23, 1881
Died Aug. 22, 1899

Henry F. Hoyt
Born July 28, 1845
Died Nov. 3, 1906

His Wife

Martha A. Hoyt
Born Oct. 12, 1852
Died Dec. 28, 1928

Baby Clifford

William A. Jecks
Born Oct. 27, 1854
Died Feb. 8, 1914

His Wife

Alice E. Jecks
Born Jan. 21, 1879
Died Dec. 13, 1928

C. R. Medlin
Born Dec. 14, 1839
Hurt Nov. 8, 1882
Died July 28, 1888

Catharine Clem
Born Mar. 20, 1856
Died Nov. 5, 1908

William Clem
Born Oct. 19, 1840
Died July 31, 1915

Charley J. Portrum
Born Sept. 16, 1878
Died Aug. 19, 1893

Daniel J. Robertson
Born June 2, 1889
Died Jan. 3, 1929

Daniel J. Robertson Jr.
Born Apr. 21, 1914
Died Mar. 2, 1916

Homer Robertson
Born Aug. 3, 1908
Died Feb. 12, 1909

Andy J. Robertson
Born Sept. 13, 1869
Died June 19, 1913

Sarah C. Imman, Wife of
Daniel J. Robertson
Born May 6, 1849
Died Dec. 28, 1881

Rachel Sams, Wife of
Daniel J. Robertson
Born July 29, 1867

Joseph E. Crane
Died June 23, 1876
28 yrs. 10 mo. 16 da.

Albert S. Sullenberger
Born June 30, 1812
Died Aug. 1, 1884

Margaret R. Livingston
Wife of A. S. Sullenberger
Born Dec. 9, 1822
Died July 14, 1900

Jonnie W. E.,,Son of
J. W. & S. C. Luttrell
Born Dec. 1, 1869
Died July 27, 1872

Charley O., Son of
J. W. & S. C. Luttrell
Born Jan. 18, 1872
Died Aug. 7, 1872

J. L. Mc Gimpsey
Born at Fonta Flora, N. C.
June 17, 1849
Died at Morristown, Tenn.
Nov. 13, 1921
Confederate 8, N. C.

M. V. Russell Mc Gimpsey
Born July 9, 1859
Died July 8, 1925

Humphreys

Father-Aug. 21, 1842
Feb. 11, 1914

Mother-May 30, 1861
Oct. 26, 1934
Jesus called them home.

John L. Milam
Born Jan. 25, 1848
Died Feb. 4, 1918

Geneva, Dau. of B. M. &
M. J. Thompson
1905-1907

William H. Cameron
Born Aug. 29, 1886
Died Nov. 2, 1919

His Wife

Mattie C. Landrum
Born June 9, 1873
Died Sept. 4, 1935

Lucian H., Son of
E. M. & Mollie E. Miller
Born Dec. 10, 1896
Died Jan. 3, 1915

Alice A., Dau. of
J. D. & M. A. Miller
Born Sept. 6, 1869

Robert Y. La Prade
1900 - 1931
Jr. O. U. A. M.

Francis Russell La Prade
1864 - 1933

Marcus Y. La Prade
1859 - 1926
Jr. O. U. A. M.

James Calvin Michell
Died May 6, 1935
Aged 73 yrs. 1 mo. 10 da.

Mary Ida Bradley
Born Oct. 23, 1887
Died Aug. 24, 1885

William Bradley
Born Feb. 3, 1853
Died Jan. 5, 1930

Charles Arthur Orndorff
June 20, 1930
Aged 75 yrs. 8 mo. 2 da.

In Memory of Milton Shields
Born Dec. 16, 1804
Died Dec. 20, 1866

In Memory of Priscilla J.
Wife of Milton Shields
Born Jan. 4, 1821
Died Mar. 5, 1886

Lucy Penelope, Dau. of
M. & P. J. Shields
Born Jan. 5, 1845
Died Oct. 17, 1859

Sarah, Wife of Geo. A.
Russell
Born Oct. 14, 1828
Died Sept. 17, 1879

John C. Russell
Born June 23, 1827
Died May 12, 1914
Confederate Soldier
Member of Co. G. 61
Tenn.

His Wife

Barshia M. Baker
Born Nov. 24, 1831
Died Aug. 12, 1885
U. C. V.

Joseph M. Russell
Born Feb. 5, 1834
Died in 1863
Co. G. 2 Tenn.
Engineer Corp.

Samuel G. Chapman
Born Feb. 19, 1812
Died Oct. 21, 1857

Geo. T. Reynolds
Born Nov. 18, 1872
Died

His Wife

Dellia H. Noe
Born June 1, 1879
Died Oct. 27, 1908
Age 49 yr. 4 mo.

Phebe A. Jenkins
Born May 8, 1882
Died

Z. H. Hayworth
Born Apr. 11, 1845
Died Jan. 29, 1902

John W. Scott
Born Nov. 8, 1870
Died Aug. 11, 1893

Mary Shields, Infant
dau. of John B. &
Carrie Shields
Died Aug. 7, 1867

Nancy Roddie
Born Jan. 10, 1834
Died Aug. 8, 1904

W. B. Roddie
Born Mar. 10, 1865
Died Dec. 19, 1915

Annie Roddie
Born Feb. 11, 1875
Died June 18, 1898

John Rice
Died in his 94th year.

J. M. Rice
Born Jan. 8, 1834
Died Apr. 22, 1880

In Memory of Mary M.
Wife of Jacob Livingston Sen.
Born May 21, 1785
Died May 1, 1865
Age 80 yr.

Jacob Livingston
Born May 15, 1773
Died Dec. 5, 1854

Alice Maude, Wife of
J. S. Tucker
Born July 31, 1840
Died June 22, 1887

Frank Y. Long
Born Mar. 23, 1849
Died Aug. 13, 1899

William W. M. Bayless
Son of R. M. & S. R.
Bayless
Born June 23, 1858
Died Feb. 1, 1862

Willie L., Dau. of
Mary J. & John H.
Danieley
Born Dec. 9, 1879
Died Nov. 19, 1898

Lula, Dau. of Mary J.
& John H. Danieley
Born Feb. 12, 1878
Died Oct. 18, 1898

Josie, Dau. of A. B. &
M. A. Phipps
Died Aug. 29, 1890
Aged 13, yr. 28 da.

(Pg. 8)

Mary A., Wife of
 Wyatt Stubblefield
Dec. 14, 1823
Apr. 21, 1883

Wyatt Stubblefield
Born Aug. 4, 1810
Died Jan. 31, 1892

Mary Loudeama, Dau. of
 R. R. & E. F. Range
Born Apr. 21, 1906
Died May 13, 1906

D. A. Purkey
Born Aug. 16, 1881
Died Sept. 15, 1917

Nancy A. Lawless, Wife of
 William Purkey
Born Jan. 6, 1846
Died Dec. 19, 1907
Farewell dear Mother, sweet
 thy rest.

William Purkey
Born May 24, 1844
Died Mar. 23, 1919

Margaret, Wife of
 Lewis Black
Born Nov. 6, 1848
Died July 12, 1907

Son of S. E. & B. E.
 Black
Born May 10, 1891

James Estes
Born Feb. 5, 1805
Died Dec. 18, 1887
Age 82 yr. 10 mo. 3 da.

Catharine Estes
Born Sept. 29, 1809
Died Dec. 12, 1886
Age 77 yr. 2 mo. 13 da.

Phebe, Wife of
 John Noe
Died Aug. 13, 1876
Age 77 yr. 2 mo. 9 da.
There is rest in Heaven.

Rachel Noe
Born May 19, 1818
Died May 22, 1880

Willie Erastus, Son of
 J. B. & Ida M. Chandler
Aug. 10, 1890
Died Jan. 24, 1891

J. J. Huston
Born Feb. 24, 1831
Died July 2, 1899

His Wife

Rebbeca Ann Cox
Born Feb. 14, 1834
Died June 1, 1878

Benjamin Cox
Born Mar. 15, 1786
Died Dec. 3, 1870

Mother
Tiney Coffman
Born Mar. 10, 1862
Died Apr. 14, 1930
At Rest

Eula Kimbrough
Dec. 25, 1935
Aged 45 yr. 4 mo. 26 da.

Dortha Lee Kimbrough
June 9, 1934
Age 14 days.

John J. Jenkins
Age 73 yrs.

His Wife

Rhoda Jenkins
Age 63 yrs.

David Devore
Born Apr. 3, 1831
Died Sept. 11, 1908

Caroline, Wife of
David Devore
Born Mar. 18, 1833
Died Apr. 22, 1903

C. M. Inman
Born Feb. 17, 1858
Died Aug. 4, 1911

His Wife

Eliza J. Jackson
Born Jan. 1, 1857
Died July 28, 1929

Charley H., Son of
C. M. & A. E. Inman
Born Feb. 7, 1889
Died June 25, 1890

Sarah E., Dau. of
C. M. & A. E. Inman
Born Aug. 2, 1882
Died July 18, 1882

W. R. Cubine
Born May 2, 1858
Died May 29, 1909

Geo. K. Williams
Died Sept. 8, 1859
Age 23 years

Marion Mefford
Born Feb. 10, 1821
Died Nov. 29, 1882

Rowena M. Mefford
Born June 23, 1825
Died July 14, 1864

James C. Johnson
Born July 29, 1828
Died Aug. 2, 1882

Mary Burnett, Wife of
S. J. Sullenberger
Born Feb. 20, 1844
Died June 8, 1898

Samuel Sullenberger
Born Apr. 1, 1846
Died Apr. 29, 1919

Thomas Robertson
Born Oct. 27, 1833
Died May 27, 1905

His Wife

Eliza J. Robertson
Born Jan. 28, 1839
Died May 11, 1926

Margarette Mims
June 20, 1864
Jan. 15, 1866

Jervis M. Mims
Jan. 12, 1828
July 15, 1865
Murdered by a Yankee
Mob.

David N. Sears
Died Aug. 31, 1872
Aged 62 yrs.

Montague A. Whitt
Born in Tasewell Co. Va.
Oct. 14, 1834
Died June 20, 1879

Wiley E. Read
Born Sept. 10, 1795
Died July 26, 1869

Mattie F. Carmichael
Born Oct. 4, 1867
Died Nov. 10, 1926

Maria W. Carmichael
Born May 5, 1853
Died May 3, 1924

Daniel L. Carmichael
Born July 23, 1864
Died Apr. 12, 1922

Sarah Eveline Lathim
Wife of James T.
Carmichael
Born May 1, 1829
Died Sept. 3, 1879

Mary Eva Carmichael
Wife of Dr. F. M. Roberts

Born Apr. 11, 1851
Died May 25, 1899

Henry Clay Carmichael
Born June 11, 1859
Died Dec. 1, 1902
Aged 43 yr. 5 mo. 20 da.

Thomas H. Carmichael
Born Dec. 21, 1856
Died July 7, 1917

In Memory of Hannah H.
Wife of Alexander Williams
Born Oct. 14, 1817
Died July 22, 1881

Alexander Williams
Born May 26, 1807
Died Nov. 5, 1879

Mollie C., Wife of
D. B. Noe
Born Mar. 1, 1840
Died Apr. 9, 1870

Gid Arlona, Dau. of
J. S. & M. E. Williams
Born Feb. 4, 1881
Died July 27, 1881

Addie M. Williams
Born Feb. 13, 1881
Died Oct. 23, 1881
Age 26 yrs. 8 mo. 8 da.

Catharine E. Mc Gee
Born Sept. 23, 1844
Died Oct. 26, 1888

Geo. W. Black
Born July 16, 1861
Died July 12, 1881

Walter D. Mims
Born Nov. 4, 1861
Died Aug. 4, 1863

Willie C. Mims
Born Nov. 14, 1859
Died Sept. 1, 1860

William C., Son of
J. M. & S. J. Mims
Sept. 1, 1860
Age 2 mo. 13 da.

Samuel Sitzler
Born Nov. 28, 1816
Died May 4, 1892

Hannah Sitzler, Wife of
Samuel Sitzler
Born Oct. 26, 1814
Died Dec. 19, 1860

Keziah Sitzler
Born Oct. 26, 1827
Died Feb. 2, 1895

Ruth, Wife of Wm. Darnell
Born Nov. 13, 1854
Died Sept. 4, 1881

William Darnell
Born Jan. 4, 1817
Died July 20, 1854

Elizabeth Harris.
Consort of Wm. Harris
Died Oct. 13, 1854
Age 50 yrs. 6 mo.

Martha M. Carriger
Consort of Jas. P. Carriger
Born Feb. 3, 1825
Died June 9, 1899

James P. Carriger
Born May 11, 1821
Died July 29, 1886

Hester A., Wife of
Jas. P. Carriger
Born Sept. 26, 1829
Died Feb. 11, 1895

Mattie F. Carriger
Born Aug. 20, 1862
Died May 12, 1878

Shadrach Inman
Born Jan. 11, 1809
Died July 30, 1885

Eliza J. Riggs, Wife of
S. Inman
Born May 17, 1822
Died Oct. 8, 1860

M. Barnes
Born June 2, 1814
Died Apr. 12, 1850

Geo. C. Speck
Born Sept. 13, 1804
Died Mar. 10, 1847

Dr. Thomas J. Speck
Born Aug. 16, 1836
Died Apr. 26, 1910

Martha Carter Speck
Born Sept. 24, 1837
Died Feb. 1, 1922
At Rest

Julia Wright, Wife of
 G. W. Anderson
Died Dec. 11, 1891
Age 70 yrs.

J. M. Mims
Born Jan. 1808
Died July 1865

James Darnell
Born June 13, 1800
Died Oct. 3, 1874

Annie E. Foster , Wife of
 C. B. Holley
Born July 29, 1850
Died June 19, 1888
She is not dead, but sleepeth.

Our Boy

Son of A. E. & C. B. Holley
Born Mar. 29, 1882
Died Apr. 2, 1882
Our lamb is safe.

Salliea, Dau. of C. B. &
 A. E. Holley
Born June 7, 1871
Died Dec. 21, 1871

Larkin, Son of
 Larkin & Sarah Foster
Born June 19, 1861
Died May 5, 1873

Thomas, Son of
 Larkin & Sarah Foster
Born Mar. 28, 1865
Died May 15, 1875

Larkin Foster
Born Apr. 8, 1821
Died Nov. 15, 1883

Sarah W. Foster
Born Mar. 20, 1821
Died Aug. 26, 1888

Frank I., Son of
 D. S. & Sinda Howard
Born Sept. 14, 1880
Died Aug. 1, 1888

Johne Foster, Son of
 H. & F. Hankee
Died Oct. 25, 1887
Age 6 yr. 2 mo.

Annie E., Wife of
 Dan M. Purkey
Born May 20, 1869
Died Nov. 5, 1921

Stephen J. Ammons
Born Apr. 27, 1882
Died Aug. 5, 1912

Rev. J. M. Ammons
Born Dec. 5, 1843
Died Apr. 7, 1905

James E. Hutton
Born June 15, 1844
Died Apr. 9, 1872
"Gone but not forgotten"

Thomas, Son of S. &
 Lizzie Foster
Born Mar. 23, 1875
Died Aug. 26, 1890

Sallie A., Dau. of
 S. & Lizzie Foster
Born Nov. 22, 1881
Died Apr. 27, 1892

Louis H. Felknor
Born Mar. 1, 1852
Died Oct. 14, 1906

Coy E. W., Son of
 J. R. & Laura Fulton
Born Aug. 22, 1895
Died Oct. 25, 1899

Wm. Fulton
Born in County Tyrone
 Ireland
Died May 24, 1893
Aged about 72 yrs.

Sidney Ervan, Son of
A. C. & H. M. Jenkins
Born Jan. 2, 1895
Died June 26, 1896

A. C. Jenkins
Born Aug. 3, 1858
Died Aug. 11, 1904

Harry Mefford
Born May 22, 1824
Died Apr. 16, 1902

His Wife

Sarah J. Thompson
Born Nov. 18, 1821
Died Aug. 21, 1900

Juliette C. Thompson
Born Nov. 15, 1849
Died July 21, 1896

Gideon G. Thompson
Born July 28, 1832
Died Jan. 4, 1900

Margaret G. Havely
Born July 8, 1850
Died June 14, 1923

H. Rice Thompson
Born Dec. 24, 1834
Died Nov. 27, 1909

Charley T., Son of
R. K. & Lennie Robertson
Born Oct. 29, 1905
Died Aug. 9, 1906

Rufus K. Robertson
Born Aug. 13, 1870
Died-

His Wife

Lennie Robertson
Born July 5, 1876
Died June 1, 1928

William Darnel
Born May 8, 1829
Died Jan . 16, 1916

Louisa Jane, Wife of
Wm. Darnel
Born Nov. 7, 1837
Died Dec. 24, 1912

W. N. Landrum
Born Oct. 18, 1835
Died Mar. 2, 1915

Nancy S. Landrum
Born Sept. 28, 1845
Died Sept. 15, 1920

John W. Graham
Jan. 20, 1930
Age 63 years.

Annie B. Rayle
Born July 18, 1881
Died July 13, 1906

Elisha G. Rayle
Feb. 26, 1866

Walter Higgins, Son of
G. W. & Nora Higgins
Born June 25, 1903
Died July 21, 1921
"Gone but not forgotten."

Jr. O. U. A. M.
B. P. Burger
Born Jan. 11, 1890
Died Oct. 19, 1926

Sallie Brown, Wife of
J. J. Epperson
Born May 19, 1837
Died July 13, 1906

I. W. Burger
Born Sept. 15, 1857
Died June 28, 1902

H. C. Kenley
Born Dec. 19, 1840
Died Mar. 2, 1914

Eliza J. Solomon, Wife of
H. C. Kenley
Born Sept. 6, 1842

Eliza J. Estes, Wife of
William Fulton
Born June 2, 1835
Died Mar. 11, 1917

Willis G., Son of
Albert W. & Mae L. Noe
Born Oct. 24, 1919
Died Aug. 2, 1926

Myrtle Joe, Dau. of
J. E. & Berta Gibson
Born Apr. 2, 1921
Died May 10, 1921

Miss Laura Johnston
Died Oct. 11, 1862 in
the 19th year of her age.

David B. Michell
Born Nov. 11, 1888
Died Dec. 22, 1926

James C. Michell
Born Apr. 6, 1857

His Wife

Eliza F. Michell
Born June 23, 1848
Died Dec. 30, 1917

Geo. W. Michell
Born Aug. 17, 1917
Died Aug. 18, 1917

Tommie C., Son of J. C. &
E. F. Michell
Born Feb. 5, 1891
Died Sept. 3, 1906

Mildred Nell, Dau. of
W. F. & K. E. Michell
Born Jan. 28, 1926
Died July 4, 1926

Mary Ruth Michell
Born Sept. 26, 1918
Died June 21, 1927

M. E. Miller
Born Feb. 3, 1821
Died Aug. 18, 1897

Mary J., Wife of
L. H. Felknor
Born Nov. 16, 1857
Died Apr. 6, 1894

Sallie C. Thompson, Wife of
H. R. Thompson
Born Nov. 27, 1853
Died Oct. 31, 1923

C. L. Burnett
Born Apr. 7, 1884
Died Feb. 25, 1907

Milton S. Burnett
Born Feb. 20, 1844
Died Apr. 29, 1916

Myrtle S. Burnett
Born Dec. 1, 1890
Died Sept. 9, 1912

Mary A. Burnett
Born Oct. 4, 1855
Died-

Willie A. Burnett
Born Feb. 24, 1895
Died Feb. 10, 1917
In Gods Care.

Sarah J., Wife of
Chesley J. Burnett
Born July 27, 1823
Died Jan. 15, 1900

Chesley J. Burnett
Born Jan. 5, 1817
Died Oct. 16, 1894

Daisy Everet
Born July 9, 1883
Died Aug. 24, 1907

Jas. R. Rayle
Born Dec. 7, 1830
Died Nov. 25, 1900

Sarah J. Rayle
Born Dec. 25, 1840
Died Oct. 11, 1916

(Pg.14)

W. F. Kenley
Born Feb. 19, 1870
Died Nov. 29, 1906

John Jones
Born Apr. 7, 1835
Died Nov. 11, 1913

Samuel Thomas Shields
Born Apr. 30, 1851
Died May 1, 1906

His Wife

Lucy Word Shields
Born Mar. 15, 1851
Died Mar. 21, 1909

Kate N. Shields
Born Jan. 24, 1880
Died May 21, 1912

James C. Rymer
Born Mar. 2, 1878
Died June 19, 1928

His Wife

Ida Reynolds Rymer
Born Jan. 20, 1877
Died-

Lena May Rymer

Mary Kate Rymer

Mary A. Reynolds, Wife of
R. A. Rymer
Born May 2, 1832
Died Aug. 1, 1914

Martha W. Warren
Feb. 9, 1932
Age 72 years

S. E. White
Born Nov. 24, 1870
Died Aug. 10, 1906

Mildred M., Dau. of
Oscar & Effie Sams
Born Jan. 6, 1926
Died Oct. 10, 1927

Robert R. Stump
Died Aug. 23, 1936
Age 66 yrs.

Mrs. Charles T. Swaimn
Died Nov. 28, 1935
Age 67 yrs. 5 mo. 7 da.

Charles T. Swaimn
Died July 12, 1930
Age 66 yrs. 11 mo. 15 da.

Lou L. Swaim, Wife of
Rev. M. P. Swaim
Born May 2, 1840
Died Aug. 28, 1901

Infant dau. of
Geo. E. & Bessie Taylor
Born Nov. 17, 1909
Died Dec. 8, 1909

Infant son of
Geo. E. & Bessie Taylor
Born Dec. 25, 1908
Died Jan. 20, 1909

Katharine, Dau. of
Geo. E. & Bessie Taylor
Born Nov. 23, 1903
Died May 28, 1905

W. F. Sullivan
Born May 10, 1854
Died Oct. 25, 1913
I will bless the Lord at
all times; His praise shall
continually be in my mouth.

Nancy A., Wife of James Kistler
Born Aug. 7, 1826
Died Sept. 2, 1904

J. Sim. Coffey
Born Feb. 14, 1876
Died May 27, 1913
"Gone but not forgotten."

Laura B. Repass, Wife of
D. A. Thompson
Born Dec. 2, 1865
Died June 11, 1920

D. A. Thompson
Born Nov. 10, 1860
Died Feb. 10, 1934

Infant son of D. A. &
Edith Pearl Thompson
Died Apr. 6, 1920

Margaret, Dau. of
J. L. & D. P. Mc Kinney
Born July 26, 1920
Died May 3, 1921

Bettie A. Johnson
Born June 9, 1892
Died Aug. 5, 1895

Jane Haws, Wife of
J. C. Johnson
Born Sept. 13, 1834
Died May 23, 1909

John H. Gregg
Born Feb. 13, 1835
Died Nov. 30, 1915

Kate A., Wife of
John H. Gregg
Born Dec. 12, 1844
Died Apr. 14, 1884

Agusta A., Dau. of
J. H. & K. A. Gregg
Born Oct. 10, 1866
Died Dec. 15, 1891

John R., Son of
J. A. & S. E. Gregg
Born Oct. 27, 1907
Died Feb. 28, 1908
U. C. V.

J. W. Barlow
Co. A. 23, Va. Reg.

Lizzie Barlow
Born May 13, 1862

Jno. Watts
Co. E.

Little Dora Ann, Dau. of
J. E. & Josephine Thompson
Born May 27, 1869

Calvin Seals
Born Oct. 26, 1845
Died Dec. 5, 1903

Hiram, Son of J. R. &
Plinea Sams
Born June 22, 1876
Died Sept. 16, 1905

Hugh O., Infant son of
S. O. Noe
Died Dec. 25, 1879
Age 10 mo. 14 da.

Anna C. Pryde, Dau. of
John & Mary A. Pryde
Died Oct. 15, 1874
Age 16 yrs. 8 mo. 16 da.

Virginia M., Wife of
A. M. C. Taylor
Died Dec. 4, 1867
Age 28 yrs. 8 mo.

Robert B. Pryde, Son of
John & Mary A. Pryde
Died Sept. 28, 1864
Aged 16 yr. 7 mo. 12 da.

Rev. C. T. Carroll
Born Feb. 27, 1842
Died July 13, 1918
"I have fought a good fight,
I have finished my course,
I have kept the faith."

Lucinda Swan, Dau. of
Rev. C. T. Carroll
Born Mar. 28, 1880

Died Mar. 6, 1885

Virginia Belle, Dau. of
Rev. C. T. & E. E. Carroll
Born Mar. 29, 1883
Died July 27, 1883

Elizabeth Ester Shields
Wife of Rev. C. T. Carroll
Born Feb. 4, 1844
Died Dec. 20, 1910

Connie W., Dau. of
Mike & Mary Purkey
Born Nov. 8, 1873
Died Nov. 24, 1882

Harvey Lee Purkey
Born Aug. 27, 1871
Died Mar. 10, 1903

Mary E., Wife of
Mike Purkey
Born June 22, 1843
Died Oct. 20, 1913

Mike Purkey
Born 1842
Died Jan. 20, 1914
"My Trust is in God."

James Bullon Moore
Died in 1867

Rebecca Russell Moore
Born July 8, 1825
Died April 1866

Alice B., Dau. of
J. C. & B. M. Russell
Born May 28, 1858
Died Oct. 3, 1869

In Memory of
G. W. Cunningham
Died Feb. 22, 1873
Age 58 years

D. M. P. Newell
Born June 6, 1823
Died Mar. 2, 1873

Lula V., Dau. of
Mike & Mary Purkey
Born Aug. 11, 1866
Died Nov. 7, 1882

Thomas A. Scott
Born Oct. 23, 1828
Died June 5, 1880
"Blessed are the dead
which die in the Lord"

Thos. P. Whitt
Born 1865- Died 1871
"Our little lamb is safe"

J. E. Thompson
May 14, 1828- Dec. 25, 1891

(Pg. 16)
Jas. R., Son of
M. & P. J. Shields
Nov. 1, 1848

Milton R., Son of
M. & P. J. Shields
Born Sept. 3, 1853
Died Oct. 3, 1854

Mary Jane, Daughter of
M. & P. J. Shields
Born April 9, 1842
Died Sept. 6, 1859
"The righteous shall
inherit eternal life"

Lida A. Houston
Born April 6, 1864
Died Mar. 2, 1934

Rev. James Thompson
Born 1795
Died April 23, 1870
Aged 75 years

Janet Thompson, Wife of
James Thompson
Died 1863
Age 64 years

Rev. John M. Crismond
Born Apr. 27, 1875
Aged 70 Years

Sacred to the Memory of
Robert J. Taylor, son of
Redden and Nancy W. Taylor
Born 19th Oct. 1837
Died 16th Oct. 1847
"This tribute of formal affection
was erected to his memory
by his parents"

Eliza T., Daughter of
D. & S. J. Wood
Died June 1, 1862
Aged 22 years

Mary, Wife of J. R. Albert
Born Mar. 1, 1848
Died Sept. 9, 1884

Ollivia A., Daughter of C. A. & J.
Albert, Born Oct. 1, 1861
Died Apr. 8, 1878

HAMBLEN COUNTY
MACEDONIA CEMETERY
(Page 1)

Macedonia Baptist church is located about six miles north of Morristown, just a few yards to the left, off the old Tate Springs Pike. The church can easily be seen from the pike.

Copied by Willard Noe, May 12, 1937

Dave W. Noe
Died July 8, 1936
Age 60 yr.

George Thomas Harbin
Died July 27, 1934
Age 70 yr. 6 mo. 12 da.

Delbert B. Holler
Dec. 2, 1875
Apr. 28, 1934

His Wife
Sarah Punch Holler
Aug. 5, 1880 -

Mrs. Ethel W. Helton
Died May 1, 1932
Age 34 yr. 2 mo. 17 da.

Claud Allison, Son of
Roger & Essie Noe
Born & Died June 25, 1928
"Gone to be an angel"

Eva Jane Burchell
Born & Died Oct. 27, 1922

Robert Ruble Burchell
Oct. 27, 1922
June 30, 1926
"Gone but not forgotten."

Mrs. Sarah Lee Chaney
Died May 19, 1933
Age 29 yr.

Floyd R. Burchell
Died Aug. 20, 1934
Age 24 yr. 6 mo. 27 da.

Susie Burchell Kelley
Died Jan. 10, 1937
Age 17 yr.

Ida Mae, Dau. of Andrew &
Julia Helton
Born June 27, 1897
Died Feb. 8, 1912
"In God I trust,
I wish to be there,
I lie in the morning light."

J. A. Helton
Aug. 20, 1840
Dec. 2, 1915
"I am going home."

Eliza Noe, Wife of
J. A. Helton
Born Jan. 11, 1846
Died May 1, 1915

Bessie Collins
Born Jan. 12, 1888
Died Nov. 22, 1908

George Earnest Noe
Oct. 15, 1892
Mar. 25, 1931

His Wife
Irene Grigsby Noe
July 31, 1904 -

HAMBLEN COUNTY
MACEDONIA CEMETERY
(Page 2)

Lucile Marie, Dau. of
G. E. & Irene Noe
Dec. 28, 1929
May 10, 1930

James A. Camper
Died Apr. 26, 1933
Age 60 yr. 7 mo. 2 da.

Pleas Lawless
Born Jan. 28, 1846
Died Jan. 3, 1926
"Asleep in Jesus."

Mabel M., Dau. of
Andy & Minnie Lawless
Sept. 24, 1906
Sept. 25, 1911

Eliza Lawless, Wife of
Pleas Lawless
Born Mar. 18, 1853
Died July 5, 1921
"Asleep in Jesus"

Geneva Paralee, Dau. of
Mr. & Mrs. Pleas Lawless
Born May 7, 1896
Died July 6, 1918

Clint Gentry
Born May 6, 1895
Died Jan. 3, 1929
World War Vet.

George W. Witt
Died Aug. 11, 1936
Age 70 yr.

Carrie Elizabeth Dawson
Oct. 11, 1931
Age 58 yr. 7 mo. 2 da.

Glenn Noe
Oct. 10, 1904
Mar. 1, 1919

Issac Noe
Born Aug. 7, 1860 -

Mary Pane, Wife of
Isaac Noe
Born Apr. 25, 1859
Died July 12, 1899

Mary B. Williams, Wife of
J. P. Williams Jr.
Born Sept. 29, 1854
Died Jan. 4, 1928
"A tender mother, and a faithful
    wife."

Joseph Harbin
1854 - 1928

Margaret, Wife of
John Harbin
Feb. 2, 1923
Age 81 yr.

John Harbin
Born May 1826
Died Dec. 8, 1908

Martha Spoons
Jan. 14, 1858
July 6, 1904

Mary Eva, Wife of
C. P. Smith
Apr. 18, 1868
Mar. 4, 1914

W. S. Treece
Born Oct. 14, 1829
Died July 19, 1915

Jane, Wife of W. S. Treece
Born Apr. 13, 1829
Died Mar. 11, 1897

HAMBLEN COUNTY
MACEDONIA CEMETERY
(Page 3)

Daniel R. Treece
Born Feb. 18, 1872
Died Apr. 4, 1926
"Gone but not forgotten."

Maggie J., Dau. of
Andrew & Julia Helton
Born Apr. 7, 1896
Died Oct. 19, 1897

Andrew Helton
July 8, 1870 -

  His Wife
Julia Helton
Apr. 30, 1873
Apr. 24, 1913

Bessie Olivena, Dau. of
D. C. & Oma Smith
Born Aug. 8, 1923
Died Nov. 19, 1924
"Gone from mother's arms to Jesus"

Dan Helton
Born Mar. 4, 1842
Died Jan. 16, 1926
Age 84 yr.

Leah Chaney Day
Nov. 9, 1934
Age 43 yr. 1 mo. 7 da.

Pleasant Holt
July 20, 1856
Jan. 28, 1928

  His Wife
Nancy Holt
July 10, 1861
Nov. 13, 1935

  "At Rest"
Laura Noe, Wife of Samuel Noe
Born May 4, 1886
Died Apr. 21, 1925

Samuel Noe
Died Mar. 19, 1933
Age 53 yrs.

Infant dau. of
Mr. & Mrs. Will Holt
Jan. 24, 1930
    "At Rest"

John Holt
Born Aug. 8, 1884
Died Feb. 25, 1921
"In God We Trust"

Sarah J. Treece
Died Jan. 16, 1926
Age 80 yr.

S. A. Cox
Nov. 14, 1860
Apr. 23, 1936
"In my Father's house are many
Mansions"

Margaret J. Harville
Mar. 27, 1896
Died Apr. 5, 1916

Mary A. Helton, Wife of
D. P. Noe
Feb. 16, 1843
May 10, 1920

Arthur S. Riggs
May 4, 1877
May 12, 1934

  His Wife
Willie Kate Carmichael
Jan. 19, 1889 -

G. W. Carmichael
1843 - 1915

D. L. Carmichael
Born Feb. 17, 1839
Died Mar. 29, 1898

HAMBLEN COUNTY
MACDEONIA CEMETERY
(Page 4)

Julia A. Noe, Wife of
D. L. Carmichael
Born June 25, 1849
Died Dec. 13, 1898
"Weep not Dear children,
God doeth all things well."

Sallie E. Carmichael
Aug. 28, 1871
July 10, 1923

Juliet C. Fain, Wife of
J. L. Noe
Born Apr. 1, 1836
Died Oct. 16, 1915

James T. Noe
Feb. 7, 1841
Apr. 6, 1899

His Wife
Nancy C. Holt
Jan. 17, 1847
May 21, 1913

Will C. Noe
Aug. 24, 1874
July 14, 1914

John R. Treece
Born in 1841
Died Apr. 25, 1918
Age 77 yr.

D. A. Goodson
Mar. 11, 1848 –

His Wife
L. C. Goodson
Sept. 9, 1848
Aug. 30, 1926

Amanda L. Goodson
Born Mar. 2, 1880
Died Mar. 27, 1921
"At Rest"

"Baby Boy", Son of
Rev. J. M. & Nannie Anderson
Born Aug. 13, 1892
Died (?)

Eliza M. Ray, Wife of
Thos. R. Holt
Began Life Jan. 3, 1849
Passed to Spirit Life
June 12, 1923

Thomas R. Holt
Began Life July 5, 1842
Passed to Spirit Life
Nov. 30, 1911

Jennie M. Noe
Mar. 18, 1878 –

David E. Noe
F. L. T.
Aug. 18, 1873
Jan. 30, 1922

Ina C. Noe
Jan. 29, 1909
May 31, 1910

Shields & Maynard, Infant Sons of
D. E. & J. M. Noe
May 5, 1896
Died July 11, 1896

Sue J. Johnson
Nov. 7, 1849
July 23, 1906

Robert J. Daniel
Born Dec. 21, 1828
Died Oct. 17, 1896

Bess Frances Carmichael, Wife of
James W. Charles
Dec. 7, 1892
Dec. 7, 1923

HAMBLEN COUNTY
MACEDONIA CEMETERY
(Page 5)

Samuel Carmichael
Born Oct. 19, 1835
Died Feb. 28, 1893

Elizabeth J. Carmichael
Born Nov. 29, 1836
Died Apr. 14, 1896

G. W. Noe
Born Mar. 4, 1823
Died Dec. 31, 1891

John F. Noe
May 20, 1836
June 15, 1912
"At Rest"

Joseph R. Noe
Mar. 27, 1844
May 31, 1914
Confederate Soldier of the 61st
Tenn. Regament

   His Wife
Sarah C. Noe
Nov. 5, 1853
Oct. 17, 1934

Bruce G. Noe
May 17, 1891
Feb. 7, 1926

Jack Spoon
Died Nov. 26, 1929
Age 75 yr.

William Helton, Son of
J. & Martha Helton
Age 60 yr. (?)

Thomas J. Cooper
1844 - 1928
Confederate Vet.

   His Wife
Allice G. Greenlee
1849 -

James Daniel Noe
Aug. 7, 1864
June 9, 1935

   His Wife
Mary Helton
Mar. 16, 1871
July 17, 1935
"We will meet again."

Allice Purkey, Wife of
J. F. Purkey
Born June 6, 1869
Died Apr. 19, 1914

Hubert Bruce, Son of
Mr. & Mrs. George Noe
Born Dec. 23, 1903
Died Oct. 1, 1913

Cordia, Wife of
G. W. Noe
Born Jan. 2, 1872
Died Mar. 1, 1916

Sallie N. Holt
Born Dec. 11, 1880
Sallie N. Hacker
Died May 1, 1902

Alice Hazlewood, Wife of
R. T. Hacker
Born Mar. 11, 1881
Died Oct. 12, 1903

D. W. Davis
Born Mar. 30, 1850
Died Aug. 9, 1911

Rev. J. C. Hacker
Born Sept. 8, 1840
Died July 31, 1902

Lewis M., Son of
J. C. & Susan Hacker
Born Nov. 5, 1873
Died Mar. 20, 1900

HAMBLEN COUNTY
MACEDONIA CEMETERY
(Page 6)

Carrie Belle Gilliam
Died July 8, 1937
Age 34 yr. 2 mo. 6 da.

Katie, Wife of
Jake Harbin
Born in 1851
Died May 17, 1914

Adeline Harbin
Born Feb. 17, 1879
Died Apr. 30, 1896

James P. Cox
Born Mar. 14, 1830
Died Feb. 2, 1894

Orlena E. Noe, Wife of
J. P. Cox
Born Nov. 14, 1835
Died Nov. 17, 1893

Lemey E. Harbin
Born May 7, 1889
Died July 24, 1909

Cordelia Cox, Wife of
E. G. Bayle
Born June 10, 1871
Died Aug. 31, 1892

Demorris, Wife of Laborn Collins
Born Jan. 15, 1856
Died Dec. 8, 1889

Louisa Chaney, Wife of
J. H. Cox
Born Aug. 18, 1875
Died Aug. 3, 1900

Cornelia E. Noe
Born Feb. 15, 1841
Died May 28, 1899

Isaac B. Noe
Born Nov. 18, 1829
Died Dec. 5, 1888
(Double rock)

Reed Payne
Born Nov. 29, 1828
Died Apr. 16, 1891

Sarah E., Wife of
Joseph P. Williams
Born Dec. 16, 1831
Died Mar. 17, 1914

Joseph P. Williams
Born Oct. 28, 1828
Died Mar. 15, 1907

Sterling Long
Born May 22, 1859
Died Jan. 17, 1898

J. D. Long
Born June 8, 1827
Died Nov. 20, 1892

Lula, Wife of
J. J. Long
Born July 25, 1862
Died Oct. 17, 1899

Cynthia Johnnie Long, Wife of
Edward L. Bowman
Born Mar. 5, 1882
Died Nov. 28, 1914

John J. Long
Died Apr. 12, 1932
Age 76 years

Viley Cooper, Wife of
P. E. Helton
Born Mar. 8, 1857
Died Sept. 30, 1914

Sallie Treece
Born June 18, 1821
Died June 12, 1898

Joseph Cooper
Born July 15, 1849
Died Feb. 1, 1918

HAMBLEN COUNTY
MACEDONIA CEMETERY
(Page 7)

His Wife
Harret Cooper
Born July 14, 1840
Died Aug. 5, 1919

James W. Hill
Born Jan. 17, 1848
Died Oct. 26, 1928

His Wife
Catharine Payne
Born Apr. 12, 1853
Died Apr. 28, 1913

David Helton
Born Nov. 18, 1816
Died Aug. 5, 1861

Daniel Jones Taylor
Born Mar. 8, 1830
Died Apr. 12, 1904

Margaret Jane Taylor, Wife of
Daniel J. Taylor
Born Apr. 10, 1831
Died Feb. 27, 1915

HAMBLEN COUNTY

MC FARLAND CEMETERY

What is known as the Mc Farland Cemetery is located about six and one half miles south east of Morristown on the Springvale pike on a farm now belonging to J. L. Rhodes. The farm for many years belonged to the Mc Farlands, but evidently other families in the community buried in the plot, who were not family connections. Buried in this grave yard is Col. Robert Mc Farland, the only known officer of the Revolutionary War buried in Hamblen County, and for whom the Robert Mc Farland Chapter Sons of the American Revolution, is named. His grave is unmarked except by a marker from a local Funeral Home which has recently been placed; decendants of his living in Morristown knowing the location of his grave. A sketch of Col. Mc Farland copied from the minutes of the Chapter of the American Revolution bearing his name, accompanies this record.

There are many more unmarked than marked graves in the cemetrery.

Copied by Margaret H. Richardson, Oct. 31, 1936

In Memory B. F. Richardson
Born Mar. 1, 1851
Died Aug. 20, 1880
Aged 29 yrs. 5 mo. 20 da.

Our Father
Thomas M. Jones
Born Aug. 3, 1817
Died Dec. 26, 1890
Erected to his memory by his
 children, R. M. Jones and
 E. M. Speck

Penelope West
Died Apr. 24, 1826
Age 18 yrs. 11, mo. 5 da.

Elizabeth Hill, Wife of
 Robert Hill
Died May 9, 1833
Aged 54 yrs. 5 mo. 28 da.

Robert Hill
Died Feb. 26, 1832
Age d 51 yrs. 4 mo. 1 da.

Anne Ramsey Hill, Wife of
 John W. Hill
Died Aug. 22, 1834
Age 20 yrs. 10 mo. 3 da.

Abram Wade, Son of
 William & Phebe Maskall
Born Oct. 23, 1824
Died Dec. 14, 1841

Phebe Maskall, Wife of
 William Maskall
Born Oct. 17, 1794
Died Oct. 20, 1845

William Maskall
Born Dec. 21, 1790
Died June 23, 1869

Alvinzi Alonzo, Son of
 Harvey and Mary Andruss
Born Dec. 16, 1830
Died Dec. 1, 1847

HAMBLEN COUNTY
Mc FARLAND CEMETERY

(Pg. 2)

Jacob Hoback
Born Apr. 22, 1773
Died Oct. 23, 1845

Robert Mc Farland
  (Sketch accompanies record)

James Cunningham
Born Mar. 31, 1818
Died Jan. 21, 1885

Elizabeth, Consort of James
  Cunningham
Died ? 26, 1860
Age 29 yrs. 4 mo. 2 da.

In Memory of our Mother
Mary A. Mc Farland, Consort of
  Robert Mc Farland
    (Who lies near White Hall)
    Madison County Kentucky)
Born Feb. 11, 1799
Died Feb. 23, 1866

Sacred to the memory of
Levinia M. Jones, Consort of
  Thos. M. Jones, And Dau. of
  Robt. & Mary Mc Farland
Died Apr. 17, 1850
Age 24 yrs. 1 mo. 2 da.

A SKETCH OF THE LIFE OF COL. ROBERT Mc FARLAND
THE SECOND, FOR WHOM THIS CHAPTER IS
NAMED

The Robert Mc Farland Chapter, Sons of the Revolution, at the annual meeting March 25th, 1918 voted unanimously to designate March 15th, which is the birthday anniversary of Col. Robert Mc Farland, as the annual meeting date of this chapter, in memory of the only officer of the Revolution whose remains rest in Hamblen County soil, he having been buried on the old plantation near Springvale, Tennessee.

Col. Robert Mc Farland was a boy of seventeen at the beginning of the Revolutionary war and rode by his father's side to the battle of King's Mountain.

He was born in the Shenandoah Valley in Virginia, March 15th, 1759 and died February 5th, 1837. He married Margaret Mc Nutt, the first white child born south of the French Broad river, His father was an officer in the Colonial army, and father and son were pioneers in the Wautauga settlement. He was the father of Col. Robert Mc Farland, the third, who served his country in the war of 1812. His grandson, Col. Robert Mc Farland the fourth, served with the Confederate army in the Civil war and was afterward Judge of the Supreme court of Tennessee and lived in Morristown.

Sir John Mc Farland, of Arrouquah, Scotland, born there in 1708 and who came to Virginia in 1746, was the American head of this family and the grandfather of Robert Mc Farland, the second.

William Calloway's list of loyal Americans gives his name and oath of allegiance to Virginia.

The old Presbyterian church in Augusta county, Virginia, in which Sir John was an elder, is standing today.

This history is given as the reason why this chapter is named the Robert Mc Farland Chapter, Sons of the Revolution.

Taken from the Minute Book of Robert Mc Farland Chapter.

Copied December 29, 1936-- Ada Ruth Noe

HAMBLEN COUNTY

TOMB STONE RECORDS

MORELOCK CEMETERY

Located about a mile and a half east of Morristown. Turn to the
left at the old Fair Grounds and follow the road which will turn
to the right back of the Fair Grounds and continue till reaching
the cemetery. The ground for the cemetery was given by Jonathan
Morelock early in the 19th century and adjoined Read's Chapel,
an early Methodist church. The first person buried in the graveyard was Archibald Martin and at the time he was buried it was
all a forest. There is no trace of the chapel now. A descend-
ent of old Jonathan Morelock living near the cemetery stated that
the chapel was used by the Union soldiers during the war and that
they finally burned it. The cemetery is still used and is well
kept for a country graveyard.
Quoting PRICE'S HISTORY OF METHODISM:-
About the year 1808 while on his vast itinerancy, Bishop O. H. As-
bury with his assistant, Henry Boehm, held a meeting at a neat pine
chapel, known as Read's Chapel. This structure was built by and
named for Phelps Read of Grainger County.
Copied by Williard Noe, Nov. 1936

O. D. Purkey
Born April 13, 1861

His Wife, Mary O. Purkey
Born Nov. 15, 1865
Died July 5, 1926

Infant of R. E. and
Reta Curl
Born and died Oct. 15, 1916

John M. Curl
Born July 4, 1830
Died

His Wife, Elizabeth
Born April 2, 1847
Died April 2, 1912

Wilbur R., Son of J. A. and
Leatha Garretson
Born Feb. 3, 1914
Died Oct. 1, 1919

Sam B. McAlister
Born Dec. 7, 1870
Died April 26, 1932

Thomas, Son of S. B. and
L. J. McAlister
Born Oct. 4, 1899
Died Aug. 13, 1913

Ruby Mae, Dau. of S. B.
and L. J. McAlister
Born May 17, 1910
Died Oct. 1, 1911

Rev. H. W. Bussey, Son of
H. T. and N. O. Bussey
Born Aug. 3, 1870
Died Dec. 11, 1897
"Blessed are the pure in
heart for they shall see
God."

(Pg.2)

In Memory of
Martha M. Morelock
Born July 26, 1849
Died Oct. 10, 1849
Aged 2mo. 15 days

In Memory of
Elizabeth A. Morelock
Born Oct.27,
Died May 16, 1860
Aged 33 yrs. 6 mo. 20 da.

In Memory of
George W. Morelock
Born Sept. 25, 1829
Died June 13, 1865
Aged 35 yrs. 8 mo. 18 da.

Sacred to the Memory of
Jane Shannon
Born May 15, 1755
Died Dec. 19, 1828

Gone but not forgotten
Elizabeth Robertson
Born Jan. 27, 1846
Died Sept. 30, 1891
Her happy soul has winged its way,
To one pure bright eternal day.

Lunda J., Wife of
Dr. M. B. Williams
Born Feb. 23, 1874
Died May 25, 1915
Aged 41 yrs. 3 mo. 2 da.
Asleep in Jesus.

Our Baby

Infant son of
Dr. M. B. & Lunda J. Williams
Born & Died Mar. 26, 1904

Infant of J. I. & S. J. Purkey

Infant of J. I. & S. J. Purkey.

Sallie J., Wife of
J. I. Purkey
Born Apr. 27, 1856
Died Mar. 15, 1883

J. I. Purkey
Born Feb. 9, 1855
Died Sept. 6, 1922

George W. Purkey
Born Jan. 15, 1854
Died Mar. 6, 1888

David Purkey
Born May 10, 1822
Died Jan. 28, 1885

Our Mother

Mollie E. Purkey
Wife of David Purkey
Born Aug. 10, 1825
Died Aug. 28, 1906

My Wife

Amey Morelock
Born Dec. 18, 1804
Died July 2, 1878

Johathan Morelock Sen.
Born Oct. 15, 1804
Died May 14, 1876
Age 71 yrs. 8 mo.

Joseph B. Morelock
Born Aug. 26, 1839
Died Sept. 16, 1876
Age 37 yrs.

Jacob Thomas
Born Feb. 16, 1842
Died Jan. 6, 1919

Lucy J., Wife of Jacob
Thomas
Born June 24, 1827
Died Aug. 13, 1889

Lucinda G., Wife of
J. N. Mc Alister
Born Dec. 30, 1828
Died May 12, 1881
Enclosed with an
iron fence.

James T. Oliver
Born July 9, 1875
Died Dec. 1, 1889

Gone to Rest
William B. Lackey
Born July 3, 1859
Died May 10, 1880

William M. Reynolds
1863

Lue M. Purkey, Wife of
William M. Reynolds
1870

Cornelia A. Long
Born June 1, 1866
Died Dec. 14, 1886
"Gone but not forgotten."

Mary Long
Born May 27, 1838
Died Jan. 4, 1887
I know that my Redeemer
liveth.

Emma E. Scales
Born Jan. 8, 1868
Died June 19, 1925
Age 53 yrs.
At Rest

Charlie R., Son of
T. J. & Emma Scales
Born Sept. 22, 1891
Died Apr. 11, 1911
The gates of Heaven for
Him have opened wide.

Scared To the Memory of
Jacob Garretson, Son of
Winifred P. Garretson
Born July 9, 1819
Died June 6, 1811

Job Garretson
Born Mar. 14, 1796
Died Apr. 15, 1850

Eugene, Son of
L. D. & F. E. Snyder
Born Aug. 25, 1920
Died Sept. 6, 1921

Jane Mc Carary
Born Aug. 17, 1876
Died Feb. 5, 1914

Sacred to the Memory of
George Washington, Son of

Chesley & Katherine
Rogers
Born Oct. 23, 1844
Died Feb. 25, 1849

Sacred to the Memory of
Archebald Martin, of Ga.
Who died on the 5th of
July 1813
Age 35 yrs.
Rest is obblerated.

"Gone but not forgotten"
Elizabeth Robertson
Born Jan. 27, 1846
Died Sept. 30, 1891
Her happy soul has winged
its way,
To one pure bright eternal
day.

Lunda J., Wife of
Dr. M. B. Williams
Born Feb. 23, 1874
Died May 25, 1915
Age 41 yrs. 3 mo. 2 da.
Asleep in Jesus.

Our Baby

Infant son of
Dr. M. B. & Lunda J.
Williams
Born & Died Mar. 26, 1904

Sara, Dau. of
Thomas & Sara Mc Alister
Born Jan. 25, 1885
Died Feb. 17, 1885

Sarah, Wife of
Thomas Mc Alister
Born Feb. 1850
Died June 30, 1885

T. M. Mc Calister
Born June 3, 1843
Died Dec. 4, 1917

Anna, Wife of
John Robertson
Died May 2, 1873
Aged about 60 yrs.
"I shall be satisfied when
I awake with thy likeness."

(Pg.4)

John Robertson
Born May 21, 1795
Died Feb. 20, 1868
"The battle fought, the
victory won, glory to
his name."

James, Son of John &
Annie Robertson
Born Jan. 15, 1850
Died Sept. 21, 1909
"Saved from earthly taint
and sin."

Wm. Robertson
Died Aug. 8, 1884
Aged 62 yrs. 1 mo.

My Husband

James H. Gray
Born June 10, 1824
Died Nov. 13, 1881
Age 57 yrs. 5 mo. 3 da.

Our Father

H. W. Taylor
Born Sept. 22, 1803
Professed Relegion
July 1822
Joined the Baptist at
Bethel South 1826
Ordained to the Ministry
Baptised 1406 Persons
Died June 5, 1888

Our Mother

Alice G. Grantham, Wife of
H. W. Taylor
Born May 7, 1808
Died Mar. 29, 1900

Scared to the Memory of
Sarah, Consort of
John Garretson
Born July 11, 1809
Died Aug. 14, 184?

The grave of Lucy Cain
Consort of Hugh Cain
Born May 12, 1811
Departed this life
Dec. 6, 1852

Dollie M. Byrd
Born July 21, 1840
Died Sept. 29, 1917

F. P. Riggs
Born July 25, 1823
Died?

H. E. Riggs
Born June 14, 1824
Died May 24, 1844

Mary Ann Smith
Born Aug. 26, 1826
Died June 22, 1841

Richard F. Taylor
Born Mar. 7, 1844
Died Apr. 11, 1865

N. G. Taylor, Son of
H. W. & A. G. Taylor
Born Dec. 6, 1833
Died June 4, 1909

Sacred to the Memory of
Benjamin Mc Cravy
Born Sept. 12, 1799
Died Sept. 8, 1840

Louisa A. C. Hodges
Died July 5, 1858
Rest ielligible

Elizabeth Hodges
Born Oct. 29, 1795
Died June 9, 1866
Age 71 yrs. 7 mo. 10 da.

Mollie P. Miller
Born Sept. 26, 1868
Died Jan. 19, 1924

Henry R. Miller
Born Nov. 28, 1864
Died Sept. 4, 1912

William R., Son of
H. R. & M. P. E. Miller
Born Jan. 30, 1896
Died Nov. 25, 1902

(Pg.5)

Mary Rachel, Dau. of
H. R. & M. P. E. Miller
Born Jan. 14, 1889
Died Aug. 14, 1889

D. R. Garretson
Born Mar. 16, 1836
Died Dec. 28, 1917

Rachel Miller
Born July 22, 1818
Died June 29, 1896

Ellen, Dau. of D. R. &
Rebecca Garretson
Born Dec. 17, 1878
Died Oct. 9, 1895
Age 16 yrs. 9 mo. 22 da.

Geo. W. Miller
Born Jan. 26, 1818
Died July 19, 1899

Annie E., Dau. of D. S. & M. A.
Miller
Born Apr. 24, 1889
Died Aug. 3, 1889

Sara A. Garretson
Wife of T. J. Rayl
Born Oct. 7, 1868
Died Oct. 13, 1917

Hannah Malissa, Wife of
A. J. Morelock
Born Oct. 18, 1850
Died May 13, 1920

Mattie E., Dau. of T. J. &
Sara A. Rayl
Born Feb. 12, 1898
Died Sept. 19, 1898

A. J. Morelock
Born Aug. 3, 1824
Died Aug. 4, 1895

Jas. D. Morelock
Born May 31, 1866
Died Sept. 1908
"A precious one we loved is
gone, A voice we loved is
stilled, A place is vacant
in our home."

Mae, Dau. of A. J. &
H. M. Morelock
Born June 11, 1880
Died June 20, 1887

Lillie M. Morelock, Wife of
H. B. Helton
Born July 6, 1889
Died Oct. 24, 1918

Josie Richards, Wife of
J. D. Morelock
Born Dec. 6, 1872
Died

Little Infant son of
G. W. & Minnie
Born & Died Nov. 2, 1905

Infant son of Jas. D. &
Josie Morelock
Born & Died Jan. 20, 1894

Roy Reed, Son of
T. C. & A. M. Garretson
Born June 2, 1904
Died Oct. 6, 1904

Mary Purkey
Born Nov. 15, 1865
Died July 5, 1928

Alice M., Wife of
T. C. Garretson
Born Sept. 18, 1876
Died Sept. 18, 1904

Minnie, Wife of Homer Black
Born Jan. 18, 1880
Died Feb. 3, 1904

Rebecca Garretson
Born Feb. 23, 1846
Died June 26, 1927

Howard S., Son of S. I. &
C. V. Luttrell
Born Jan. 20, 1893
Died Feb. 19, 1894

Willie, Son Of
S. I. & C. V. Luttrell
Born June 6, 1877
Died 1878

Nettie Shirley Oliver
Died Jan. 26, 1936
37 yr. 3 mo. 2 da.

Nellie Lena Oliver, Wife of
R. E. Oliver
Born Aug. 2, 1898
Died Oct. 16, 1918

Henry Richard Jenkins
Died Mar. 16, 1931
Age 60 yr. 11 mo. 27 da.

William Chapman
Born June 8, 1873
Died June 9, 1918

W. B. Richards
Born Dec. 30, 1878
Died Aug. 15, 1906

Lizzie E. Richards
Died Mar. 3, 1925

Nancy A., Wife of Newton
    Richards
Born Jan. 30, 1839
Died Oct. 29, 1914
Aged 75 yr. 8 mo. 29 da.
"A true wife and a good mother
    at rest."

Newton Richards
Born June 28, 1846
Died June 22, 1918
Age 71 yrs. 11 mo. 22 da.

Mary D. Mendenhall, Wife of
M. C. Williams
Born Jan. 13, 1838
Died Nov. 13, 1912

Melvin C. Williams
Born Oct. 3, 1838
Died June 4, 1916
Our Parents, has gone to a
  Mansion of rest to the glorious
  land by the Fliety blest.

Albert M., Son of
M.C. & M. D. Williams
Died July 7, 1889
Aged 8 yr. 2 mo. 7 da.
"Gone but not forgotten."

Stuard H. Barrett
Born Mar. 31, 1890
Died Oct. 12, 1918

"Asleep in Jesus"
Robert Henry Miller
Born May 30, 1906
Died May 5, 1926

Charlie T. Miller
Born May 16, 1908
Died June 29, 1914

Laura Miller
Born Oct. 22, 1901
Died May 19, 1913

Earl E. Miller
Born Aug. 18, 1910
Died May 15, 1914

Bertie P. Miller
Born Nov. 29, 1903
Died Mar. 14, 1913

Luesa C. Purkey
Born July 26, 1842
Died July 25, 1883

Susannah, Dau. of
G. & Nancy Livingston
Born Nov. 25, 1861
Died July 28, 1891
"Blessed are the dead that
  die in the Lord."

Benjamin N., Son of
N. B. & Nancy Morelock
Born Mar. 6, 1882
Died Dec. 13, 1904

Nancy, Wife of Nathan B.
    Morelock
Died Apr. 23, 1924
Age 88 yrs. 1 mo. 3 da

Augustus B. Long
Born Feb. 10, 1835
Died Apr. 22, 1897

Clarence R., Son of
 D. W. & C. K. Long
Born Jan. 15, 1904
Died Dec. 30, 1904

        My Husband

Levi Long
Born Aug. 13, 1845
Died Jan 23, 1901
Age 55 yrs. 5 mo. 10 da.

Alford Long
Born Aug. 13, 1809
Died May 17, 1891

Susan Long, Wife of
 Alford Long
Born May 25, 1811
Died July 20, 1894

T. M. Mc Alister
Born June 3, 1843
Died Dec. 4, 1917

Andrew J. Purkey
Born Aug. 29, 1857
Died Aug. 11, 1858

Nathan B. Morelock
Born Mar. 1, 1836
Died Aug. 11, 1919
Confederate Soldier
Member of Co. G. 43 Tenn. Reg.

Delia, Dau. of N. B. & Nancy
 Morelock
Born Nov. 16, 1870
Died July 2, 1889

Emma H. Morelock
Born 1843
Died 1866

HAMBLEN COUNTY
MORRIS FAMILY CEMETERY

Located just back of the W. H. Mullins residence on South Cumberland Street, Morristown, Tennessee.

This is the burying ground of the Morris family, pioneer settlers, and for whom Morristown was named. It was never a public cemetery, tho there were connections and friends of the Morris family buried there.

There are a great many unmarked graves, but due to the over grown condition, it is impossible to estimate how many. Most probably the graves of Gideon Morris, a Revolutionary soldier, and his wife, Jane, are in this plot.

It remains the property of the family, and is enclosed with an iron fence.

Copied by Margaret Helms Richardson, Morristown, Tennessee
May 15, 1937

Harvey Mefford
Born Feb. 18, 1830
Died Aug. 17, 1898
(His wife is buried at
his feet, stone fallen.)

Thomas M. Mc Bride
Born Nov. 15, 1841
Died June 12, 1897

Mary, Wife of
Abraham Spoon
Born in Randolph, N. C.
Oct. 28, 1779
Died Mar. 22, 1882

In Memory of
Marcus Mc Bride
Born July 20, 1818
Died 1852
Aged 33 yrs. 1 mo. 7 da.

Sacred to the Memory of
John Morris
Born Nov. 26, 1809
and departed this life
Aug. 3, 1850
Aged 40 yrs. 8 mo. 8 da.

Sacred to the Memory of
John Morris
Born Nov. 18, 1770
Departed this life
Jan. 1843

In Memory of
Rachel Morris, Wife of
John Morris
Born 28th of Feb. 1786
Died April 2, 1862

In Memory of
Rachel, Dau. of
John & Rachel Morris
Born June 11, 1826
Died April 21, 1844

In Memory of
Mary Mc Bride, Dau. of
John & Rachel Morris
Born 31st Jan. 1816
Died 15th Nov. 1842
Aged 26 yrs.

Drew Morris
Born Mar. 4, 1856
Died Aug. 23, 1916
"He died as he lived, a
Christian."

HAMBLEN COUNTY
MORRIS FAMILY CEMETERY

Alice, Wife of
Drew Morris
Born Jan. 11, 1858
"A tender mother, a
faithful wife."

Nancy Long
Died Apr. 20, 1888
Aged 63 years

Mollie Morris
Died Sept. 26, 1914
"A great intellect, just,
generous, kind hearted, a
life of toil and self denial
that she might help others.
The Bible she read and knew.
This verse was her guide "Do
unto others as you would they
would do unto you."
(Erected by her sister Hannah.)

John Morris
Born May 30, 1818
Died May 23, 1884

Elizabeth Morris, Wife of
John Morris
Born Sept. 3, 1837
Died Apr. 27, 1907

HAMBLEN COUNTY

TOMB STONE RECORDS

MORRISTOWN CITY CEMETERY

Located in the town of Morristown, Tennessee.

Copied by Williard Noe, October 1936.

In Memory of Ella Gratton
Payne, Wife of Dr. Geo.
Kempton Turner
Born in Lynchburg, Va.
Dec. 14, 1848
Died July 27, 1894

George Kempton Turner, M. D.
Surgeon C. S. A.
Born in Lynchburg, Va.
April 22, 1845
Died March 26, 1898
"I will find the light and
in the light will die."

W. P. Rogers
Born October 20, 1827
Died Jan. 13, 1879

William N. Carson
Born Dec. 6, 1837
Died July 10, 1873

Wirtie Wooten Caldwell
Born August 1, 1881
Died Dec. 12, 1893
Age 12 Years

Allen A. Corry,
Born Feb. 2, 1848
Died Dec. 18, 1885

Martha J. Corry
Born Jan. 25, 1850
Died Oct. 25, 1880

Caroline Alice Mee
Wife of B. B. Arwood
Born Sept. 24, 1856
Died April 4, 1901

W. S. Mee
Born Nov. 12, 1859
Died July 10, 1899
6th U. S. Volunteer Inft. Co. E.
"Sleep, Soldier, sleep:
Thy warfare is over."

Louis Zehrbach
Born July 16, 1850
Died March 20, 1913

Margaret Anna Zehrbach
Born April 30, 1858
Died Dec. 30, 1923

Perlie Maria Zehrbach
Born Nov. 10, 1885
Died June 8, 1911

Edward Henry Zehrbach
Born May 10, 1874
Died Sept. 30, 1892

James A. Townsend
Born Aug. 29, 1841
Died Aug. 15, 1915

His Wife, Stacy Hawkins
Born Oct. 4, 1850
Died Dec. 27, 1927

Rebecca E., wife of
Joseph Grigsby
Born June 15, 1842
Died Aug. 20, 1923

Lena, Dau. of Joseph
and Rebecca Grigsby
Born Dec. 5, 1861
Died Dec. 2, 1879

HAMBLEN COUNTY

MORRISTOWN CITY CEMETERY
(Page 2)

Charles Grigsby
Born Aug. 20, 1878
Died July 20, 1909

Joseph Grigsby
Born Oct. 23, 1838
Died Dec. 22, 1892

Isaac Nave Browne
Born Feb. 19, 1843
Elizabethton, Carter Co.
Tennessee
Died Aug. 9, 1914
Morristown, Hamblen Co.
Tennessee.

Elizabeth Andes Brown
Born July 8, 1848
Harrisburg, Rockingham Co.
Virginia
Died Oct. 26, 1930

Mary Jane, Daughter of Dr. M.
and Srah A. Carriger
Born Oct. 4, 1855
Died July 14, 1866

Sallie A., wife of M. J. B.
Roberts
Born July 22, 1860
Died Aug. 26, 1890

Mrs. Martha M. Rhoton

Fannie J. Spillman
May 12, 1845
Married Edward M. Grant May29, 1866
Married Rev. Rufus M. Hickey
Sept. 28, 1870
Aug. 28, 1892

Rev. Rufus M. Hickey
Born Aug. 28, 1820
Died Nov. 5, 1903

Julia Oaks
Born April 18, 1838
Died Feb. 14, 1920

Calvin F. Cunningham
Born May, 1, 1818
Died May 2, 1866

Mary H. Cunningham
Born March 1, 1839
Died May 31, 1902
"Sometime, Somewhere:
We'll understand."

W. H. Graddon
Born June 19, 1852
Died May 28, 1885

Ida, Wife of R. D. Craig
Born June 4, 1862
Died Nov. 7, 1890
Age 28 years, 5 Mos. 3 days

In Memory of Caswell C. Stuart
Born June 22, 1824
Died May 10, 1875
Age 50 years, 10 Mos. 18 days

Frank Stubblefield
Born Nov 20, 1848
Died April 18, 1916

His Wife, Annie Carmichael
Born Nov. 19, 1855
Died Feb. 5, 1900

Thomas C. Cain
Born Jan. 19, 1842
Died July 10, 1916

His Wife, Elizabeth Kenner
Born Aug. 24, 1842
Died March 9, 1913

Mary Kate Michael
Born May 11, 1871
Died April 20, 1891

Columbia J. Linn
Wife of Elijah Michael
Born July 6, 1840
Died July 28, 1923

HAMBLEN COUNTY

MORRISTOWN CITY CEMETERY
(Page 3)

John W. Harle
Born Feb. 2, 1820
Died Oct. 17, 1893

Penelope D., Wife of
J. W. Harle
Born July 30, 1830
Died Sept. 16, 1901

John W. Harle, Jr.
Born July 14, 1873
Died Aug. 25, 1895

S. A. Toney,
Born March 8, 1836
Died Oct. 1, 1879

Mollie Pettigrew
Born Feb. 9, 1868
Died March 19, 1902

Lewis Pettigrew
Born Feb. 23, 1866
Died Jan. 30, 1897

Robert Pettigrew
Born July 25, 1873
Died Mar. 14, 1906

Lee Roy Pettigrew
Born Nov. 17, 1892
Died June 15, 1894

Charles Pettigrew
Born Sept. 3, 1858
Died Aug. 19, 1898

Infant of C. W. and
Sallie Pettigrew
Allice Pettigrew Winfrey
Born Feb. 12, 1861
Died Mar. 26, 1886

Charles Lee Townsend
Born Mar. 5, 1859
Died July 26, 1924

Little Willie, Son of
J. A. and S. S. Townsend
Born Aug. 1, 1878
Died Dec. 7, 1879

Little Freddie Townsend
Born Feb. 1, 1876
Died Oct. 16, 1879

William F. Hodge L863- 1910

Edith Gammon, Dau. of W. F. and
M. A. Hodge
Born Sept. 30, 1887
Died July 27, 1892

Barton M. Hodge

In Memory of Mrs. Cynthia Gose
Mother of Mrs. J. M. Glenn
Departed this life Mar. 27, 1897
Aged 86 Years

Ida Florence, Dau. of
John and Susan Andes
Born Feb. 27, 1857
Died July 31, 1890

John Andes
Born Jan. 13, 1823
Died Mar. 7, 1877

Isaac B. Dooley
Born April 19, 1858
Died May 21, 1926

Mary L. Andes, Wife of
Isaac B. Dooley
Born Feb. 11, 1867

George A. Dooley, Son of
Isaac and Mary Dooley
Born Jan. 22, 1894
Died June 3, 1920
2nd Lieut. Signal Corps,
357th Aero Squadron

HAMBLEN COUNTY

MORRISTOWN CITY CEMETERY
(Page #4)

James Galloway Hodges,
Capt. Co. H. 60th Tenn.
C. S. A. 1837- 1908
And His Wife
Mary Angeline Witt
1839-1916

David Witt Hodges
Born Jan. 25, 1880
Died Aug. 6, 1890

W. P. Carriger
Born Oct. 31, 1850
Died Mar. 17, 1886
"My faith is implicit;
there is not a cloud
between me and my
Redeemer."

W. Pinkney, Son of
W. P. and M. R. Carriger
Born Sept. 8, 1885
Died Feb. 19, 1886

Miss Aurelia Carriger,
Daughter of Dr. M. and
Sarah Carriger

Dr. M. Carriger
Born Mar 4, 1818
Died Sept. 27, 1884

Sarah A. Jack
Wife of Dr. M. Carriger
Born Mar. 10, 1825
Died Dec. 30, 1903

Rufus Eldredge Rice
Born April 22, 1826
Died April 10, 1882

Catharine Chilton Rice
Born Mar 4, 1825
Died April 25, 1903

Harriet Amanda Rice
Born Aug. 5, 1854
"She exchanged her cross
for a crown Jan. 26, 1927

Lynn D. Rice
Born Dec. 1886
Died Feb. 1920

James A. Rice
Born Mar. 31, 1849
Died Mar. 29, 1918

Cora, Wife of J. O. Rice
Born May 1, 1860
Died July 9, 1887
"God be with you till
we meet again."

Our Darling
James Orville Rice
Born Dec. 31, 1887
Died Mar. 15, 1895

Herbert B., Son of
H. W. and Elizabeth Shields
1884- 1906

Ben J. Van Huss
Born May 12, 1812
Died April 3, 1900

Michael C. Van Huss
Born May 27, 1864
Died Dec. 20, 1907

Ira Harris
Born Aug. 31, 1832
Died May 24, 1875

Mary A. Wife of
Ira Harris
Born Dec. 15, 1835
Died Nov. 11, 1877

Salamis L. Harris
Born Sept. 24, 1857
Died Nov. 18, 1888

Mack Allen
1854- 1916

Laura Allen
1863- 1915

HAMBLEN COUNTY

MORRISTOWN CITY CEMETERY
(Page 5)

Alex Robinson
Born Jan. 8, 1865
Died Mar. 3, 1917

Sue R. Crouch, Daughter of
William H. Crouch
Died Mar 26, 1919

John A. Stubblefield
Died June 11, 1918

His Wife, Lillie Crouch
Died Nov. 17, 1916

Abbie Leva, Daughter of
A. and Azalia Johnston
Born Dec. 13, 1893
Died May 6, 1894

Sue Masengill Thomas
Wife of A. B. Wells
Born Oct. 20, 1886
Died May 29, 1927

James B. Wells
Born Feb. 12, 1817
Died Jan. 20, 1909

Harriet A. Wells
Born Dec. 27, 1820
Died April 12, 1894

May Arlene Wells
Born May 13, 1878
Died Jan. 26, 1920

Edward J. Wells
Born May 23, 1852
Died Jan. 4, 1928

Fred A. Lilienkamp
Born June 25, 1848
Died June 6, 1911

Nancy A. Johnston
Born Oct. 30, 1860
Died Sept. 17, 1906

Andrew Johnston
Born Sept. 1, 1847
Died April 18, 1915

Mary Johnston
Born May 2, 1863
Died Dec. 17, 1906

Carrie Frances, Dau. of
J. M. and L. S. Williams
Mar 15, 1894

Marion Milton, Dau. of
J. M. and L. S. Williams
April 16, 1897
Nov. 29, 1920

James Milton Williams
April 7, 1861
His Wife, Lyvia Sabinia Bailey
July 13, 1867

J. Bailey Williams, Son of
J. M. and L. S. Williams
June 2, 1890
Oct. 24, 1906

Ellen Eames
Born Feb. 23, 1824
Died Nov. 6, 1876

Curtis Eames
Born Feb. 11, 1826
Died June 11, 1878

William R. Galding
Born March 29, 1853
Died March 15, 1875

Joseph Brown
July 28, 1819
April 25, 1903

Mary F. Brown
Jan. 9, 1820
Feb. 5, 1907

HAMBLEN COUNTY

MORRISTOWN CITY CEMETERY
(Page 6)

Radford B. Noe
Born Oct. 24, 1879
Died June 24, 1911

Margaret Ann, Dau. of
Robert and Annie M. Russell
Born April 7, 1910
Died April 17, 1910

T. Cain Butler
Nov. 8, 1881
Oct. 1912
"None knew him but
to love him."

J. Rheton Noe
Born July 26, 1849
Died Sept. 7, 1916

Dr. W. L. Crawford
Born Feb. 9, 1874
Died Nov. 27, 1900

Thomas F. Farmer
Born Oct. 1872
Died April 26, 1915

His Wife, Marie Farmer
Born Oct. 27, 1869
Died

Mary Louise Oaks Fellows
Jan. 14, 1870
Sept. 12, 1923

Thomas Hadden, Son of
W. S. and Mollie Fellows
Born June 4, 1901
Died May 19, 1903

Edna Lee, Daughter of
W. S. and M. L. Fellows
Born March 19, 1906
Died Oct. 24, 1906

Earnest Willie, Son of
W. S. and M. L. Fellows
Born Jan. 30, 1896
Died Jan. 31, 1896

Mary Nelle, Dau. of
H. R. and Grace Arwood
Sept. 1, 1919
March 21, 1920

Dickie Thompson
Born Nov. 26, 1906
Died Aug. 17, 1908

J. Curry Thompson
Born March 10, 1863
May 30, 1916

Viola Thompson
June 17, 1886
Oct. 18, 1919

W. T. Martin
Born at Lafayette, Montgomery Co.
Virginia Feb. 12, 1861
Was Killed by falling slate
in Bird Eye Coal Mines at
Halsey, Kentucky July 12, 1899
"Be at rest, Brother, we are
coming."

Infant Son of W. T. and
Mary Martin
Born and died June 30, 1897

Louvenia A., Dau. of D. and E.
Finch
Born Sept. 1, 1865
Died April 28, 1897

James Lyon Galbraith
Born Feb. 3, 1843
Died Sept. 1, 1917

Anna Dantzler Galbraith,
Wife of J. L. Galbraith
Born in Heidelburg, Miss
June 11, 1861
Died Jan. 22, 1908

Jennie B. McFarland
Died April 25, 1887
Aged 52 Years

In Memoriam
Robert McFarland
Died Oct. 2, 1884
Aged 52 Years
"He Made Home Happy."

G. G. Williams
Born Mar. 29, 1851
Died Oct. 22, 1903

Sarah Williams
Born 1847
Died 1923

Oscar E. Williams
Born Jan. 30, 1875
Died July 24, 1897
"At Rest."

Jodie, Wife of W. R. Toney
Dec. 26, 1871
April 14, 1899

Minnie Pearl, Dau. of
W. R. and J. A. Toney
June 2, 1895
Oct. 5, 1899

Wilburn, Son of W. R. and
J. A. Toney
Dec. 26, 1871
April 14, 1899

Oscar D. Yoe
Jan. 29, 1852
Mar. 8, 1901

Ruth Elizabeth, Dau. of
Mr. and Mrs. Drew Hammond
Born Aug. 9, 1912
Died Oct. 2, 1912

Edith Lee, Dau. of Mr. and
Mrs. Drew Hammond
Born March 13, 1911
Died April 12, 1911

Gertrude Savilla, Dau. of
Mr. and Mrs. Drew Hammond
Sept. 25, 1909
March 20, 1910

James Rollie, Son of D. S. and
M. L. Hammond
Born Sept. 4, 1902
Died Oct. 11, 1904

In Memory of my Husband
Charles D. Moss
July 6, 1853
Feb 2, 1892
Aged 38 Years, 4 Mos. 26 Days.
"Prepare to meet they God"
Amos 4- 12

Jenny Miles Hammond
Nov. 23, 1888
June 12, 1889

Anna McFarland
Oct. 28, 1860
May 13, 1913

Mary E. Russell, Dau. of
Armanda Parker
Died Mar. 6, 1911
Aged 19 Years

Vina Jones
July 28, 1867
April 29, 1929

Robert Lee, Son of
W. M. and M. M. Simmons
March 2, 1920
June 15, 1921
"Gone to be an angel."

Ernest F. Simmons
Aug. 26, 1902
Jan. 13, 1930
"We will meet again."

Annie May Estes
Born June 1, 1919
Died Oct. 7, 1920
"Budded on earth to
bloom in heaven."

John L. Standish
Died Nov. 5, 1925
Aged 65 Years

167

HAMBLEN COUNTY

MORRISTOWN CITY CEMETERY
(Page 8)

Mary H. Standish
Born June 28, 1825
Died Nov. 29, 1907

W. G. Lacy,
Aug. 13, 1856
March 7, 1916

Edgar A. Lacy
March 24, 1879
Jan. 29, 1906

Eddie L. Anderson
Born Sept. 24, 1883
Died Jan. 13, 1906
"To peace in heaven."

Willie K. Hodges
Born Aug. 16, 1856
Died Feb. 3, 1905
"Blessed are the pure in
heart for they shall see
God."

Little Mary Agnes, Dau. of
W. K. and M. V. Hodges
Born March 23, 1905
"Budded on earth to bloom
in heaven."

James B. McCrary
Born Nov. 21, 1837
Died Oct. 18, 1883
"We will meet again."

James M. Rayl
Born Feb. 6, 1862
Died July 18, 1926

Edna Helton Rayl
Born April 1, 1868

Thomas P. Brooks
Born Feb. 7, 1829
Died Aug. 20, 1893

N. T. Gourley, Co. F. 8 Tenn. Cal.
Born Feb. 14, 1856
Died Dec. 1, 1918

His Wife,
Mary J. Brooks
Born Feb. 7, 1834
Died Aug. 22, 1924
"Gone but not forgotten."

Addie Mae Lock, wife of
H. L. Lock
Born July 9, 1909
Died Nov. 20, 1929

Beulah Mae, Dau. of H. L.
and Addie Mae Lock
Born June 30, 1928
Died Jan. 2, 1929

Gertie R. Daughter of
Amanda Parker
Born July 13, 1895
Died June 8, 1910

Annie Bell, Daughter of
M. E. and I. T. Cates
Born Aug. 7, 1902
Died Mar. 3, 1905

Catharine, Daughter of
Rufus and Lillie Mabe
Born July 7, 1898
Died Nov 18, 1901
Aged 3 Years, 4 Mos. 11 Days

Mollie F. Mabe
Born July 24, 1872
Died March 16, 1902

Charlotte E. Mabe
Born June 7, 1863
Died July 2, 1906
"The Gates of heaven for
her shall open wide."

Ida Mabe
Died Sept. 25, 1936
Aged 48 years, 1 Mo. 11 Days

William A. Mabe
Born June 8, 1869
Died Dec. 30, 1915

HAMBLEN COUNTY

MORRISTOWN CITY CEMETERY
(Page 9)

Lula E. Rayle
Born July 13, 1896
Died Feb. 4, 1904

"A Good Man is Gone."
J. F. Palmer
Born March 5, 1855
Died May 21, 1895
Aged 40 Years, 20 Mos. 17 Das.

Caroline Cox, Wife of
H. A. Crawford
Born Oct. 31, 1898
Died Dec. 27, 1893
"A precious one from us is
gone, a voice we loved is
stilled."

Lelia Mae, Wife of H. W.
Trobaugh
Born July 15, 1863
Died July 6, 1903
Aged 39 Years, 11 Mos. 21 Days.

Sallie A. O'Kelly
Born Oct. 29, 1880
Died May 30, 1907

Mary E., Wife of
E. D. Miller
Born June 5, 1869
Died Aug. 23, 1898

Rose Lee Mabe, Wife of
R. C. Dukes
Born Aug. 11, 1890
Died May 29, 1909
"She was the sunshine of
my home."

Eliza Jane, Wife of
W. P. McGinnis
Born Feb. 4, 1841
Died Dec. 29, 1890

W. P. McGinnis
Born July 3, 1837
Died Nov. 19, 1891

John Dice, Son of
J. H. and S. A. Davault
Born May 9, 1892
Died June 14, 1892
"Budded on earth to bloom
in bloom."

Nellie D., Wife of Geo. S. Crouch
Born May 25, 1851
Died April 13, 1890
Aged 39 Years

Lillie, Daughter of Geo. S.
and Nellie D. Crouch
Born Aug. 27, 1880
Died Oct. 29, 1905

William McLaurin Cowan
Born Feb. 2, 1876
Died May 15, 1921

Kate Crouch Cowan
Born March 30, 1874

Dr. D. A. Neilson
Born Mar 25, 1825
Died June 18, 1899

Lena Myrtle Palmer
Born Feb. 5, 1895
Died Feb. 25, 1895

Dorcas A., Wife of
A. Rowe
Aged 52 Years

Abraham Rowe
Aged 80 Years

Ella Johnson
Born Nov. 15, 1834
Died Oct. 10, 1875

Little Nettie, Dau. of
S. B. and E. E. Noe
Born March 3, 1883
Died June 3, 1883

HAMBLEN COUNTY

MORRISTOWN CITY CEMETERY
(Page 10)

Texanah Wilmeth, Wife of
W. C. Luttrell
Born Dec. 25, 1832
Died Aug. 31, 1896
"She lived the life of the
godly; and died the death
of the righteous, and is
waiting her loved ones to
come home."

S. Miranda Harris, Wife of
Foster Whiteside
Born July 22, 1838
Died Oct. 30, 1907

C. H. Whiteside
Born Nov. 15, 1862
Died March 11, 1891

J. A. Whiteside
Born Oct. 14, 1872
Died Oct. 15, 1893

Foster Whiteside
Born Jan. 24, 1836
Died June 21, 1897

Katie Lou, Dau. of Jake
and E. H. Witt
Born Sept. 18, 1892
Died July 18, 1893

Sarah McGuire Sharp
Wife of James B. Sharp
Born Oct. 5, 1824
Died Nov. 17, 1902

Joseph Y. Luttrell
Born May 11, 1869
Died Dec. 4, 1892

J. W. Luttrell
Born Feb. 8, 1816
Died Nov. 14, 1892
Ages 76 years, 9 Mos. 5 Days

Emily C., Wife of
A. R. Dickinson
Born May 20, 1823
Died Sept. 13, 1883

A. R. Dickinson
Born July 11, 1816
Died Oct. 15, 1902

Thomas J. Russell
Born July 11, 1840
Died Dec. 26, 1908
"God taketh care of
his own."

W. H. Fellows
Born Oct. 12, 1837
Died Jan. 23, 1974

Little Roy, Son of
M. M. and N. M. Ennis
Born Jan. 8, 1906
Died Sept. 14, 1906
"Another little angel
before the heavenly throne."

In Memory of
Martin Butts
Born Jan. 18, 1818
Died June 7, 1874

Frances Angle, Infant Dau. of
T. M. and Marguerite Walden
Aged 6 weeks and 3 Days

E. C. Bruce
Born Oct. 5, 1824
Died Sept. 15, 1887

Letitia Bruce
Born Sept. 4, 1824
Died Jan. 20, 1905
"They fall as a ripe shock
of corn,"ready for the garner
of the Lord."

William T. Hamilton
Born Sept. 20, 1876
Died April 25, 1906

Bettie Horner, Wife of
A. J. Bruner
Feb. 17, 1925

HAMBLEN COUNTY

MORRISTOWN CITY CEMETERY
(Page 11)

Dr. A. J. Bruner
Born Mar. 4, 1847
Died Feb. 17, 1904

Mary Elizabeth, Wife of
Dr. A. Bruner
Born June 4, 1841
Died Feb. 17, 1903

Rev. John H. Kennedy
Born Aug. 16, 1848
Died Dec. 1, 1898
A member of Holston Con-
ference, his last words,
"He doeth all things well."

Frances E. Bryan, Wife of
Rev. J. H. Kennedy
Born Sept. 17, 1844
Died April 3, 1912
"Precious in the sight
of the Lord is the death
of his saints."

Just a little while
Elizabeth J. Sherrill
Wife of R. A. Owen
Born Dec. 23, 1856
Died Oct. 9, 1913
"Willing rather to be
absent from the body
and to be present with
the Lord."

Arthur Shields, Son of
L. M. and H. N. Cartwright
Born Aug. 3, 1891
Died Aug. 19, 1891

Rev. R. N. Price
July 3, 1830
Feb. 6, 1923

Myra Sue Price
Asheville, N. C.
Sept. 2, 1867
Morristown, Tenn.
June 7, 1900

Mary Baird Price
Lenoir, N. C.
Oct., 18, 1862
Harriman, Tenn.
Aug. 19, 1895

W. T. Helms
Knoxville, Tenn.
May 14, 1851
Morristown, Tenn.
Aug. 9, 1904

Mrs. Mattie M., Wife of
Dr. R. S. Tidwell
Died July 29, 1893
Aged 43 Years, 5 Months and
29 Days
"A Precious One from us is Gone,
A Voice We Loved is Still."

STEWART
C. W. W.
H. E. S.
J. E. S.

Chas. D. Orr
Born June 26, 1856
Died Sept. 27, 1909

Edithe Cocke
July 20, 1911
Dec. 20, 1913

Lucy M., Wife of
J. M. Honey
Born Feb. 14, 1844
Died March 4, 1892

In Memory of
J. M. Honey
Native of Cornwall, England
Died in Middlesboro, Ky.
Oct. 5, 1901
In His 65th Year

Linus B. Brown
Dec. 5, 1851
Aug. 16, 1895

HAMBLEN COUNTY

MORRISTOWN CITY CEMETERY
(Page 12)

John C. Crowell
Born in New Jersey
April 12, 1814
Died Mar. 14, 1891

Harriet L. Crowell
Died April 5, 1873

Edith M. Crowell
August 8, 1873
Sept. 15, 1892

In Memory of
Elizabeth B. Crowell,
Wife of S. B. Crowell
Died July 7, 1875
Aged 30 Years

Stephen B. Crowell
Born Mar. 20, 1817
Died Aug. 28, 1886

Elizabeth B. Crowell
Born Sept. 12, 1807
Died Feb. 27, 1886
"She lived for Others"

Lillian M., Daughter of
C. G. & C. Crowell
Feb., 9, 1883
Oct. 17, 1889

Caroline Jane, Wife of
John D. Crowell
Born Nov. 7, 1815
Died Aug. 4, 1891
"At Rest"

Pearl Crowell, Wife of
O. P. R. Fox
Born 1869
Died 1898

Ethel, Daughter of
O. P. R. & P. C. Fox
Born 1890
Died 1901

Alexander H. Gregg,
Born 1834
Died 1900

Helen M. Gregg,
Born 1840
Died 1902

Frank Hammond, Son of
O. F. & Emma M. Hammond
Born June 28, 1896
Died April 28, 1929

Bobby, Son of
J. J. & N. A. Sikes
1884-1885

Alex Anderson
Born Mar. 23, 1861
Died Sept. 19, 1893
"A Good Man is the Noblest
Work of God."

Our Baby
Nellie Anderson
Born & Died 1893

M. B. Lane
Died Oct. 12, 1839
Aged 69 Years
"Oh Death, Where is Thy Sting?"

Minerva T. Lane
1832-1904
"A Good Woman Gone."

Louvenia, Daughter of
D. & E. Finch
Born Sept. 1, 1865
Died April, 28, 1897
"A Precious One from us is Gone."

John R. Shields,
May 23, 1889
Aug. 21, 1909

HAMBLEN COUNTY

MORRISTOWN CITY CEMETERY
(Page 13)

Minnie C., Wife of
Joe M. Seneker,
Dec. 15, 1874
June 26, 1890

Nannie A. Gammon
Born June 29, 1837
Died June 15, 1891

Kate King Davis
Oct. 13, 1877
May 13, 1903

DeWitt Clinton Davis
April 2, 1835
Mar. 11, 1920

Dora D. Davis
Jan. 12, 1851
Dec. 29, 1911

Nancy Black
Died April 25, 1920
Aged 73 Years

David Black
Died Oct. 16, 1919

Annie May Black

Samuel B. Black
Died Dec. 1928
Aged 67 Years

Thomas E. Farner
Born Oct. 1872
Died April, 1915

His Wife
Nannie Farner
Born 1869- Died
"A Precious One from Us
    is Gone,
A Voice We loved is Still,
A Place is Vacant in our Home,
Which Never can be Filled."

Our Mother
Martha Farner

Our Sister
Miss Carrie Farner

Lewis G. Rhea
1871- 1926
Age 55 Years

Tommy, Son of
J. T. & Mary Akers
Aug. 22, 1904
Feb. 7, 1906
"Of Such is the Kingdom
of Heaven."

"To the Memory of Joy
Only Child of Stephen Ira
and Lucie Helms Gilchrist
Born Dec. 23, 1903
Died June 11, 1906

Roy Pearce
1899-1923

Jane Rader
Born Jan. 6, 1809
Died Mar. 20, 1887
"We will meet again."

Malissa, Wife of
William Rader
Died 1889
"She was a devoted Wife &
taught her two little boys
the way to heaven."

Mary Read

Twin Children of
G. R. & Lizzie Whittington
May 1896- '96
"A little time on earth
was spent,
Till God for them an angel
sent."

HAMBLEN COUNTY

MORRISTOWN CITY CEMETERY
(Page 14)

Robert Hamilton Earle
Oct., 2, 1852
July 9, 1920

Sallie Foute Earle
Dec. 15, 1858
June 14, 1922
"After life's fitful fever
They sleep well."

Ralph R. Shields
Born Oct. 9, 1873
Died June 37, 1890

Mary R., Wife of
Hugh W. Lynn
Born Dec. 12, 1850
Died May 12, 1879

At Rest
Flo, Wife of Dr.
J. B. F. Dice
Feb. 6, 1906

In Memory of
Nancy A. Turley, Wife of
Wm. McFarland
Born Aug. 25, 1829
Died Feb. 25, 1883

Little Jack, Infant Son of
T. C. & D. V. Dooley
July 21, 1906
May 30, 1907
"From God to God."

Jane Renfro Herndon, Wife of
D. A. Neilson
Dec. 8, 1821
Feb. 24, 1876

Wm. A. Lyle
Born Aug. 31, 1811
Feb. 31, 1879

James K. Lawless
Oct. 6, 1843
Feb. 2, 1911
U. C. V.

His Wife
Louisa A. Norman
Sept. 16, 1846
Apr. 4, 1909
"Thy Will be Done."

Dr. H. C. McCall
Born Dec. 1826
Died March 1083

Lizzie Tate, Wife of
Dr. H. C. McCall
Born Dec. 12, 1836
Died Sept. 4, 1883

Edward Oscar Tate
Born Mar 7, 1845
Died Mar. 20, 1905

Father
Samuel B. Tate
Born Aug. 22, 1797
Died Aug. 13, 1865

Mother
Caroline M. Tate
Born Nov. 5, 1809
Died April 7, 1818

Stephen W. Tate
Born Jan. 30, 1830
Died Feb. 23, 1855

Harriet K. Tate
Born April 21, 1833
Died July 24, 1873

Mrs. Virginia T. Huffmaster
Born Sept. 15, 1834
Died July 2, 1858

Margaret J. Tate
Born Nov. 29, 1838
Died July 16, 1854

Carrie, Wife of
E. O. Tate
Born Oct. 20, 1843
Died Oct. 12, 1890

HAMBLEN COUNTY

MORRISTOWN CITY CEMETERY
(Page 15)

William Tate
Born Aug. 22, 1800
Died July 10, 1859

Selina F. Henry, Wife of
J. H. Trent
Born June 19, 1843
Died March 26, 1890

Capt. J. H. Trent
Company "A"
1 Tenn. Cav.

Little Florence, Infant
Daughter of J. H. & S. F. Trent
Born Feb. 7, 1873
Died April 13, 1873

My Mother
Naomi Trent
Born Jan. 7, 1801
Died Dec. 26, 1871

Jessie, Wife of
Robert McFarland
Born July 4, 1869
Died Feb. 12, 1899

Robert McFarland

Infant Son of
A. T. & Merrill Stowe Helms

Arthur C. Helms
Born Oct. 29, 1859
Died Feb. 1904

Nellie Trent Helms Abernathy
Died July 29, 1912

Last three graves not marked
Information given by
Margaret Helms Richardson
Morristown, Tenn.
Graves are on Crowall lot.

HAMBLEN COUNTY
CATHERINE NENNEY CEMETERY
(Page 1)

Catherine Nenney Baptist Church is located about 1 mile west of
Whitesburg on the old pike going toward Russellville.
Copied by Rebecca Colyer, May 11, 1937

54 graves marked with field stones or stakes
17 unmarked graves

Louis Monroe Courtney
Born Aug. 10, 1867
Died Dec. 6, 1934

Opha Beckner Courtney
Born June 19, 1876
(still living)

"Our Darling"
Vance, Dau. of
S. S. & L. B. Rhea
Born Sept. 16, 1905
Died Oct. 11, 1905
"Gone but not forgotten"

Odessall, Dau. of
S.S. & L. B. Rhea
Born May 8, 1910
Died Feb. 26, 1917
"Gone but not forgotten"

Sam Rhea
Born Sept. 7, 1880
(still living)

His Wife
Lillie Belle Rhea
Born July 13, 1883
Died Jan. 11, 1934

Margaret N. Cooper
Born June 27, 1916
Died Sept. 5, 1923

Charles Deadrick Williams
Born Dec. 21, 1854
Died May 22, 1924

His Wife
Ruth Elizabeth Williams
Born June 28, 1858
Died Aug. 2, 1918

Flora Haun
Born Feb. 25, 1895
Died Nov. 27, 1918
"Remember me as you pass by,
as you are now so once was I,
as I am now so you must be,
Prepare for death and follow me"

Louise Burchell, Wife of
J. G. M. Dyer
Born Jan. 25, 1865
Died Oct. 20, 1908
"At Rest"
"A wife devoted, a mother
affectionate, a friend ever
kind and true."

Minnie Thomas, Wife of
Martin Rhea
Born Sept. 16, 1877
Died Jan. 16, 1910
"The gates of Heaven for her
have opened wide."

Catherine R. Courtney, Wife of
J. C. A. Haun
Born July 22, 1869
Died Nov. 30, 1920
"She was kind and affectionate
wife, a fond mother, and a
friend to all."

HAMBLEN COUNTY
CATHERINE NENNEY CEMETERY
(Page 2)

Ezekiel Rhea
Born Jan. 6, 1849
Died Aug. 31, 1927

His Wife
Ellen Haun
Born Oct. 7, 1856
Died Feb. 25, 1926
"We will meet again."

Jesse, Son of E. & Ellen Rhea
Born Jan. 5, 1888
Died Sept. 8, 1917
"Gone but not forgotten."

Robert Thomas, Son of
Lee & Bobbie Rhea
Born Jan. 12, 1916
Died Sept. 20, 1917
"Budded on earth to bloom
in Heaven."

Mattie P. Wolfe
Born May 28, 1865
Died Feb. 26, 1929

Horace, Son of
David Parrish & Wife
Born May 11, 1909
Died Aug. 18, 1910
"Our little earnings have
gone but not forgotten."

Mack Parrish
Born Oct. 12, 1902
Died Dec. 27, 1927
"At Rest"

Mary E. Parrish
Born Mar. 5, 1871
Died Jan. 23, 1929
"Sweetly sleeping"

Thomas Parrish
Born July 12, 1871
Died Mar. 12, 1925
"He was a kind and loving
father, an affectionate husband
and a friend to all." "At Rest"

J. J. Parrish
Born Feb. 21, 1838
Died Apr. 12, 1930

His Wife
Elizabeth Parrish
Born Sept. 10, 1843
Died July 21, 1920
"Blessed are the dead which
die in the Lord."

William R. Parrish
Born Oct. 14, 1880
Died Jan. 24, 1915
Age 34 yrs. 3 mo. 10 da.
"Asleep in Jesus, Oh how sweet
Till we meet again."

Fred C., Son of
J. C. & Mattie Parish
Born Oct. 23, 1921
Died May 30, 1922

Infant Son of
J. C. & Mattie Parrish
Born & Died May 4, 1920
"Gone to be an angel."

David Pangle Estes
Born Nov. 13, 1928
Died Feb. 26, 1934
"Just a rose bud from our home
has gone to bloom in God's
garden above."

Hellen Joyce, Dau. of
John & Flora Day
Born May 30, 1925
Died July 20, 1925
"Gone so soon."

Fred M. Parrish
Born Apr. 23, 1890
(still living)

His Wife

HAMBLEN COUNTY
CATHERINE HENNEY CEMETERY
(Page 3)

Ida Collette Parrish
Born June 4, 1893
Died Nov. 10, 1925
"The Lord giveth, The Lord
taketh, Blessed be the name
of the Lord."

Joseph P. Courtney
Born Mar. 14, 1859
Died June 28, 1922

His Wife
Mary Ann Moore
Born Feb. 8, 1853
(still living)

Kenneth Ray, Son of
C. W. & Lockie Hamilton
Born Mar. 13, 1920
Died Sept. 15, 1926
"Asleep in Jesus."
He was killed in a school hack.

Mattie Walker
Died Dec. 5, 1936
Age 55 yr.
(undertakers marker.)

G. A. Walker
Born Nov. 15, 1899
Died Mar. 18, 1926
"Just in the morning of his
day, In youth and love he died."

Henry D. Susong
Born June 16, 1895
(still living)

His Wife
Nannie Susong
Born Dec. 24, 1903
Died Nov. 3, 1931

Charles R. Cline
Born Apr. 2, 1875
Died Dec. 1, 1924

Hugh M. Courtney
Born Dec. 13, 1876
Died Mar. 6, 1918
"A precious one from us has
gone a voice we loved is stilled
a place is vacant in our home
which never can be filled."

Mary E. Smith
Born June 18, 1880
Died Oct. 7, 1909

B. A. Beckner
Born June 17, 1855
Died Sept. 11, 1925

His Wife
Sarah E. Beckner
Born July 2, 1855
(still living)

Mary E. Burchell, Wife of
William H. Fowler
Born Aug. 16, 1868
Died Dec. 11, 1935

Infant Huston Carroll, Son of
H. G. & Una V. Beckner
Born & Died May 15, 1921
"Gone to be an angel."

Infant Margarette, Dau. of
H. G. & Una V. Beckner
Born Feb. 27, 1923
Died Feb. 28, 1923
"Gone to be an angel."

Infant Son of
H. G. & U. V. Beckner
Born & Died Feb. 13, 1924
"Gone to be an angel."

Tessie Paxton
1908 - 1937

HAMBLEN COUNTY
CATHERINE NENNEY CEMETERY
(Page 4)

Charles Wallace, Son of
C. W. & I. E. Morell
Born June 17, 1910
Died June 8, 1911

Mary Jane Gorden
Died Aug. 22, 1934
Age 78 yr. 9 mo. 30 da.
(undertakers marker)

Fay Leana, Dau. of
W. P. & M. N. Gorden
Born Apr. 1, 1906
Died Apr. 3, 1906

Cassie B. Legg, Wife of
W. C. A. Marshall
Born Dec. 31, 1883
Died Jan. 19, 1906
"Our mother from Home is gone."

T. N. Hale Jr.
Died Dec. 10, 1936
Age 47 yr. 11 mo.
(undertakers marker)

"Safe in the arms of Jesus"
Eva, Dau. of
J. C. & N. L. Dean
Born Sept. 13, 1900
Died June 15, 1908

In Memory of Wm. A. Dean
Departed this life Dec. 8, 1905
He was raised to the subline
Degree of a master Mason Feb. 15, 1871
He was born Nov. 30, 1836
"The Sunshine and rain pass over him
and he is not distrubed for he sleeps
in that peace which the world cannot
ever take away."

Albert Carl, Son of
T. J. & S. E. Cassell
Born Sept. 6, 1900
Died July 8, 1916
"Dear little Carl, thou hast left us and
our loss we deeply feel. This the Lord
has bereft us of one we loved so well."

Myrtle V., Dau. of
T. J. & S. E. Cassell
Born Nov. 25, 1897
Died Nov. 16, 1914
"Farewell, Myrtle, O how
we miss you, home is sad
and lonely now, while you
are in that home so bright
and fair. May God help one
and all to meet you there."

Marjorie M. Cassell
Born Jan. 23, 1929
Died Oct. 16, 1934
"Safe in the arms of Jesus"

Walter L. Ivy
Born Sept. 10, 1861
Died Feb. 14, 1920
"Gone but not forgotten."

Mary Adalin Dean Ivy
Born Dec. 23, 1841
Died Oct. 30, 1914
"Come Ye Blessed."

Martha M. Dean, Wife of
A. W. Farmsworth
Departed this life
April 26, 1909
Age 62 yrs. 2 mo. 3 da.
"Asleep in the arms of
Jesus."

The daughter baby of
T. E. & M. G. Dean
Born June 15, 1903
Died Sept. 26, 1904

Mollie G. Trobaugh, Wife of
T. E. Dean
Born Nov. 1, 1877
Died June 20, 1909

Ollie I. Haun Walker
Born Aug. 29, 1869
Married Dec. 4, 1902
"She was a devout Christian,
a devoted wife and a loving
friend."

Benjamine B. Marshall
Born Dec. 28, 1850
Died Jan. 20, 1928

His Wife
Sarah E. Marshall
Born Apr. 27, 1860
Died Apr. 16, 1920
"Gone but not forgotten."

T. A. Shields
Born Apr. 11, 1872
(still living)

His Wife
Lucie E. Marshall
Born Jan. 29, 1878
Died May 12, 1929
"We will meet thee again."

Mary Josephine Haun, Wife of
James Beck
Born June 7, 1874
Died May 21, 1905
Was a Member of Catherine
Nenney Church.

Minnie Orlena, Dau. of
Samuel & Lizzie Rush
Born Sept. 22, 1888
Died Aug. 12, 1916
"Gone but not forgotten."
"At Rest"

Charles Alvie, Son of
E. M. & Ada Rednour
Born June 27, (?)
Died Mar. 22, 1928
"Jesus loves me this I know."

John Roger, Infant Son of
J. B. M. & Vergie Kirkpatrick
Born Jan. 25, 1913
Died Feb. 27, 1913
"Budded on earth to bloom in
Heaven."

Clyde J. Shipley Jr., Son of
Mr. & Mrs. Clyde J. Shipley
Born Oct. 6, 1919
Died Dec. 1, 1924

James M. Burchell
Born Oct. 12, 1839
Died June 1, 1915
Age 75 yr. 7 mo. 19 da.
Volunteered in the Federal
army Apr. 15, 1862, Mustered
out Apr. 15, 1865, Private Co.
1st Reg. Tenn. Vol. Cav.
"Remember me as you pass by
As you are now, soh once was I
As I am now so you must be,
Prepare for death and follow
me."

Mary Ann, Wife of
J. M. Burchell
Born Mar. 19, 1849
Died Mar. 30, 1919
"At Rest"

Dan L. Horner
Co. A. 1 Tenn.

Mother
Sallie Horner
Born Apr. 14, 1858
Died Dec. 19, 1919
"She was the sunshine of
our home."

Maggie Beckner, Wife of
Robert Rhea
Born Apr. 23, 1847
Died May 24, 1914
"Gone but not forgotten."

Eliza J. Beckner, Wife of
W. S. Dyer
Born Apr. 29, 1844
Died Mar. 24, 1914

HAMBLEN COUNTY
CATHERINE NENNEY CEMETERY
(Page 6)

William S. Dyer
Born Jan. 6, 1841
Died Mar. 9, 1920
"At Rest"

Mary E. Roddy, Wife of
Jacob H. Haun
Born Dec. 25, 1866
Died Sept. 21, 1906
"As a wife devoted, as a
mother affectionate, as a
friend ever kind and true."

Charlie W. Long
Born Sept. 8, 1884
Died Apr. 24, 1935

    His Wife
Josie A. Murdock
Born Nov. 18, 18 81
(still living)
"We shall meet thee again."

C. W. Whetsell
Born Oct. 6, 1868
(still living)

    His Wife
Nannie C. Whetsell
Born Oct. 24, 1869
Died Mar. 3, 1930
"At Rest"

Thomas S. Courtney
Born May 18, 1867
Died May 9, 1935

William J. Courtney
Died Apr. 23, 1935
Age 68 yr.
(undertakers marker)

Henry C. Talley
Born Sept. 13, 1869
Died Aug. 14, 1932

Nannie Talley, Wife of
H. C. Talley
Born Aug. 1, 1871
Died Dec. 26, 1933

Son of, Orlie T. Talley
Born Aug. 8, 1906
Died Dec. 24, 1935

James Clyde Thomason
Born Jan. 25, 1931
Died Dec. 23, 1932
"Asleep in Jesus."

William A. Vinyard
Born Oct. 7, 1885
Died Mar. 23, 1934

    His Wife
Ida M. Heath
Born Dec. 25, 1887
(still living)
"At Rest"

William C. Orrick
Born Jan. 29, 1879
Died July 31, 1933

Harriet Haun
Died Feb. 28, 1937
Age 72 yrs.
(undertakers marker)

Rebecca Moore
Born May 8, 1869
Died Jan. 29, 1932
"At Rest"

Joe H. Melton
Born Jan. 5, 1865
Died Mar. 6, 1929
"At Rest"

Donald W. Beckner
Born Sept. 5, 1934
Died May 2, 1936

HAMBLEN COUNTY

TOMB STONE RECORDS

NOE'S CHAPEL CEMETERY

MET H ODIST

Located two and one half miles north of Morristown, Tennessee on the old Tate Springs Pike.

The cemetery is fenced in and kept in very good condition by the members of the community.

Copied by Williard Noe October 1936.

In Memory of Isaac Newton,
Son of J. M. and M. O. Wright
Born March 17, 1871
Died July 12, 1904

Samuel G. Medlin
June 30, 1866

His Wife, Malinda Jane
Medlin
Feb. 5, 1869
March 7, 1928

Henry C. Medlin
Born Feb. 29, 1844
Died Oct. 19, 1891

William E. Cox
Born Nov. 23, 1826
Died Jan. 12, 1902

His Wife, Sallie Cox
Born Nov. 16, 1833
Died March 20, 1905

Bessie Lee, Dau. of
J. H. and J. B. Medlin
Born March 15, 1895
Died Aug. 20, 1896

Floyd Shields, Son of
Mr. and Mrs. J. H. Medlin
Born Feb. 10, 1903
Died Feb. 13, 1913

Matilda Noe, Wife of
H. C. Medlin
Born Aug. 19, 1838

Virginia Chamberlain, Wife of
G. W. Utsman
Born Aug. 28, 1852
Died Dec. 13, 1906

Luther Chamberlain
Born Dec. 15, 1822
Died March 20, 1910

Martha Tarterson, Wife of
Luther Chamberlain
Born 1833
Died April 3, 1909

Ollie Lena, Dau. of
Lewis and Katie Chamberlain
Born Oct. 4, 1898
Died Nov. 4, 1915

L. N. Chamberlain
Born Aug. 6, 1859

Mary Kate Noe, Wife of
L. N. Chamberlain
Born Oct. 14, 1862
Died March 13, 1927

Helen Louise, Dau. of
Moss and Maude Chamberlain
Born March 25, 1915
Died July 3, 1917
"Thy will be done."

Maude Elizabeth Chamberlain
Died June 16, 1936
Age 42 Years, 4 Mos. 1 day.

HAMBLEN COUNTY

NOE'S CHAPEL CEMETERY
(Page 2)

Bell, Daughter of
John and Laura Chamberlain
Born Nov. 31, 1886
Died Nov. 9, 1887
"In after times we will
meet her."

Erastus S. Taylor
Born Oct. 13, 1888
Died Oct. 8, 1919

Herbert R. Taylor
Born Dec. 25, 1908
Died May 24, 1929

Richard M. Shockley
Tennessee Private 157
Depot Brigrade
Died Dec. 26, 1926

Andy Cross
Born Feb. 22, 1858
Died June 24, 1914
"The gates of heaven for
him have opened wide."

Bessie Oma, Dau. of
J. D. and M. E. Noe
Born Jan. 9, 1895
Died Feb. 10, 1895

Infant Son of J. D. and
M. E. Noe
Born Jan. 17, 1889
Died Feb. 6, 1889

Mrs. T. H. Noe
Born Nov. 15, 1859
Died Dec. 17, 1915

Rev. T. H. Noe
Born Dec. 4, 1857

Infant of B. A. and J. E. Noe
April 10, 1894

Little Carroll, Son of
B. A. and J. E. Noe
Born Sept. 5, 1895
Died Oct. 11, 1895

Clark Noe
Born May 23, 1885
Died July 18, 1909

B. A. Noe
Born June 10, 1861
Died Oct. 7, 1929

His Wife, Jennie E. Pettigrew
Born Nov. 16, 1863
Died April 7, 1926
Charter Member of Noe's Chapel

Infant Daughter of Hal B. and
Maude Noe
Born and died Aug. 13, 1921

Forest C. Noe,
Born Jan. 18, 1890
Died Jan. 23, 1919

Medlin Drury
Born Sept. 25, 1825
Died Nov. 28, 1903

Thelma Fay, Dau. of
J. W. and M. Noe
Born Dec. 29, 1911
Died Jan. 14, 1912

Joseph G. Noe
Born Feb. 13, 1865
Died Oct. 18, 1894

John B. Gray
Born March 24, 1826
Died Feb. 13, 1926

James Roy Gray
Born July 28, 1888
Died June 2, 1935

HAMBLEN COUNTY

NOE'S CHAPEL CEMETERY
(Page 4)

Earl James, Son of E. F.
and S. E. McCrary
Born Aug. 10, 1896
Died Oct. 15, 1900

Henry, Son of E. F. and
S. E. McCrary
Born April 12, 1903
Died June 6, 1905

Infant Daughter of
E. F. and S. E. McCrary

Lula McCrary
Born April 15, 1876
Died Mar. 3, 1908

Sallie E., Wife of
E. F. McCrary
Born Sept. 7, 1877
Died Nov. 29, 1911

Infant of W. C. and
Ethel Johnson
Sept. 22, 1917

David S. Howard
Jan. 17, 1849

His Wife, Lucinda Howard
Oct. 26, 1846
Jan. 11, 1917

Charlie Jr., Jinks
Born and died Feb. 9, 1927

Mary Holder
Died Jan. 4, 1932
Aged 69 Years
"Gone, but not forgotten."

Elbert Holder
Born June 13, 1854
Died June 35, 1915

James G. Cole
Born June 12, 1888
Died Jan. 5, 1925

His Wife, Maude Cole
Born Sept. 1, 1878

Lou Emma, Daughter of
H. G. and Anna Collins
Born and died Feb. 24, 1908

Mary J. Lester, Wife of
Charles W. Cassell
Born Dec. 2, 1863
Died June 21, 1896

Carroll T., Son of
C. W. and M. J. Cassell
Born Sept. 14, 1895
Died Feb. 18, 1897

Jedie S., Wife of
J. A. Noe
Born Nov. 7, 1857
Died Nov. 12, 1899

Mary M., Wife of
Levi Greseclose
Born March 9, 1850
Died March 29, 1905

Mary Agnes, Dau. of
Bob and Bessie Moore
Born July 6, 1923
Died Oct. 4, 1926

William Hopper
Born Dec. 20, 1849
Died April 20, 1927

Viola Hopper
Born Sept. 3, 1874
Died

Pearl Hefner Gray
Born July 28, 1895
Died Dec. 1, 1918

Infant Son
Nov. 26, 1918

Jane Hodge
Born Aug. 27, 1841
Died Sept. 6, 1918

Mary Nelson, Dau. of
W. R. and Flora Noe
Born Nov. 25, 1913
Died June 26, 1915

Julia M. Noe
Born April 29, 1837
Died March 7, 1893

Thomas M. Noe
Born Nov. 22, 1829
Died Feb. 25, 1904

David S. Noe
Born Jan. 7, 1833
Died Jan. 1, 1916

His Wife, Orlena Noe
Born Sept. 1, 1837
Died Oct. 19, 1909

Albert Hampton Noe
Born July 2, 1861
Died Feb. 17, 1913

Mary M. Noe
Born Jan. 30, 1855
Died Oct. 2, 1911

Leona, Dau. of
A. H. and M. H. Noe
Born Oct. 21, 1894
Died Sept. 14, 1906
"Gone to be an angel."

David M. Noe
Born Jan. 6, 1886
Died Jan. 23, 1916

Dollie F. Noe, Dau. of
A. H. and M. H. Noe
Born July 22, 1897
Died July 23, 1914

Joan Adams
Born Sept. 6, 1876
Died Aug. 9, 1919
"Asleep in Jesus."

Emeline J. Adams
Born April 2, 1842
Died March 15, 1921
"At Rest."

PURKEY

Sallie, Mother
Born Aug. 28, 1849
Died May 25, 1892

Dan, Father
Born Jan. 8, 1847
Died Jan. 23, 1921

Leneta
Born Aug. 24, 1891
Died June 19, 1892

Margaret McKinney
Born Nov. 16, 1815
Died Sept. 23,

Erastus H., Son of
Isaac and Mary Noe
Born Dec. 18, 1885
Died Nov. 19, 1918

Albert S. Noe
Born July 30, 1878
Died Oct. 21, 1918

J. L. Noe
Born April 28, 1830
Died Oct. 22, 1904
"Weep not, he is at rest."

Caroline, Wife of
J. L. Noe
Born March 27, 1834
Died Aug. 22, 1899

HAMBLEN COUNTY
PANTHER SPRINGS CEMETERY
(Page 1)

At Panther Spring Methodist Church, about five miles west of
Morristown, on the road leading to Panther Spring. There are
approximately 200 unmarked graves. Two Confederate soldiers are
buried in the north west corner of the cemetery, names unknown, but
marked by the Sam Davis Chapter U. D. C.

Panther Spring was a community of importance, long before Morristown was of any consequence. Many prominent, well-to-do families
lived in this locality.

The church is just a little way from the spring, which is one of
Nature's beauty spots. The name of the spring comes from the story
of a bear and panther which had a battle to the death, back in the
hills. The panther dragged his wounded body to this spring and there
died. The bear went a little farther down the valley and died at another spring, which is called Bear Spring.

There is a huge block of limestone in the water at Panther Spring,
which was left by the Indians, a deep hole is hollowed out in the center, with smaller depressions on each side, and it was here they beat
their corn to meal, the small depressions were for the stones they
used to beat the corn.

Inscriptions copied by Willard Neet of Morristown, Tennessee
Completed October 6, 1937

Sampson H. Robertson
Born July 14, 1855
Died 1916

Pauline Freelove, Wife of
S. H. Robertson
Born July 31, 1864

Otho L., Dau. of
S. H. & P. F. Robertson
Born Sept. 8, 1887
Died June 21, 1910

Rev. C. W. C. Harris
Born May 9, 1809
Died July 26, 1886

Harriet N. Harris
Born Jan. 29, 1822
Died Mar. 31, 1885

E. A. Ellis
Born Sept. 7, 1855
Died Dec. 29, 1860

Caroline Line, now Walker
Born Nov. 15, 1827
Married Aug. 15, 1867
Died May 23, 1872

Adaline M. Watkins
Born July 18, 1809
Died May 27, 1874

Oscar R., Eldest son of
O. R. & A. M. Watkins
Born July 30, 1833
Died July 8, 1855

Mary A. Wylie
Born Mar. 10, 1838
Died Nov. 21, 1858

HAMBLEN COUNTY
PANTHER SPRINGS CEMETERY
(Page 2)

Virginia V., Wife of
Dr. J. P. Hunter
Born Mar. 14, 1843
Died Oct. 4, 1892

John D. Mc Farland
Born Nov. 21, 1804
Died Mar. 20, 1876

Sherman R. Mc Farland
Born Dec. 15, 1837
Died Dec. 13, 1901

Margaret M. Mc Farland
Born May 2, 1840
Died April 24, 1915
(Husband and Wife)

Dr. J. H. Everett
Born Oct. 21, 1836
Died Nov. 26, 1881
"Let me die the death of the
rightous."

Nancy E. Senter, Wife of
Dr. J. H. Everett
Born Mar. 4, 1844
Died Jan. 18, 1903
"We don't know what tomorrow will
bring forth, But ask the Lord, He
will tell you what to do."

Cornia M. Smith
Died Jan. 9, 1862
Aged 5 years

Julia B. Smith
Died July 30, 1878
Aged 1 year

Isabella J. Smith
Died Dec. 23, 1863

Jonanna F. Smith
Died Feb. 12, 1872

Christena, Wife of
G. W. Bacon
Born Jan. 23, 1823
Died Feb. 17, 1876

Homer V., Son of
Geo. A. & B. W. Hodge
Born Nov. 3, 1870
Died Nov. 31, 1870

Julia T., Wife of
M. W. Hodge
Born Feb. 22, 1856
Died Apr. 1, 1887

Willie E., Son of
J. W. & Julia T. Hodge
Born Dec. 16, 1884
Died Nov. 12, 1898

Velma Ruth Quinn
Born May 24, 1929
Died Dec. 6, 1929

James A. Wood
Died April 10, 1874
Age 9 mo. 7 da.

James Wood
Died Aug. 9, 1876
Age 83 yr. 5 mo. 25 da.

Nancy A., Wife of
James Wood
Born Dec. 9, 1809
Died Apr. 11, 1883

Senter

S. S. S.
Born Mar. 13, 1886
Died Oct. 13, 1919

M. A. S.
Born Nov. 3, 1846
Died Nov. 27, 1922

HAMBLEN COUNTY
PANTHER SPRINGS CEMETERY
(Page 3)

W. T. S.
Born Apr. 12, 1847
Died Dec. 28, 1927

Mary L. Franklin Nee Senter,
Dau. of Rev. W. T. & Nancy Senter
Born Apr. 17, 1836
Died Jan. 15, 1913
  "At Rest"

Sallie Everett Roberts
Died Sept. 14, 1937
Age 59 yrs. 5 mo. 6 da.

        Senter

Enclosed by Iron fence.

Sacred to the Memory of
Robert Mc Clannahan
Hoo Dearted This Life
July 14, 1852
"He lived 40 years in the
Methodist Church."

Maria Jane Mc Farland, Wife of
Dr. C. S. Harris
Born Aug. 6, 1813
Died Aug. 10, 1879

Dr. C. S. Harris
Born June 13, 1802
Died Aug. 26, 1883

    "Our Bettie"
Daughter of C. S. & M. J. Harris
Born June 20, 1855
Died Mar. 1, 1867

(Records given by Mrs. John E. Helms,
of Morristown, Tenn., whom is a
grand-daughter of Dr. C. S. Harris)

Michael H. Harris, Son of
Dr. Crampton S. Harris and
Maria Jane Harris
Born June 6, 1851
Died May 31, 1867

Effie Maria Whiteside, Dau. of
Foster & Sara Miranda Harris
    Whiteside
Born Jan. 14, 1861
Dies Nov. 19, 1862

John Crampton Harris
Born Sept. 22, 1872
Died Sept. 23, 1873

Michael E. Harris
Born Sept. 6, 1869
Died Nov. 5, 1870
(Sons of John C. &
    Mary B. Harris.)

Sarah Ann Harris, Dau. of
Dr. John Crampton Harris,
  and his wife
Sarah Ann Reagan
(Sister of Dr. Crampton S.
        Harris)
Born 1814
Died June 6, 1880

HAMBLEN COUNTY
RIGGS GRAVEYARD
(Page 1)

Located on the farm of Hardee Dougherty, half a mile north of Russellville on the Three Springs Road. It is supposed that Jesse Riggs is buried by his wife. Sam Riggs, the father of Jesse, is buried in an unmarked grave on an adjoining farm. Before the Riggs owned the land, it was owned by Galbreath and Long and Eckels have owned it since the Riggs, but it has been in the Dougherty family many years. Hardee Dougherty lives in the old Riggs house, which has been greatly improved. This information was given by Hardee Dougherty.
Copied by Rebecca Colyer, Russellville, Tennessee, May 10, 1937

Mary Riggs, Consort of
Jesse Riggs
Born 1797
Died Sept. 1845

Mary Taylor, Dau. of
Jesse & Mary Riggs
Born 1821
Died 1845

HAMBLEN COUNTY
ROCKY POINT CEMETERY
(Page 1)

Located at Rocky Point Baptist Church, eight miles south east of Morristown, road to the Church is indicated by a sign post on the Springvale Road near the State Fish Hatchery.

Rocky Point Church was built about 1885, the principal participants in building it being Messrs. Luther B. Bewley, Nep Hale, and Andrew Huggins. The first pastor was Rev. Henry Hale.

This information give by Miss Frances Bewley, of Johnson City, daughter of Luther B. Bewley.

There are 12 unmarked graves, 18 graves marked with field stones, 2 graves marked with stakes.

Copied by Rebecca Calyer, Russellville, Tennessee, April 23, 1937

W. M. Thomason
Born Dec. 13, 1879
Died May 30, 1918

Clara L. Williams
Born Aug. 31, 1919
Died Nov. 24, 1923

Mildred M. Williams
Born Dec. 13, 1921
Died Nov. 18, 1922

Charles F. Williams
Born Feb. 5, 1916
Died Mar. 9, 1922

Woodrow W. Williams
Born Sept. 5, 1918
Died June 17, 1919

Mary Farley, Dau. of
C. D. & P. J. Williams
Died Oct. 24, 1905

Mariah, Wife of
C. P. Williams
Born Sept. 12, 1846
Died May 16, 1897
"Farewell dear Mother, sweet thy rest." "Gone to Rest"

C. P. Williams
Born Aug. 8, 1846
Died Jan. 2, 1891

M. Lizzie, Dau. of
C. P. & M. J. Williams
Born July 29, 1871
Died June 3, 1891
"At Rest."

A. E. Hale
Born Jan. 15, 1846
Died Mar. 27, 1891

Mary Maude Williams

Wife of Jesse Marshall
Born May 3, 1861
Died July 2, 1906
"Precious in the sight of God are the death of his Saints."

Mary Gertrude Huggins
Born March 15, 1896
Died July 4, 1902
Aged 6 yrs. 3 mo. 19 da.
"We had a little treasure once she was our joy and pride, We loved her Oh! perhaps too well for soon she slept and died."
"Lead Kindly Light."

"Lead Kindly Light"
Robert Chesley Huggins
Born May 25, 1901
Died July 17, 1902
Aged 1 yr. 1 mo. 22 da.
"Precious darling he has left us yes, forever more but we hope to meet our loved one on that bright shore."

HAMBLEN COUNTY
ROCKY POINT CEMETERY
(Page 2)

Mother
Minnie Pearl, Wife of
W. H. Higgins
Born April 9, 1878
Died April 11, 1922
"She left her home on earth
to forever live in Heaven."
"A sweet and gentle voice from
Jesus said come."

Lieut Lewis Clyde Wisecarver
Born June 1, 1893
Died Feb. 13, 1922

"Our Beloved"
Vergie L. Horton
Born Mar. 24, 1916
Died July 16, 1933
"At Rest"

Issac E., Son of
Denney and Martha A. Williams
Born 1871

James Hale
Born June 19, 1813
Died Dec. 19, 1889
"Oh death where is thy sting,
Oh grave where is thy victory."

Mary Ann Hale, Wife of
James Hale
Born July 9, 1820
Died May 16, 1875
Aged 54 yrs. 10 mo. 7 da.

Sarah E., Wife of N. Hale
Born Sept. 21, 1847
Died July 1, 1896
Aged 48 yrs. 9 mo. 25 da.

N. Hale
Born May 30, 1844
Died Feb. 19, 1911
Aged 66 yrs. 8 mo. 19 da.

Loyd, Son of
N. & S. E. Hale
Born June 30, 1893
Died Nov. 10, 1897

Mayme Lee, Dau. of
V. M. & E. F. Cox
Born Oct. 30, 1902
Died Nov. 23, 1902
"Gone to be an angel."

Herman Cox, Son of
H. M. & F. N. Cox
Born April 15, 1906
Died Feb. 23, 1907

Florence N. Nichols, Wife of
H. M. Cox
Born Nov. 6, 1866
Died Jan. 27, 1917
"Gone but not forgotten."

Ester B. Cox, Wife of
J. F. Courtney
Born Aug. 27, 1889
Died June 9, 1918
"The gates of Heaven for her
shall open wide."

Dixia E. Perry
Born June 20, 1905
Died Oct. 14, 1918
"Asleep in Jesus."

Nancie E., Wife of
J. M. Morrison
Died June 14, 1909
Aged 75 years

HAMBLEN COUNTY
RUSSELLVILLE CEMETERY
(Page 1)

Located in Russellville, on the main highway going east to Greene-
ville. The land was bought from Mr. Nenney. On the account of over-
grown condition it is hard to determine the number of unmarked graves.
Copied by Rebecca Colyer, Russellville, Tennessee, Apr. 28, 1937

Monroe Jenkins
April 28, 1920
July 11, 1936
"Asleep in Jesus."

Jacob M. Bewley
Feb. 16, 1844
Nov. 6, 1910

His Wife
Martha Jane Parvin
Oct. 28, 1850
Sept. 10, 1912

William Senter Bewley
Aug. 28, 1840
Died Sept. 28, 1895

Cap. W. S. Bewley

Emmerson C. Bewley
Born May 25, 1846
Died May 28, 1864

Rev. J. A. G. Bewley
Feb. 18, 1850
Age 41 yr. 6 mo. 5 da.
He professed Religion joined
the Methodist Episcopal Church
in the year of 1827 and was
called to the Gospel Ministry
in which he labored to the time
of his death.

Martha A., Wife of
Jackson Miller
May 10, 1832
Dec. 10, 1867
"Sweet be thy rest dear Mother,
We will meet thee again."
Erected by Mary E. Miller, Wife of
I. T. Foster, In memory of her mother.

Jas. O. B. Miller
Sacred to the memory of
James Miller

Son of S. & S. Miller
Dec. 30, 1823
July 14, 1847
Age 23 yrs. 6 mo. 14 da.

J. A. Bewley
Mar. 7, 1833
May 15, 1909

R. B. Bewley
June 9, 1879
Sept. 5, 1929

James V. Anderson
Mar. 31, 1805
July 27, 1873
Age 68 yr. 3 mo. 28 da.

Clara Atkins Anderson
March 26, 1855
May 5, 1897
"We will meet thee again."

L. A. Wall
Died Aug. 20, 1914
Age 77 yr.
"Reached in Heaven"

Ethel Ruth, Dau. of
A. E. & B. G. Potter

Evan Potter
Co. C. 8 Tenn. Cav.

O. G. Bradley

HAMBLEN COUNTY
RUSSELLVILLE CEMETERY
(Page 2)

In Memory of
Luthenery, Wife of
C. M. Haberl
Born Oct. 18, 1822
Died Aug. 31, 1877

Thomas Nugent
Born April 1, 1849
Died April 17, 1877
"In peace we rest."

S. E. Couch
Nov. 17, 1870
Nov. 23, 1872
Age 2 yr. 6 mo.

Una V. Couch
Aug. 10, 1867
Feb. 23, 1870
Age 2 yr. 6 mo. 13 da.

The grave of William Crocket Cain
Feb. 13, 1838
Departed this life May 1, 1865

Hugh Cain
May 5, 1801
Departed this life Apr. 27, 1864

Florence R. Cain
Oct. 4, 1860
Sept. 11, 1864

Olivia Annie Cain
Jan. 29, 1859
Sept. 14, 1864

Blanche Cain
Sept. 25, 1875
Died Apr. 18, 1883
"Blessed are the early dead."

John W. Cain
July 18, 1828
Oct. 25, 1892
"Death thou art infinite, It is
life is little."

Minerva Weems, Wife of
J. W. Cain
Sept. 28, 1834
July 14, 1902
"Blessed are the dead which
die in the Lord, that they
may rest from their labor
and their works do follow
them."

Issac Minnich
Born Nov. 17, 1826
Mar. 26, 1893

Emelina Oaks
May 6, 1843
April 25, 1897
"Earth has no sorrow that
Heaven can not rest."

Luvenyer, Dau. of
Issac & E. A. Minnich
May 12, 1868
Sept. 16, 1868

American A. Minnich

Eva A. Minnich

Rice Oaks
Sept. 28, 1794
Oct. 14, 1873
Age 78 yr.

Patience L., Wife of
Rice Oaks
Jan. 14, 1802
Aug. 27, 1877
Age 74 yrs.

Infant son of
Adalphus & Beuelah White
Born May 17, 1897
Died June 9, 1897

188

189

Beuelah Cain, Wife of
Adalphus White
Born Aug. 15, 1862
Mar. 25, 1897
"In after time we'll meet her."

Infant son of
Adalphus & Beuelah White
Born & Died Mar. 28, 1896

Narcissa Catharine Cain
Nov. 29, 1866
Mar. 14, 1916
"Blessed for they shall see God."

Herbert G. Hays
July 24, 1878
Sept. 2, 1886
"A smile has passed which
filled my (?)"
B
Baxter Bean
Dec. 1, 1829
Mar. 8, 1899

Charles Evans
Oct. 1, 1824
Died Mar. 3, 1902

Henry K., Son of Charles & Sarah
M. Evans
Mar. 11, 1867
May 22, 1890

Sarah M. Evans
Oct. 5, 1837
June 4, 1920

Dau. of R. H. & M. A. Irwin

William E., Son of
J. P. Bowlin
Feb. 8, 1874
April 8, 1889

Odie Mae, Dau. of
J. P. & N. E. Bowlin
May 27, 1893
Mar. 22, 1894

Mary J., Wife of
J. D. Bowlin
Born Sept. 12, 1848
Died May 23, 1890
"She died as she lived
trusting in the Lord."

Blanche, Dau. of
Charles & Sara M. Evans

Lemuel Cox
Died Mar. 17, 1890
Aged 74 yr.

His Wife
Mary R. Miller
Age 77 yr.

Cordelia, Wife of
J. H. Pierce
Born Feb. 20, 1855
Died Sept. 13, 1877
Aged 22 yr. 5 mo. 23 da.

James W., Son of
J. H. Pierce
Sept. 12, 1877
Oct. 11, 1877
Age 29 da.

Hope Woodson Taylor, Son of
John & Martha Miller
Sept. 5, 1876
Jan. 2, 1915
Member of the Russellville
Baptist Church
"There will be no goodbys in
Heaven."

In Memory of my Beloved Dau.
Sallie Miller
Aug. 17, 1874
Aug. 5, 1908
"Jesus can make a dying bed
feel soft as downy pillows,
are which on his breast I
rest my head and breath my
life out sweetly there."

Walter, Son of
John & Martha Miller
Born Feb. 5, 1888
Died Feb. 23, 1905
"One by one we are gathering
home."

Martha, Wife of John Miller
Born Apr. 27, 1840
Died July 20, 1887
"Precious in the sight of God
is the death of his Saints."

M. G., Infant Son of
Joseph & Mollie Wall
Aug. 3, 1916
Sept. 5, 1916

Thomas White

Father
J. B. Newell
Dec. 12, 1818
Mar. 17, 1895

Mary A. E. Newell
Born Apr. 5, 1821
Died Mar. 14, 1900
"The gates of Heaven for her
shall open wide."

Augusta A. Ford, Wife of
Frank W. Ford
Mar. 24, 1875
Dec. 8, 1903
"The gates of Heaven for her
shall open wide." "At Rest"

Martha Annie Elizabeth Ford
Jan. 13, 1847
Jan. 16, 1901
"Farewell dear Mother, Sweet
thy rest."

Father
C. L. Ford
Dec. 25, 1836
Dec. 3, 1903
"The peace of the Lord be
always with you."

Frank W. Ford
Nov. 22, 1875
June 4, 1923
"At Rest"

J. R. Bewley
Dec. 11, 1849
Aug. 15, 1886

Howard, Son of
R. F. & M. V. Bewley
Oct. 19, 1899
Died Dec. 26, 1899

R. F. Bewley
Born Jan. 5, 1877
Died Aug. 26, 1910
"Gone but not forgotten"

W. M. Miller
Died June 22, 1899
Age 81 yr.

His Wife
Lucy Cox
Age 41 yr.
"Gone but not forgotten"

William E. Creech
Born Apr. 19, 1848
Died July 4, 1907
"May he rest in peace."

HAMBLEN COUNTY
RUSSELLVILLE CEMETERY
(Page 5)

"Gone Home"
Nancy, Wife of
William W. irmillion
Born in Russell County Va.
April 5, 1818
Died Mar. 27, 1880
Age 61 yr. 11 mo. 20 da.

In Memory of
Minerva, Wife of
E. R. Cole
March 17, 1835
March 12, 1880

Mary P., Wife of
Wm. White
April 16, 1866
Feb. 21, 1877

Lafayette S. White
Jan. 5, 1868
Mar. 12, 1871

Lizzie A. Lynch
April 4, 1856
Aug. 20, 1864

Catherine B. Lynch
May 12, 1823
Aug. 10, 1864
"Sleep on dear mother and
take thy rest, God hath
called thee he knows best."

Passed on to the spirit Land
April 2, 1879
George W. Lynch
Born Sept. 9, 1814
"Rest weary one rest Thy labors
are o'er, But thou art of last,
only gone before."

Sara A., Wife of
J. H. Johnson
Sept. 27, 1824
Mar. 28, 1869

John H. Johnson
June 25, 1815
Jan. 25, 1871

Allen L. Trobough
Dec. 14, 1847
June 5, 1863
Age 15 yr. 5 mo. 21 da.

James F. Trobough
July 26, 1842
Sept. 2, 1859
Age 17 yr. 1 mo. 6 da.

Hannah, Wife of
Allen Trobough
Born Oct. 11, 1816
Died Mar. 26, 1885
"The morning cometh."

Joseph V. S., Son of
Elizah E. & Nancy Miller
May 14, 1864
July 12, 1866

In Memory of
George Squibb
April 10, 1799
Oct. 14, 1852
Age 53 yrs. 6 mo. 4 da.

Annie C. F., Dau. of
C. E. V. & Sophia
Sept. 29, 1856
Feb. 28, 1858

M. J., Wife of
J. H. Couch
Born Sept. 23, 1829
Died June 28, 1902
Age 72 yr. 9 mo. 5 da.
"Farewell dear Mother"

Joseph Couch

TOMBSTONE RECORDS

HAMBLEN COUNTY

ST PAUL CEMETERY

Located about six Miles South of Morristown to the right,
and in sight of the Old Road leading from Morristown to
Newport, thru what is known as the Lowland Section.
There are several graves marked with Field Stones and
about 175 with Stones.   St Pauls Cemetery is a Presbyterian
Cemetery.
Copied by F. R. Moreland, Dandridge, Tenn. July 23, 1937.

Hannah Jones
Born 1857
Died 1932

Rapts Jones
Born 1857
Died 1934

W. A. Davis
Born 1865
Died 1936

Hugh Williams
Born April 21, 1889
Died March 20, 1926
"Gone but not forgotten"

Mollie Quinn
Born Dec. 28, 1896
Died Feb. 24, 1931
"A dear Mother and
a Faithful friend"

Dortha Hunley
Born Jan. 5, 1906
Died July 20, 1907

Mary D. Hale
Born Sept. 24, 1868
Died Sept. 17, 1904
"How desolate our home
barren of thee Darling we miss thee"

Herman Buckner
Born 1897
Died 1934

Jean Buckner
Born 1925
Died 1926

Charles Davis H.
Born Jan. 23, 1871
Died Oct. 23, 1925
"Sleeping in Jesus"

William Rightsell
Born March 14, 1845
Died Sept. 20, 1930
Pvt. Co. "D" 4 Tenn Inf"

Alonzo Buckner R.
Born Nov. 1905
Died April 10, 1928
"Asleep in Jesus"

Robert W. Buckner
Born Feb. 27, 1872
Died Nov. 23, 1926
" At Rest"

Leland D. Milligan
Born Aug. 10, 1863
Died May 22, 1925

(Hamblen County St Paul Cemetery P. 2)

James D. Cooper
Born Sept. 16, 1906
Died Sept. 5, 1926

Kate Cooper
Born Oct. 34, 1874
Died June 9, 1928

Ebenezer Fagan- Co. E 6 U. S. V. Inf.
Born July 13, 1878   Sp. Am. War
Died July 11, 1929

Sarah Hunley Inman
Born Aug. 26, 1856
Died June 35, 1892

Rufus Inman
Born 1857
Died 1936

John Inman
Born 1856
Died 1930

Mollie Inman
Born 1867
Died 1927

Lizzie Felkner Smith
Born Nov. 3, 1876
Feb. 23, 1928
   "We Trusted in Jesus"

Marjorie Milligan
Born June 9, 1922

Allie Ruth Inman Milligan
Born June 23, 1898
Died Aug. 24, 1922

John Willie Stroud
Born Nov. 14, 1923
Died July 12, 1927

Mrs. S. W. Felknor
Born 1872
   Died - -

Hobert K. Moyers
Born Nov. 2, 1896
Died Dec. 17, 1897

Thaddues McCorkle
Born Oct. 26, 1862
Died June 1, 1905

Lafhyette McCorkle
Born Oct. 25, 1862
Died Oct. 25, 1899

A. M. Falknor
Born Jan. 37, 1830
Died Nov. 12, 1899

Francis Milligan
Born Aug. 36, 1898
Died Dec. 1, 1907

Ida McClister
Born 1891
Died 1924

Clyde Hale
Born Jan. 28, 1884
Died Oct. 18, 1918

G. S. Hale
Born May 23, 1840
Died July 1, 1915

Kate Smith Hale
Born Nov. 8, 1847
Died Feb. 7, 1922

Hazel Felknor
Born Nov. 9, 1913
Died Dec. 4, 1913

S. W. Felknor
Born May 19, 1872
Died April 5, 1926

Donald M. Felknor
Born Dec. 23, 1908
Died July 23, 1925
"Blessed are the pure
in heart for they shall
   see God"

(Hamblen County St Paul Cemetery P. 3)

Jane Riggs
Born Oct. 18, 1834
Died Aug. 8, 1903

A. A. Bayless
Born Aug. 1, 1843
Died July 25, 1924

Ira B. Bruce
Born Aug. 15, 1880
Died Nov. 29, 1903

Caroline A Bruce
Born Oct. 23, 1867
Died - no date

G. W. Angle
Born Sept. 4, 1843
Died Jan. 4, 1922
Eliza Angle
Born July 26, 1865
Died Aug. 30, 1930

Polina Jane Canter
Born Jan. 23, 1822
Died July 22, 1909

J. A. Conkin
Born Sept. 6, 1872
Died May 37, 1902
"Gone but not forgotten"

Florance A. Riggs Conkin
Born Aug. 25, 1875
Died March 18, 1905
"Resting in hope of a
Glorious Resurrection"

W. A. Penland
Sept. 29, 1873
Died July 24, 1911

Minnie Penland
Born May 17, 1880
Died Feb. 15, 1911

Clifford Penland
Born July 23, 1903
Died Aug. 4, 1906

Hazel Penland
Born March 20, 1907
Died June 18, 1907

Nettie E. Bayless
Born Dec. 2, 1863
Died April 17, 1902

Bill Penland Hale
Born Jan. 30, 1876
Died Oct. 3, 1899

Mary Bayless
Born Aug. 17, 1855
Died Oct. 11, 1897

William Felknor
Born Feb. 26, 1820
Died Dec. 15, 1898

Margaret Tompson
Born April 18, 1826
Died Dec. 20, 1908
"Asleep in Jesus blessed
sleep from which no one ever
wakes to week"

J. Minnis Felknor
Born Feb. 6, 1828
Died Dec. 11, 1912

Katherine F. Felknor
Born Sept 25, 1846
Died April 19, 1920

Frank Cleo Felknor
Born July 21, 1905
Died May 25, 1906

Laura A. Felknor
Born April 3, 1875
Died Aug. 10, 1905

(Hamblen County St Paul Cemetery P. 4)

Mary Felknor Smith
Born July 22, 1824
Died May 4, 1858

Mary Addeline Smith
Born May 1, 1858
Died Jan. 31, 1937

Looney Peck Smith
Born Feb. 14, 1820
Died May 19, 1897

Sadie T. Felknor
Born Feb. 9, 1902
Died June 20, 1902

Infant Son Felknor
Born & Died July 20, 1895

Maggie Felknor
Born Sept. 30, 1874
Died Nov. 6, 1893
"Weep not for me, for
I am waiting in Glory"

Maud A. Felknor
Born Sept. 12, 1887
Died Nov. 11, 1887
Rosa A. Felknor
Born Jan. 12, 1872
Died Dec. 22, 1881
"Taken from a world of
care an everlasting
bliss to share"

Pauline Felknor
Born Aug. 2, 1842
Died Aug. 7, 1888
"And so shall we ever
be with the Lord"

William McCarkle
"Who was born in Wadesboro,
N. C. May 23, 1831 and
Died at Hartford, Conn.
Nov. 18, 1899

Emily T. McCarkle
Born Dec. 1, 1837
Died July 19, 1894

Isaac A. Thomas
Born Apr. 10, 1870
Died Aug. 24, 1893

Elizabeth Thomas
Born Nov. 15, 1833
Died July 29, 1913
"Resting in hopes of
a Glorious Resurrection"

Florence Britt
Born July 28, 1865
Died May 7, 1937

Dave M. Britt
Born June 11, 1864
Died - -

Ella Kate West
Born Aug. 26, 1918
Died Nov. 16, 1919

Mary Hazel West
Born Nov. 7, 1919
Died March 2, 1920
"At Rest"

Sarah West
Born Apr. 11, 1860
Died Jan. 23, 1935

William Baker
Born Nov. 27, 1833
Died Oct. 27, 1858

Fannie Baker
Born March 9, 1806
Died Oct. 10, 1883
"Blessed are the dead
Who die in the Lord"

(Hamblen County St Paul Cemetery P 5)

Jennie Baker
Born Jan. 15, 1844
Died Feb. 13, 1863

Rosa M. Cox
Born Dec. 15, 1863
Died June 27, 1923
"Rememberence of Wife & Mother"

W. D. Smith
Born July 15, 1823
Died July 4, 1900
"At rest with Loved Ones"

Obediah Reams
Born Dec. 4, 1835
Died Oct. 19, 1861

Joseph B. Brown
Born Aug. 6, 1864
Died April 5, 1900

John Brown
Born June 1, 1827
Died April 24, 1897

Susan D. Brown
Born June 17, 1828
Died Feb. 21, 1892

Charles D. McCalister
Born May 23, 1851
Died April 6, 1911
"How Desolate our home
bereft of thee"

John G. McCalister
Born March 12, 1830
Died Nov. 5, 1900

Lizzie McCalister
Born Jan. 3, 1846
Died July 20, 1883

William McCalister
Born Jan. 28, 1796
Died Feb. 11, 1879

Addie McCalister

Eliza J. McCalister
Born July 21, 1837
Died June 10, 1914

James A. McCalister
Born June 23, 1838
Died June 9, 1862

George D. McCalister
Born Feb. 15, 1834
Died Feb. 23, 1916
"Thou Art gone but
not forgotten"

Sarah Catherine McCalister
Born Feb. 10, 1843
Died Aug. 10, 1920

James H. McCalister
Born Apr. 22, 1844
Died May 15, 1920

Madge Rosamond McCalister
Born July 10, 1888
Died Aug. 31, 1889

Sarah McCalister
Born Feb. 15, 1842
Died Feb. 16, 1908

David McCalister
Born Feb. 9, 1820
Died Oct. 23, 1889

Maria Helm McCalister
Born Sept. 19, 1816
Died Jan. 12, 1897

William P. McCalister
Born Jan. 19, 1851
Died Feb. 19, 1871

Nancy F. Griffin Moyers
Born Feb. 27, 1845
Died Sept. 29, 1901

(Hamblen County St Paul Cemetery P. 6)

James Moyers
S. Born Sept. 18, 1838
Died Dec. 2, 1905

John T. Moyers
Born Aug. 25, 1877
Died Sept. 18, 1877

Rightsell Effie
Born Oct. 23, 1868
Died Feb. 8, 1871

C. D. Rightsell
Born April 20, 1852
Died April 23, 1915

Robert W. Rightsell
Born Sept. 10, 1859
Died - -

Nettie Thomas C.
Born Oct. 14, 1856
Died May 21, 1909
" The Gates of Heaven
for her shall open wide"

Samuel H. Riggs
Born May 1, 1848
Died July 19, 1918
" He was faithful
to every duty"

Rebecca Jane Riggs
Born April 16, 1855
Died July 19, 1918

Mrs. O. J. Moss
Born May 27, 1836
Died Apr. 28, 1896

James Manson C.
Born 1822
Died 1898

Catherine Manson
Born 1826
Died 1898

Mary Manson
Born 1862
Died 1906

Benjamine F. Allen
Born May 6, 1867
Died Apr. 3, 1929

William G. Allen
Born Dec. 30, 1890
Died June 13, 1910

C. N. McCurley
Born March 1864
Died June 5, 1935

Thomas P. Bible
Born 1853
Died 1916

Billie J. Bible
Born 1863
Died 1919

Mattie Talley E.
Born Dec. 26, 1852
Died April 17, 1925

A. T. Talley
Born Apr. 13, 1849
Died April 8, 1923

Mary S. Talley
Born Oct. 19, 1856
Died June 24, 1916

Julia A. Talley
Born Jan. 9, 1886
Died Aug. 24, 1900

Sarah Talley
Born June 5, 1839
Died July 18, 1886

Nancy Talley Owen
Born March 1, 1862
Died Oct. 5, 1912

(Hamblen County St Paul Cemetery P. 7)

S. M. Owen
Born Jan. 16, 1848
Died Nov. 24, 1925

M. D. Talley
Born Nov. 17, 1850
Died June 18, 1906

George Buhl
Born July 25, 1805
Died May 5, 1895

Elizabeth Smith
Born Nov. 23, 1825
Died Aug. 26, 1896

Rev J.T. Smith
Feb. 22, 1833
Died Nov. 27, 1882
"Blessed are the dead
which die in the Lord"

Deliah Bayless
Born Feb. 22, 1816
Died Apr. 15, 1896

Asa Bayless
Born Dec. 13, 1813
Died Jan. 27, 1893

A. F. Bayless
Born Dec. 18, 1846
Died Feb. 22, 1909

Roma Bayless
Born Feb. 18, 1849
Died Dec. 25, 1925

J.T.W. Penland
Born Sept. 3, 1845
Died March 7, 1892
" Otwill be sweet to
meet on that blessed shore"

Lee Davis
Born Apr. 13, 1886
Died Aug. 2, 1887

Mattie E. Wice Davis
Born Jan. 6, 1865
Died Jan. 7, 1906

John T. Baker
Born Sept. 30, 1876
Died Dec. 25, 1908

John Baker
Born March 1, 1838
Died Dec. 25, 1893

Mary A Baker
Born May 29, 1851
Died Aug. 12, 1875

Oscar W. Baker
Born 1882
Died 1915

Wilburn Baker
Born 1835
Died 1908

Nannie C. Davis Baker
Born 1852
Died 1924

Nellie J. Baker
Born 1871
Died 1888

S. P. Baker
Born July 26, 1851
Died June 19, 1914
" A precious one from
us has gone, a voice we
loved is stilled a
place in our home is
vacant which can never
be filled "

Kiff N. Smith
Born Oct. 21, 1897
Died July 29, 1916

(Hamblen County St Paul Cemetery P. 8)

Charles Blake Smith
Born Aug. 17, 1902
Died Jan. 14, 1923

Paralles B. Smith
Born July 15, 1842
Died Feb. 26, 1917

Mary C. Williams
Born Dec. 3, 1832
Died July 8, 1901

John F. Williams
Born Nov. 18, 1809
Died Jan. 27, 1888
"He was a member of
St Paul's Church 61
years -Heaven is my Home"

Malinda Williams
Born Feb. 36, 1807
Died March 18, 1883
" A Member of St Paul's
Church 52 years"

Cythee Will
Born 1807
Died 1885

John Wesley Reams
Born April 10, 1851
Died March 16, 1930

Dorthula Reams
Born April 15, 1853
Died Sept. 9, 1934

Peter W. Ford
Born 1822
Died 1898

M. E. Hill
Born Jan. 1, 1860
Died Sept. 2, 1885

Lutisha Hill
Born Feb. 5, 1822
Died Nov. 3, 1917
"Gone but not
Forgotten"

Andrew Hill
Born Jan. 10, 1824
Died May 2, 1906
"God knows best He
has Called Him to rest"

Mary E. Hill
Born Feb. 19, 1858
Died July 8, 1900
"At Rest"

Sally J. Hill
Born Jan. 9, 1870
Died March 11, 1900
"Death is another Life"

Lizzie C. Hill
Born Aug. 14, 1859
Died July 29, 1879
"At Rest"

William F. Blackwell
Born June 2, 1892
Died June 22, 1918

Elizabeth Cope
Born Nov. 3, 1836
Died Sept. 18, 1914
"Asleep in Jesus far
from thee thy kindred
and there groves may be,
but thine is still a
blessed sleep from which
none ever wake to weep"

Private William F. Blackwell
38 Co. 10 Train Battalion G 2nd
Depot Brigade
Born June 2, 1892
Died at Camp Pike, Little Rock
Arkansas, June 22, 1918.

(Hamblen County -St.Paul Cemetery .)

Our Dear Brother Jimmie
Son of William & Jane Baker
Born Jan. 10, 1844
Died Feb. 13, 1862
Age 18 Yrs 13 days

Nancy E., wife of
J. M. Brady
Born Oct. 20, 1861
Died May 17, 1884

In Memory of J. A. Talley
Born June 2, 1818
Died   1880

Sarah A. Talley
Born   1839
Died Nov. 1, 1879

Daniel E. Evans
Born Dec. 3, 1837
Died Sept. 23, 1874

Jacob Evans
Co. C
8th Tenn. Cav.

Easter E. Moyers
Jan. 13, 1873
Jan. 27, 1877

T. C. Brown
Co. K
32nd Ky. Inf.

Philip Brown
Co. D
8th Tenn. Inf.

S. Y. Smith
Co. C
4 Tenn. Cav.

James Mc Moyers
Co. A
Ind. Cav.

Jane, Wife of Wm. Baker
Born Mar. 9, 1808
Died Oct. 10, 1883
Age 75 Yrs. 5 Mos. 1 day

Jacob Baker
Soldiers Rest Tenn
Born Nov. 25 1840
Died Mar. 12, 1883
Aged 42 Yrs 3 mos & 15 Ds.

Solomon Overton
Died July 25, 1888

Ellender Anderson
Born Jan. 1, 1814
Died Apr. 10, 1887

John Anderson

Erected in Memory of
Hester McClister
By G. D. McClister

Erected in Memory of
John McClister
By G. D. McClister

Elihu Lynch
Co. B
1st Tenn. L. A.

J. N. Rightsell
Co. C
4th Tenn. Cav.

S. D. Timmons
Co. C
4th Tenn. Cav.

L. G. Wilson
Co. C
13th Tenn. Cav.

(Hamblen County St. Paul Cemetery P. 9)

Solomon Overton
Died July 25, 1888
"He has gone but
    not Forgotten"

Amelia Smith
Born Nov. 4, 1887
Died Dec. 28, 1893

Priscilla Hogan
Born Jan. 11, 1843
Died Dec. 22, 1921

Alex Hogan
Born July 5, 1833
Died June 25, 1908

Lethia Gentry
Born Apr. 7, 1883
Died Apr. 12, 1907

Tennis Gentry
Born Feb. 4, 1909
Died Aug. 5, 1934
" She was the Sunshine
    of our Home "

Nellie Bible Hale
Born Nov. 15, 1886
Died Oct. 23, 1907

Mattie Hale
Born Jan. 7, 1890
Died Aug. 25, 1904

Nora Pearl Hale
Born July 23, 1888
Died June 30, 1908
"There are no parting
    in Heaven"

Jesse Joseph Tompson
Born July 8, 1874
Died Dec. 16, 1933

William Frank Tompson
Born May 13, 1897
Died Dec. 13, 1919

Alice Irine Tompson
Born Nov. 22, 1874
Died Aug. 22, 1906

Joseph Tompson
Born 1842
Died 1909
"He giveth His
    Beloved Sleep"

HAMBLEN COUNTY
MARTHA SUNDERLAND CEMETERY
(Page 1)

Located about 5 miles west of Morristown on the main highway
leading from Morristown to Knoxville; can easily be seen from the
highway.
The cemetery is well kept and there are about 95 unmarked graves.
Copied by Mrs. Arlie Turner, Talbott, Tenn. May 17, 1937

W. R. Talbott
Died Feb. 1, 1937
Age 23 yrs. 10 mo. 28 da.

Allie Bell Talbott
Died Jan. 3, 1937
Age 32 yrs. 9 mo. 16 da.

Talbott
John M. Talbott
Apr. 16, 1862
Nov. 8, 1925

His Wife
Nannie J. Talbott
Aug. 21, 1858

Judith Talbott, Wife of
Oscar Talbott
Dec. 20, 1841
Feb. 24, 1915

Oscar Talbott
Born Aug. 9, 1827
Died Jan. 8, 1914
"Blessed are the dead which
die in the Lord."
Erected by his sister.

Bowen
G. M. Bowen
Oct. 18, 1829
Jan. 26, 1904
"Thanks be to God, who giveth
us the victory through our Lord
Jesus Christ."

Mary Talbott Bowen
Sept. 1, 1838

Father
Ross Talbott
Born Mar. 25, 1799
Died Dec. 26, 1871
"I will come again and receive
you unto my self, That where I
am there ye may be also."

Mother
Temperance, Wife of
Ross Talbott
Born Feb. 7, 1805
Died May 31, 1880

Alice, Wife of
T. M. Roberson
Born Apr. 16, 1835
Died July 3, 1910
"He that believeth on me, Hath
everlasting life."
Erected by her son, H. P.
Roberson.

Sunderland
J. E. Sunderland
Born July 31, 1845
Died July 21, 1912
"They shall walk with me in
white, For they are worthy."

Martha Sunderland, Wife of
J. E. Sunderland
Born Sept. 1, 1838
Died Nov. 18, 1901

W. W. Sunderland
Born Oct. 1, 1850
Died July 20, 1897
"His sun set clear and bright"
"At Rest"

HAMBLEN COUNTY
MARTHA SUNDERLAND CEMETERY
(Page 2)

Wendell H. Sunderland
Nov. 4, 1890
Dec. 28, 1924

John Gilbreath, Son of
G. R. & Elsie G. Sunderland
Feb. 18, 1915
Feb. 19, 1915

Sarah Carter, Dau. of
G. R. & Elsie G. Sunderland
Dec. 6, 1916
Jan. 16, 1917

Alma May Talbott
Aug. 14, 1917
July 1, 1918
"Budded on earth to bloom in
Heaven."

Quarles
Ora H. Quarles
1884 - 1935

C. T. Quarles
Jan. 20, 1847
Sept. 6, 1929

His Wife
Artha L. Quarles
Nov. 19, 1847
Jan. 26, 1927

Sallie Quarles
Born July 11, 1872
Died Sept. 27, 1929

Jessie Howell Quarles
Born Nov. 11, 1880
Died Oct. 7, 1900
"His sun went in the morning
When all was clear and bright,
But it shines to-day on the far
Away hill of the land where is
no night."

Ethel, Dau. of
T. L. & Tennessee Roberson
Sept. 17, 1913
Dec. 29, 1917

Tennessee Roberson
Died May 29, 1925
Age 30 yrs. 1 mo.

Charles Roberson
Died May 25, 1925

Nannie Lou Roberson
Born July 5, 1910
Died July 1, 1911

Madgie Roberson
Born Feb. 7, 1908
Died June 2, 1908

Hugh P. Roberson
May 27, 1863
Oct. 11, 1916

Mary Roberson
Died Oct. 15, 1932
Aged 48 yrs. 3 mo. 6 da.

John M. Watkins
July 15, 1822
Jan. 7, 1916

Belvadra N., Wife of
John M. Watkins
Died Feb. 5, 1865
Age 34 yrs. 4 mo.

Lou, Dau. of
J. M. & Belvadra N. Watkins
Born Feb. 7, 1863
And sweetly fell asleep
in Jesus, Oct. 6, 1898
"Blessed are the dead that
die in the Lord."

HAMBLEN COUNTY
MARTHA SUNDERLAND CEMETERY
(Page 3)

Barshie, Dau. of
J. M. & B. N. Watkins
Jan. 22, 1850
Sept. 4, 1907
"He giveth his beloved sleep"

Mary Watkins, Wife of
Dr. J. P. Hunter
Born Dec. 30, 1856
Died Mar. 29, 1915

Infant of Wirt C. & K. K.
    Watkins
Died Dec. 31, 1883

        Baer
William F. Baer
1858 - 1936

Dr. J. H. Brown
Beloved Physician
1853 - 1926

Dr. D. D. Walker
June 12, 1868
Feb. 19, 1921

        His Wife
Lizzie H. Walker
Aug. 12, 1863-

Dr. J. P. Hunter
June 14, 1844
Mar. 9, 1922

        Huff
Andrew F. Huff
May 18, 1854
Died 9, 1923

Sarah E., Wife of
Andrew E. Huff
Nov. 22, 1853 -
"God gave, He took, He will
restore."

        Hale
John B. Hale
July 31, 1872
May 13, 1919

Mae Hodge Hale
Apr. 12, 1879

John B. Hale Jr.
Jan. 2, 1909
Sept. 26, 1910

Dr. W. L. Tadlock and Wife
Ema Lawrence Tadlock
Was killed by train at
Talbott, Jefferson Co. Tenn.
May 1916, and both were
buried in the same grave.

Little John, Son of
Dr. & Mrs. W. L. Tadlock
Jan. 5, 1905
Jan. 30, 1905

Charles E. Lowry
Feb. 7, 1873
Dec. 9, 1932

Modesta Idoma, Dau. of
Charles E. & Mary B. Lowry
Mar. 21, 1899
Dec. 19, 1931

Herbert B., Son of
C. E. & M. B. Lowry
Feb. 3, 1898
Nov. 4, 1918

Lillian, Dau. of
C. E. & M. B. Lowry
July 6, 1911
Oct. 1911

HAMBLEN COUNTY
MARTHA SUNDERLAND CEMETERY
(Page 4)

Robert Okley, Son of
W. M. & Myrtle Shaver
Sept. 9, 1904
Mar. 18, 1925
"Gone but not forgotten"

Eva Lena, Wife of
J. E. Noe
Sept. 4, 1896
Jan. 29, 1927

Gray
Robert M. Gray
1871 - 1931

Ida Davis, Wife
1873 -
"In Heaven we'll part no more."

Rev. O. L. Underwood
Jan. 26, 1860
May 2, 1932

His Wife
Minnie E. Hodges
Sept. 1, 1868
May 26, 1932

Wester
Lawrence Newton Wester
Aug. 27, 1913
Apr. 14, 1923

Wade H. Wester
May 5, 1884
Nov. 4, 1920

Shanks
William M. Shanks
Aug. 24, 1857
Feb. 1, 1932

Mrs. W. M. Shanks
Died Feb. 23, 1937

Josephine Creech Shanks
Died Dec. 3, 1934

"Our Darling"
Carroll Eugene, Son of
Mr. & Mrs. J. R. Line
May 6, 1925
June 25, 1925
"Just Sleeping"

M. A. Line
Born Apr. 6, 1844
"Mother"

Joseph Line
Born Dec. 25, 1840
Died Mar. 6, 1901
"Father"
"In God we have put our trust,
we shall not be arraid."

J. Ralph, Son of
H. H. & Nellie Line
Nov. 7, 1914
Dec. 24, 1914
"Awaiting to be reunited."

Alexander Porter Line
Nov. 15, 1851
Aug. 10, 1914

His Wife
Sarah E. Line
Mar. 7, 1850
Sept. 1904

Frank Whiteside
Died July 3, 1928
Aged 77 yrs. 9 mo. 10 da.

Mrs. Frank Whiteside
Died Nov. 1, 1923

J. B. Long
Died Jan. 1, 1934
Age 78 yrs. 2 mo. 16 da.

Mrs. Anna Long
Died May 3, 1935
Age 63 yrs. 9 mo. 2 da.

HAMBLEN COUNTY
MARTHA SUNDERLAND CEMETERY
(Page 5)

Nancy N. Cockrum
Born Nov. 12, 1891
Died Jan. 27, 1935
"Gone but not forgotten"

Cockrum
Frances G. Cockrum
Aug. 15, 1887
Nov. 30, 1915

Goforth
John H. Goforth
Dec. 11, 1854
Apr. 2, 1906

Nancy C. Goforth
June 8, 1862
May 11, 1933

Baby
Lloyd Edward May
Jan. 16, 1936
Jan. 1936

A. L. Treece
Died Jan. 5, 1936
Age 68 yrs.

Holland Bradley Jr.
1929 - 1933
"Our Darling"

Mary Malissa, Wife of
J. S. Bradley
Born Sept. 22, 1870
Died Mar. 31, 1900

Infant of J. S. &
Mary M. Bradley
Born Mar. 30, 1900
"Gone to live with Jesus."

Harvey M. Rogers
May 23, 1836
Jan. 22, 1896
"At Rest"

Loyd E. Richards
Died May 19, 1924

Pauline Collins
Died Nov. 18, 1924
Age 24 yrs. 1 mo.

Essie Collins
Died Apr. 12, 1936
Age 41 yrs.

Lillie May Wood, Wife of
G. C. Wood
Apr. 25, 1894
Aug. 22, 1933

Nannie Elizabeth Rhea
Died Aug. 8, 1930
Age 53 yr. 4 mo. 1 da.

Vioma Louise, Dau. of
Mr. & Mrs. G. F. Morrell
Born & Died Dec. 28, 1926

Mary Beatrice, Dau. of
Mr. & Mrs. N. S. Morrell
Born Sept. 27, 1927
Died Jan. 30, 1928
"Gone to be an angel"

Bell Mc Carry
Born Sept. 30, 1885
Died July 18, 1926
"Peaceful be thy slumber."

Sophia Hux
Died Nov. 10, 1920
Age 68 yrs.

Alex Hux
Died Oct. 7, 1913
Age 76 yrs.

Jessie Virch, Son of
J. R. & Nora E. Bacon
July 4, 1903
Mar. 28, 1913

Mollie Hax
Died July 16, 1936
Age 65 yrs.

HAMBLEN COUNTY
MARTHA SUNDERLAND CEMETERY
(Page 6)

Bettis
Porter C. Bettis
Aug. 12, 1850
Sept. 19, 1836

His Wife
Carrie W. Bettis
May 23, 1863
Apr. 4, 1918

Mildred Anna Patterson
Born Jan. 7, 1839
Died Nov. 16, 1907

Daniel
Lessa A. Daniel
Sept. 21, 1846
Nov. 18, 1809 ?
"Blessed are the meek for they
shall inherit the earth."

"At Rest"
Eliza J., Wife of
James Daniel
Born Dec. 5, 1819
Died Nov. 30, 1901
"Farewell dear Mother, sweet
thy rest."

James H. Daniel
Born Aug. 28, 1817
Died Apr. 9, 1889

Lloyd Huskel, Son of
C. H. & E. H. Travis
Born Sept. 27, 1905
Died July 3, 1919

Sarah J. Brabston
Born Jan. 26, 1832
Died Oct. 19, 1907
"Come all you who pass by,
As you are now, So once was I,
As I am now, you soon shall be,
Prepare for death and follow Me."

Estilla H. Haynes, Wife of
C. H. Travis
Born Sept. 1, 1880
Married Jan. 3, 1900
Died Aug. 20, 1910
"Thy work ended, thy rest won."

Ida J. Rines
Nov. 18, 1873
Oct. 9, 1932
"At Rest"

Wade, Son of
T. E. & I. J. Rines
Sept. 11, 1906
June 14, 1907
"Weep not, He is at rest."

J. Lee Rines
Died Nov. 26, 1931
Age 2 mo. 15 da.

Wallace Rines
Jan. 31, 1936
Age 3 mo. 10 da.

Mrs. Mary E. Rines
Died Jan. 27, 1937
Age 80 yr. 3 mo. 12 da.

J. C. Rines
Born June 14, 1895
Died July 15, 1915

John H. Rines
Died Jan. 30, 1937
Age 65 yrs. 4 da.

Hollifield
William L. Hollifield
Mar. 19, 1899
May 18, 1928
"Father"

HAMBLEN COUNTY
MARTHA SUNDERLAND CEMETERY
(Page 7)

Rosa Lee Hollifield
Aug. 24, 1906
Dec. 6, 1925
    "Mother"

Lucinda Hollifield
Born Oct. 6, 1845
Died Mar. 19, 1918
    "Mother"
"Gone but not forgotten"

Nettie Hollifield, Wife of
John Cross
1884 - 1931
"At Rest"

John W. Gooch
Oct. 30, 1856
Feb. 18, 1924
"Gone but not forgotten"

L. T. Pearson
Born July 29, 1836
Died May 5, 1915
"Now, Lord, what wait I for(?)
My hope is in thee."

W. P. Thomas
July 5, 1884

Carrie, His Wife
June 15, 1896
June 4, 1923
"Gone but not forgotten"

Roy, Son of
E. L. & J. Z. Beverly
Aug. 6, 1907
May 28, 1908
"Budded on earth to bloom
in Heaven."

    Mother
Bettie Rader
May 2, 1844
Oct. 16, 1918

    Hurt
J. C. Hurt
Feb. 4, 1861
July 19, 1919

Martha Parker
Died Mar. 25, 1935

S. W. Paschal
Apr. 27, 1859

    His Wife
Ladie Emert
July 11, 1868
Sept. 18, 1929
"In God we trust, Good by
till we meet again."

    Father
S. G. Cockrum
June 12, 1863
Feb. 21, 1932
"Asleep in Jesus"

    Husband & Wife
C. E. Lowe
April 1, 1898

Eva Lowe, Wife of
C. E. Lowe
May 12, 1902
Sept. 22, 1935
"At Rest"
"Gone from our home but not
from our hearts."

Infant son of,
J. M. & Eliza Copeland
May 26, 1900
Aug. 27, 1900

David M. Crockrum
May 7, 1855
Apr. 11, 1923

HAMBLEN COUNTY
MARTHA SUNDERLAND CEMETERY
(Page 8)

Mrs. Margaret Miller
Died Nov. 13, 1935
Age 68 yrs. 1 mo. 22 da.

Nettie, Dau. of
J. B. & N. E. Miller
Apr. 28, 1906
Dec. 17, 1920
"Only Sleeping."

William E. Gooch
Oct. 5, 1920
Mar. 5, 1921

Lula Mae Gooch
May 10, 1918
Oct. 10, 1918

Reba, Dau. of
W. H. & A. C. Gooch
Oct. 14, 1906
July 24, 1914

"Mother"
D. J. Hurst
June 18, 1841
Feb. 18, 1906

Ezekiel Hurst
Mar. 5, 1845
Oct. 8, 1914

W. S. Jones
June 30, 1906

"Brother"
James A. Bacon
Born May, 20, 1886
Mar. 2, 1925
"Gone but not forgotten."

"Mother"
Indie V., Wife of
T. L. Bruce
Born Oct. 11, 1874
Died Mar. 2, 1907

Infant Son of T. L. &
S. P. Bruce
Born May 8, 1909
Died May 10, 1909

Roy, Son of
J. R. & N. E. Cansler
July 28, 1898
Jan. 3, 1907
"May he rest in peace."

"Our Son"
G. W. Hammond
Born in Hamblen Co. Tenn.
June 2, 1881
Died at Fort Terry N. Y.
July 23, 1907
Co. 100th Coast Art.

W. H. Hammond
July 11, 1 864
Nov. 9, 1908
"Asleep in Jesus"

W. H. Hammond
Aug. 14, 1841
Sept. 24, 1913
"May he rest in peace."

Dr. S. E. Cosson
Died Feb. 21, 1919
Age 76 yrs.

John Crampton Cosson
Died Jan. 10, 1937
Age 53 yrs. 8 mo. 6 da.

Johnie W., Son of
R. E. & L. H. Miller
June 24, 1905
July 7, 1922
"A light from our home has gone
A voice we loved is stilled
A place is vacant in our home
Which never can be filled."

HAMBLEN COUNTY
MARTHA SUNDERLAND CEMETERY
(Page 9)

Mrs. Sue Owens Newman
Died Oct. 16, 1935
Age 61 yr. 3 mo. 14 da.

Mary Newman
Aug. 24, 1900
Sept. 23, 1927

"Mother"
Flora Moore Underwood
Dec. 1, 1903
Jan. 15, 1935
"Asleep in Jesus."

E. M. Turner, Wife of
E. L. Turner
Born Sept. 13, 1853
Died Aug. 14, 1902

Edith,M., Dau. of
G. A. & M. J. Mills
April 25, 1906
Jan. 20, 1919

Infant son of
J. J? & A. E. Green
Born June 6, 1902
Died June 15, 1902

Marie Richards
Died Sept. 10, 1929

J. L. Cluck
June 5, 1852
Dec. 31, 1918

His Wife

Mary K.
Feb. 14, 1851 -

Claude M., Son of
J. L. & M. K. Cluck
Nov. 15, 1881
Dec. 10, 1898

"Father"
J. W. Bacon
Born Aug. 24, 1854
Died May 24, 1917
"We will meet again."

"Mother"
Arley Bacon, Wife of
J. W. Bacon
Nov. 24, 1858
Feb. 5, 1927
"We will meet again."

Infant Son of
J. R. & Nora E. Bacon
Born & Died Dec. 25, 1907
"Budded on earth to bloom
in Heaven."

E. L. Rice
Oct. 29, 1893
Feb. 20, 1920
"Thoe lost to sight, to memory
dear"

Lorene, Dau. of
E. L. & B. M. Rice
Oct. 19, 1917
Nov. 17, 1922
"Gone to be an angel."

Lucy J. Kenipe
Died May 17, 1936

James Gilbert Boles
1847 - 1923

Sarah Elizabeth Boles
Died Feb. 3, 1933
Age 87 yr. 3 mo. 2 da.

William Perry Boles
1884 - 1922

210

HAMBLEN COUNTY
MARTHA SUNDERLAND CEMETERY
(Page 10)

Dora E. Lane, Wife of
P. B. Burton
Born Dec. 2, 1866
Died Mar. 13, 1916

P. B. Burton
Born Dec. 24, 1851
Died Feb. 21, 1910

Arthur Bailey
Died Mar. 29, 1933
Age 64 yr. 1 mo. 25 da.

James M. Malcom
Nov. 4, 1858
Apr. 23, 1902

Gyless Willard, Son of
J. C. & C. P. Bettis
July 4, 1906
June 22, 1907

Mary Orlena, Dau. of
J. C. & C. P. Bettis
June 24, 1905 AE
2 mo. 3 da.

Thomas Reams
Mar. 5, 1855
Oct. 29, 1934

Reams
Charity A. Reams
Aug. 9, 1831
Oct. 15, 1876

George W. Reams
July 4, 1822
Nov. 11, 1899

Charity M. Reams
July 9, 1849
Oct. 8, 1921

Samuel C. Roberts
Died Oct. 28, 1936
     (Killed by a tree)
Age 22 yrs. 10 mo. 21 da.

Lena, Wife of
M. A. Roberts
Born Aug. 23, 1850
Died May 19, 1900

M. A. Roberts
Died Aug. 30, 1933
Age 83 Yrs. 29 da.

Parker
"Father"
C. C. Parker
Feb. 16, 1855
Mar. 29, 1925

Sibbie S. Parker, Wife of
C. C. Parker
Oct. 2, 1855
Sept. 1, 1922
"For I know whom I have
believed, and am persuaded
that He is able to keep that
which I have committed unto
Him against that day."

Maggie Mae,
Born Dec. 7, 1882
Died Nov. 21, 1902
"At rest where the rose blooms
with out the thorn, and flowers
are not mixed with ramblers."

"Our little Boy"
W. G. W. Son of
C. C. & S. S. Parker
Born & Died Dec. 9, 1887

Parker
In Memory of Father
John B. Parker

Mother
Margaret B. Parker

Sister
Ella Neal Parker

HAMBLEN COUNTY
MARTHA SUNDERLAND CEMETERY
(Page 11)

John B. Parker
Born Sept. 23, 1818
Died Nov. 28, 1864

Margaret B. Parker
Boen Apr. 18, 1828
Died June 30, 1877
Age 49 yr. 2 mo. 12 da.

Ella N. Parker
Born June 7, 1861
Died Apr. 3, 1867

William H. Parker
Feb. 7, 1847
Dec. 6, 1825

Dora Wright Parker
Died May 6, 1932
Age 59 yrs. 11 mos. 2 das.

Bettis
Uncle Perry A. P. C. Bettis
Born Jan. 6, 1821
Died Jan. 14, 1905
"Gone but not forgotten."

Rebecca A. Looney, Wife of
A. B. C. Bettis
Born Dec. 22, 1847
"Has gone to meet loved ones
on the other Shore."

"He giveth his beloved Sleep"
James X. Duncan U. C. V.
Apr. 14, 1842
Aug. 12, 1916

His Wife
Martha J. Duncan
Aug. 7, 1844
Sept. 19, 1916

"He giveth his beloved Sleep"
J. B. Duncan
Aug. 13, 1887
May 25, 1915

"He giveth his beloved Sleep"
J. Commodore Duncan
Born July 27, 1881
Died July 25, 1904

Howell G. Duncan
Born Jan. 7, 1884
Died Jan. 23, 1905

James
Valliee, Wife of
R. T. James
Born June 8, 1885
Died Aug. 16, 1908

James S. James
May 6, 1870
Mar. 23, 1923
"Tho lost to sight, to memory
dear."

Samuel James
Jan. 20, 1836
Aug. 25, 1912

Lizzie Read James
Oct. 11, 1844
May 16, 1919

Viola M. James
June 15, 1875
Aug. 11, 1911

Mc Millan
"Father"
S. B. Mc Millan
Oct. 4, 1866
Apr. 25, 1926

"Mother"
Minnie V. Mc Millan
June 17, 1929

HAMBLEN COUNTY
TALLEYS CEMETERY
(Page 1)

At Talleys Methodist Church, two miles north of Russellville on the Three Springs road. The land was donated by W. C. Trent.

There are about 85 graves marked with field stones or stakes, and about 50 unmarked graves.

Copied by Rebecca Colyer, Russellville, Tennessee May 4, 1937

Pleasent M. Talley
Born May 20, 1882
Died June 25, 1934

J. H. Solmon
Born Apr. 11, 1884
Died Nov. 30, 1925

Mable Horner
Born Oct. 13, 1918
Died Mar. 29, 1919

Elizabeth Horner
Born in the year of 1897
She died March the 11, 1909

Jas. Talley
Co. A. 12 Tenn. Cav.

Wm. S. Newell
Born Oct. 27, 1850
Died Oct. 3, 1880
Age 30 yr. 24 da.

Luther L., Son of
Wm. & Mary Newell
Born Oct. 31, 1878
Died Oct. 3, 1879

Ida Horner Earl
Born May 15, 1875
Died Nov. 26, 1904
Mother of Jefferson D. Earl

Thomas, Son of
James & Clara Lawson
Born May 26, 1930
Died Nov. 30, 1936

HAMBLEN COUNTY
PRIVATE CEMETERY
THOMASON

Located on a farm belonging to Mr. Ike Williams of Morristown, Tenn.
The farm being located about 2 ½ miles south of Russellville, Tenn.

Copied by Rebecca Colyer, Russellville, Tennessee
May 21, 1937

Sarah R. Thomason
Born March 3, 1840

James Thomason
Born Feb. 21, 1836
Died Oct. 6, 1889

George N. Thomason

HAMBLEN COUNTY
UNION GROVE CEMETERY
(Page 1)

Union Grove M. E. Church is located eight miles south - east of Morristown on a hill just off the Springvale pike, easily seen from the pike. It is a mile and a quarter beyond the State Fish hatchery.

It was a church where several denominations worshiped, who eventually built churches of their own. One church which grew out of Union Grove was Rocky Point Baptist, which was built in 1885.

The earliest marked grave bears the date 1872. All graves have markers except two, which are marked with wooden stakes.

Copied by Rebecca Colyer of Russellville, Tennessee
April 23, 1937

William R. E., Son of
A. C. & M. L. Haun
Born Nov. 2, 1879
Died Mar. 17, 1897

Fannie B., Dau. of
J. B. & D. M. Marshall
Born Mar. 24, 1910
Died Oct. 20, 1918
"Gone but not forgotten."

Mary C. R. Haun, Wife of
J. B. Marshall
Born Sept. 13, 1877
Died Jan. 31, 1925

James B. Marshall
Born July 26, 1880
Died Oct. 31, 1918
"A place is vacant in our
home which never can be filled."

A. C. Haun
Born March 12, 1839
Died March 8, 1925

Mourning L, Wife of
A. C. Haun
Born Sept. 16, 1840
Died July 21, 1889

Infant Son of
A. C. & M. L. Haun
June 15, 1872

Sara D. F. Haun
Born June 17, 1869
Died Sept. 11, 1889

Lara C. E., Dau. of
A. C. & M. L. Haun
Born March 28, 1875
Died June 29, 1892

Nannie M., Dau. of
A. C. & M. L. Haun
Born & Died June 9, 1893

Minnie, Dau. of
James & Mary Estes
Born July 31, 1871
Died June 16, 1878

H. J. Haun
Born Aug. 2, 1863
Died Oct. 13, 1901

Ollie L. L., Dau. of
J. A. J. & M. L. Haun
Born May 5, 1884
Died Oct. 1, 1901

S. C. E., Son of
J. A. J. & M. L. Haun
Born Mar. 25, 1886
Died Sept. 5, 1889

N. M. D., Dau. of
J. A. J. & M. L. Haun
Born Apr. 18, 1889
Died Sept. 23, 1890

George B., Son of
B. S. & C. E. Lane
Born Mar. 3, 1876
Died Apr. 14, 1896

Catharine E. Haun, Wife of
R. S. Lane
Born Jan. 4, 1837
Died July 4, 1910
Aged 73 yrs. 6 mo.
"The gates of heaven for
her shall open wide."

R. S. Lane
Born Sept. 3, 1836
Died Jan. 3, 1911
Age 74 yrs. 3 mo. 10 da.
Capt. R. S. Lane
Government marker.

Alvas, Son of
Ferry & D. E. Burton
Born April 6, 1905
Died July 16, 1905

Rufus, Son of
W. F. & M. A. Haun
Born Oct. 29, 1881
Died Nov. 13, 1882

L. R. Lane, Wife of
Jesse Marshall
Born July 6, 1875
Died Jan. 12, 1903

Infant Son of
Jesse & L. R. Marshall
Born May 5, 1900
Died May 6, 1900

Esther, Dau. of
G. E. & E. C. Marshall
Born Jan. 21, 1896
Died June 18, 1896

George E. Marshall
Born Aug. 30, 1854
Died Dec. 8, 1919

Cecil, Son of
S. B. & L. C. Easterly
Born June 25, 1900
Died Aug. 19, 1901

Charlcie Lee, Dau. of
S. B. & C. L. Easterly
Born June 29, 1896
Died July 6, 1898

Ulah Alline, Dau. of
S. B. & C. L. Easterly
Born Oct. 15, 1894
Died July 24, 1895

Jacob Haun
Born Oct. 16, 1811
Died July 1, 1888

Sara S. Courtney, Wife of
Jacob Haun
Born June 14, 1816
Died July 28, 1896

Elizabeth C. Haun
Born July 14, 1850
Died Feb. 1, 1922

George E. Haun
Born Dec. 31, 1843
Died Mar. 15, 1896

HAMBLEN COUNTY
UNION GROVE CEMETERY
(Page 3)

Rebecca A., Dau. of
G. E. & E. C. Haun
Born Dec. 7, 1868
Died Aug. 15, 1884

Mary D., Dau. of
G. E. & E. C. Haun
Born July 21, 1873
Died Sept. 11, 1884

Sara E., Dau. of
G. E. & E. C. Haun
Born April 15, 1867
Died March 6, 1891

Lena Haun
Born Oct. 24, 1875
Died July 10, 1901
"Blessed are the dead which
die in the Lord."

Claude E., Son of
G. E. & E. C. Haun
Born Feb. 11, 1888
Died Apr. 11, 1908
"Just in the morning of his
youth and love he died."

Rachel Annie, Wife of
James Golden
Born Mar. 22, 1860
Died Apr. 28, 1906
"Sleep on dear Mother take thy
rest, God has called thee he
knows best." "You will surely
wait for me beside the pearly
gates."

Charlie A., Son of
J. M. & R. A. Golden
Born April 28, 1906
Died Sept. 17, 1906
"Budded on earth to bloom in Heaven."

TOMBSTONE RECORDS

HAMBLEN COUNTY, TENNESSEE

VINYARD CEMETERY

Located One mile from Witts on the School Road and
cross concrete road East 1/2 Mile.
Copied by F. R. Moreland, Dandridge, Tenn. Oct. 11, 1937.

W. P. Swain
Born Oct. 27, 1851
Died June 12, 1921
 "Gone but not Forgotten"

Mrs. W. P. Swain
Died Nov. 27, 1936
Age 75 Years

John Wesley Blevins
Born Mar. 10, 1858
Died Jan. 28, 1908
"As a husband devoted
As a Father affectionate
as friend ever kind and true"

W. L. Witt
Born 1880
Died - No date

Loucinda Witt
Died July 6, 1913
Age 84 Years
"A brave and gallant
soldier, a true patriot
her trials have passed
her work is done"

Josie Witt
Born May 14, 1854
Died May 15, 1889
"She is now at rest
where she is learning of
Heavenly things so devine
and true when on earth she
never knew"

Amanda Gass
Born Feb. 28, 1845
Died Feb. 10, 1848

Elizabeth Mase,
Born -
Died -   No dates

William Mase
Born Mar. 15, 1802
Died Mar. 11, 1866

Rachael Mase
Born Sept. 13, 1803
Died Feb. 13, 1883

Clara Lee Blevins
Born Nov. 10, 1808
Died July 25, 1909

(Hamblen County Vinyard Cem. P. 2)

James W. Jacobs
Born Aug. 18, 1832
Died - no date

Amelia Vinyard
Born Sept. 16, 1830
Died Mar. 13, 1908
"Gone but not forgotten"

Infant Jacob
Born & Died Mar. 13, 1898

Catharine Vinyard
Born Sept. 3, 1796
Died June 5, 1838
"To die is gain"

William Vinyard
Born Feb. 3, 1795
Died Oct. 14, 1881
"Not dead but sleepeth"

Elizabeth Vinyard
Born June 30, 1828
Died May 30, 1907
"Her end was Peace"

Allen Vinyard
Died Jan. 13, 1937
Age 4 das

Isaac Anderson
Born Sept. 15, 1904
Died Dec. 4, 1905
"Sleep on sweet babe and
take thy rest, God calls away
when He thinks best"

Dora L. Vinyard
Born Sept. 15, 1878
Died Sept. 14, 1892

Nancy Richey Vinyard
Born July 31, 1855
Died June 3, 1897

James A. Vinyard
Born Oct. 3, 1858
Died May 9, 1926

Nancy J. Richey Vinyard
Born July 3, 1858
Died June 3, 1897

Mary A. McDowell Vinyard
Born Aug. 7, 1860
Died July 31, 1888

Mary Vinyard
Born Aug. 7, 1860
Died July 31, 1888

John S. Vinyard
Born July 12, 1836
Died Aug. 4, 1861

Martha Ogle
Born Aug. 17, 1881
Died Dec. 14, 1909

B. J. Smith
Born Mar. 29, 1866
Died Mar. 5, 1898
"Gone but not forgotten"

Lewis Minnich G.
Born May 22, 1893
Died July 17, 1919
"Gone but not forgotten"

TOMBSTONE RECORDS

HAMILTON COUNTY, TENNESSEE

WITTS GRAVEYARD

Located between Morristown and White Pine, Tennessee
about six miles Southeast of White Pine and off the
State Highway about 1/2 mile. Of Baptist Denomination
There are 105 Marked graves. Copied by F. R. Moreland
Dandridge, Tenn., Sept. 6, 1937.

J. F. Daniel
Born Sept. 9, 1865
Died Aug. 6, 1932

Joseph Prince
Born Feb. 19, 1866
Died Mar. 6, 1890
"Weep not wife and
children for me, for I
am waiting in Glory for
thee"

Eliza Etter
Born July 23, 1838
Died Feb. 10, 1914

James Etter
Born Nov. 15, 1838
Died - no date
"Gone but not forgotten"

Clarence Southerland
Died Oct. 29, 1932
Age 11 Yrs. 2 mo. 1 da.

Nellie Southerland
Died July 30, 1936
Age 49 Years

J. R. French
Born Jan. 23, 1887
Died Dec. 21, 1934
" At Rest"

Lucy Badgens
Born May 23, 1890
Died - no date

J. J. Goan
Born June 3, 1874
Died April 23, 1923

Hurbert Elliott
Born May 25, 1925
Died Dec. 9, 1928

Henry Peoples
Born & Died April 11, 1926

Peoples Infant Son
Born & Died Nov. 28, 1922

Sarah Black Smith
Died Aug. 2,
85 Yrs. 10 Mos.

(Hamblen County Witts Graveyard P. 2)

Charles Jones Jr.,
Born Nov. 6, 1918
Died Mar. 9, 1931
"Budded on earth to
bloom in Heaven"

R. M. Goan
Born June 3, 1874
Died April 28, 1933

Erna Leeola Goan
Born Sept. 6, 1900
Died Oct. 3, 1920
"Blessed Are they which
die in the Lord"

George Lee Horton
Died Aug. 23, 1936
Age 13 Yrs. 4 Mos. 3 Das.

Sarah J. Davis
Born 1873
Died 1931
"Asleep in Jesus"

John S. Ball
Born Aug. 23, 1848
Died Nov. 28, 1914

Nancy A. Ball
Born April 4, 1851
Died - No date
"The Gates of Heaven
for them shall open wide"

Alex P. Ivey
Born June 8, 1837
Died March 15, 1914

Sallie Kelso Ivey
Born July 17, 1860
Died Mar. 11, 1917
"In loving remembrance of
our Father and Mother
gone to Heaven"

Augustus Lennon
Born Dec. 28, 1878
Died Oct. 19, 1918

Larellia Lennon
Born Oct. 6, 1887
Died May 6, 1904
"The gates of Heaven
for her have opened wide"

George W. Lennon
Born Jan. 30, 1847
Died Sept. 15, 1905
"A dear one is gone a
voice we loved is stilled
a vacant place is in our
home which never can be
filled"

Martha A. Lennon
Born 1850
Died 1937
"Asleep in Jesus

Pryor D. Smith
Born Jan. 17, 1841
Died July 20, 1891
"Gone but not forgotten"

Floyd Smith
Born Aug. 28, 1890
Died Oct. 7, 1895

Marvin Smith
Born May 1, 1891
Died May 2, 1896

Grace Smith
Born May 1, 1896
Died July 20, 1897
"Children of Neal and
Ida Smith)

Emma Self
Born Aug. 24, 1844
Died Jan. 17, 1907

221

(Hamblen County Witts Graveyard P. 3)

Ida Mae Self
Born Feb. 19, 1877
Died July 30, 1903

W. B. Nichols
Company "G" 4th,
Tennessee Cav.

Louvinia McClanahan
Born Dec. 15, 1854
Died Nov. 2, 1930
        "At Rest"

Sallie West
Born Jan. 10, 1888
Died Mar. 14, 1914
"I am the Resurrection
and the Life"

George W. Whitaker
Company "K" 143
New York Inf."
Joseph Gillinn
Born Aug. 5, 1837
Died Mar. 1, 1907
"The Gates for him shall
open wide"

John W. Gillinn
Born July 20, 1867
Died July 23, 1911
"Gods finger touched him
and he slept, weep not he
is at rest"

Martha E. Gillinn
Born June 1, 1849
Died May 30, 1916
"Thy trials ended thy
rest now"

Willie Ruth Manis
Born Feb. 19, 1911
Died Oct. 26, 1914
    "Our Baby"

Mary Galdona Smith
Born Nov. 28, 1886
Died Feb. 28, 1920

Ralph M. Maun
Born June 10, 1919
Died June 23, 1910

Sallie K. Maun
Born Jan. 22, 1883
Died Jan. 15, 1923
    "At Rest"

Mal H. Maun
Born June 15, 1925
Died Nov. 1, 1926
    "Our Baby"

William Clark
Born Feb. 7, 1883
Died Feb. 4, 1930
    "Gone but not for-
gotten"

Grace Young Quinton
Died Sept. 23, 1931
Age 24 Yrs.

May Mink Denkins
Died May 27, 1933
Age 45 Yrs. 3 Mos. 5 da.

Robert Dailey Denkins
Born Sept. 21, 1910
Died June 21, 1925
"And when the Chief
Shephard shall appear
Ye shall receive a crown
of Glory that faddeith
not away"

Howard Lee Alley
Born June 23, 1908
Died Sept. 1, 1924
    "Gone but not forgotten"

(Hamblen County Witts Graveyard P. 4)

William S. Wright
Born Sept. 25, 1923
Died - no date

Sallie J. Wright
Born Dec. 13, 1843
Died Feb. 27, 1923

Della May Fullington
Born Mar. 26, 1917
Died Nov. 3, 1917
"Asleep in Jesus
blessed Sleep"

Jacob L. Leeper
Born Feb. 20, 1859
Died May 30, 1913
"Peace perfect Peace"

David H. Leeper
Born April 4, 1895
Died Feb. 17, 1912

Johnathan Hann
Born June 8, 1877
Died Aug. 9, 1930

R. C. Owen
Born July 23, 1859
Died June 11, 1932

Mary Estes Owen
Born Sept. 20, 1875
Died Dec. 3, 1926

Evert Stanley Owen
Born June 28, 1904
Died May 25, 1917

Richard Louis Owen
Born April 10, 1914
Died July 4, 1914

Sarah Edith Owen
Born July 7, 1906
Died June 15, 1907

Thomas Boyd Owen
Born Oct. 30, 1895
Died July 5, 1922
"Gone but not forgotten"

James Almer Owen
Born Feb. 23, 1892
Died Feb. 6, 1911

Walters Albert Owen
Born Dec. 25, 1881
Died April 14, 1904

James D. Owen
Born Jan. 18, 1850
Died Aug. 18, 1914

Maggie A. Owen
Born Feb. 11, 1855
Died Mar. 21, 1923
"God gave, He took He
will restore, He doth all
things well"

Alice L. Coan
Born July 31, 1862
Died Dec. 26, 1909
"She was the sunshine of
our Home"

Matison Leonard
Born Oct. 18, 1859
Died Nov. 11, 1902
"Blessed are the dead which
die in the Lord"

Center Lawson
Born Aug. 6, 1837
Died May 27, 1894
"An affectionate hus-
band a loving father and
a friend to all"

Harriet Lawson
Born May 12, 1847
Died Oct. 15, 1907
"The faithful are certain
of their reward"

Clethie Wilmouth
Born Jun 24, 1883
Died Dec. 19, 1893

Virginia A. Moser
Born Sept. 13, 1849
Died May 17, 1894
"For ever with thy God
and Saviour Blessed rest
sweet thy rest for ever"

Lizzie C. Moser
Born July 37, 1879
Died Oct. 3, 1895

Edith C. Moser
Born Nov. 23, 1847
Died June 19, 1896

Velda Jean Painter
Born & Died July 30, 1930

Mary Louise Painter
Born & Died June 4, 1929

Margaret McFarland
Died April 28, 1840
Age 56 Years

Andrew B. McFarland
Died May 26, 1873
Age 80 Yrs. 9 Mos. 11 das.

Daniel T. Witt
Born April 16, 1845
Died Mar. 18, 1915

Horace M. Witt
Born June 16, 1870
Died Jan. 19, 1903
"As a son devoted, as
a Brother affectionate,
As a friend ever kind and true"

Ida Jacobs Jones
Born Aug. 15, 1868
Died May 2, 1909

Louis Cline
Born June 26, 1887
Died Oct. 29, 1936
"At Rest"

Maggie L. Cline
Born Mar. 13, 1888
Died No date

Ida R. Cline
Born & Died Mar. 23, 1923

Eanos Earl Hunt
Born Jan. 13, 1907
Died Oct. 35, 1929
"Safe in the arms of
Jesus"

Willson A. Hunt
Born June 15, 1916
Died Dec. 15, 1916

Mable Howard Presley
Born Aug. 16, 1900
Died Feb. 36, 1921
"She is not dead but
sleepeth"

Gladys Lorene Presley
Born Feb. 27, 1921
Died June 16, 1935
"Gone but not forgotten"

C. F. Francisco
Born Jan. 14, 1844
Died Oct. 11, 1927

Therrsie Francisco
Born May 27, 1846
Died No date

Robert N. Owen
Born July 16, 1854
Died Oct. 12, 1926

W. B. Painter
Born Nov. 12, 1862
Died June 2, 1930

Mary Manis Painter
Born July 19, 1868
Died No date
"Resting in hope of a
Glorious resurrection"

Jane Painter
Born May 17, 1926
Died May 22, 1928
"Asleep in Jesus"

L. D. Painter
Born June 23, 1928
Died May 13, 1928
"Asleep in Jesus"

Vernetta Painter
Born Dec. 10, 1907
Died Oct. 10, 1908
"Suffer little children
to come unto me"

Eva B. Lewis
Born Jan. 18, 1866
Died Aug. 25, 1917
" At Rest"

Hettie Sneddy
Born Sept. 26, 1881
Died Nov. 15, 1911
"God takes the lives
he gives"

Infant Sneddy
Born & Died Nov. 30, 1905
"Gone but not forgotten"

Infant Sneddy
Born & Died May 31, 1902
"Another little Angle"

Frank G. Wells
Born Nov. 4, 1903
Died July 12, 1904

Millie M. Lee
Born Jan. 23, 1900
Died Feb. 24, 1901

Viola Helm
Born Nov. 19, 1888
Died Nov. 23, 1888

Lizzie Brown
Born April 21, 1863
Died - No date

Mahala Fry
Born Sept. 13, 1834
Died April 17, 1889
"At Rest"

Edwin Augustus Rice
Died Aug. 10, 1827
Age 27 Yrs. 9 Mos.

Elvira Rice
Died Aug. 11, 1834
Age 10 Years 7 Mos.

Mary B. Rice
Died July 4, 1838
Age 37 Years 7 mos. 10 das.

W. H. Tritt
Born July 26, 1848
Died Feb. 28, 1925
Co. A 2nd, Tenn. Vol. Cav.

Sarah J. Tritt
Born Oct. 1, 1861
Died - No date

Olla Mae Hash
Died Aug. 29, 1937
Age 31 Years 5 Mos. 13 Das.

George Crosby
Born Sept. 4, 1867
Died Sept. 7, 1851

Sarah Crosby
Born Mar. 2, 1778
Died May 3, 1839
"Resting in hope of a
Glorious Resurrection"

(Hamblen County Witts Graveyard P. 2)

Melissa Smith
Born March 29, 1824
Died Feb. 17, 1899
"Blessed are the Pure in
Heart for they shall see
God"

M. A. Smith
Born March 29, 1824
Died Feb. 7, 1899

John M. Hill
Born Mar. 31, 1851
Died July 14, 1883

David G. Greenhorn
Born July 3, 1838
Died March 31, 1886
(Married Lizzie Lee Mar. 20, 1878)

Florence M. Malley
Born Nov. 4, 1865
Died April 30, 1883
"Clothed in white raiment she
rests in the tomb, where Jesus
doth love his Saints is to lead"

Rhesen E. Witt
Born 1887
Died Feb. 1, 1903
"At Rest"

Alice G. Witt
Born Feb. 12, 1857
Died Oct. 2, 1886

P. J. Witt
Born Sept. 16, 1840
Died July 13, 1924

Rebecca Witt
Born April 29, 1844
Died Dec. 3, 1899

S. M. Peoples
Born Jan. 20, 1857
Died Sept. 9, 1899
"At Rest in Heaven"

Willie Dickey
Born July 5, 1883
Died April 9, 1901
"She was the sunshine of
our Home."

J. S. Fisher
Born Feb. 27, 1882
Died Aug. 10, 1909
"Farewell Dear Scott, sweet
thy rest"

Irvin Fisher
Born Oct. 12, 1886
Died June 17, 1909
"Sleep on dear one and take
Thy rest, God called thee
Home, He knows the best"

Emory Newcum
Born Sept. 16, 1904
Died Nov. 7, 1913
"Sleeping in Jesus"

Anna Mack Falkner
Born Oct. 27, 1900
Died Dec. 14, 1918

Henry Wigington
Born Feb. 15, 1851
Died - No date

Manerva Nash Wigington
Born May 15, 1850
Died Dec. 25, 1922
"Gone but not forgotten"

Mary Rouse Wigington
Born May 13, 1884
Died April 24, 1934

Sarah E. Rouse
Born Oct. 10, 1890
Died March 12, 1925

Kenneth Rouse
Born Nov. 14, 1900
Died July 4, 1922

(Hamblen County Witts Graveyard P. 8)

Sam S. Rouse
Born Sept. 13, 1851
Died June 5, 1922

Rachel M. Widner Rouse
Born April 25, 1858
Died - No date
"Gone but not forgotten"

Laura Witt
Born Aug. 7, 1867
Died Oct. 21, 1923

John W. Snodgrass
Died Sept. 21, 1937
Age 70 Yrs. 1 Mo. 1 da.

Malinda J. Baker
Born Sept. 28, 1848
Died April 13, 1937

H. Crockett Baker
Born Mar. 6, 1848
Died May 6, 1920
"An honest man is the
Noblest work of God"

Hugh Parrott
Born Aug. 7, 1858
Died Mar. 7, 1932

Bruce Messeriah
Born March 12, 1854
Died Dec. 31, 1931

Martha F. Smith
Born Dec. 2, 1856
Died July 20, 1933

Myrtle A. Reagan
Born July 12, 1918
Died March 8, 1919

Anna Baker Holt
Born Jan. 24, 1890
Died Nov. 5, 1918
"Gone but not forgotten"

Mary I. Davis
Born Nov. 10, 1848
Died May 4, 1917

Richard Harrison
Born Nov. 27, 1913
Died Mar. 23, 1914

Mary Lily Harrison
Born Nov. 23, 1911
Died Oct. 15, 1915

R. L. Black
Born Aug. 1, 1847
Died July 30, 1924

Martha Black
Born Jan. 1, 1863
Died Nov. 19, 1913

Luther A. Wood
Born May 31, 1879
Died Jan. 1, 1923

Charles P. Williams
Born Dec. 3, 1879
Died Mar. 16, 1922

George L. Williams
Born Jan. 11, 1908
Died July 7, 1908
"Suffer Little children
to come unto Me"

Virginia Nevins
Born March 15, 1879
Died Jan. 8, 1923

Charles F. Wassum
Born July 32, 1873
Died April 6, 1915

"Gone but not forgotten"

(Hamblen County Witts Cem. P. 9)

Lucy G. Wassum
Born Dec. 6, 1898
Died Sept. 26, 1906

Ella M. Brinkall
Born Feb. 4, 1889
Died June 18, 1917
"At Rest"

Andrew J. Allen
Born July 29, 1852
Died Nov. 15, 1902

Borthula Allen
Born May 13, 1858
Died June 6, 1933

Isabelle Williams
Born Feb. 23, 1875
Died Oct. 31, 1912

Robert M. Williams
Born Oct. 27, 1887
Died April 18, 1914

Thomas J. Williams
Born Jan. 27, 1896
Died Dec. 15, 1926
"Gone but not forgotten"

Thomas W. Williams
Born Aug. 17, 1913
Died July 30, 1913

Houston Williams
Born April 14, 1836
Died Jan. 20, 1913

Mary E. Witt Williams
Born Sept. 7, 1850
Died April 20, 1936

Elizabeth Allen
Born Dec. 16, 1834
Died Mar. 2, 1892

Burnsey J. Smith
Born Feb. 22, 1893
Died Oct. 18, 1893

Pleasant Witt
Born Sept. 15, 1848
Died Sept. 7, 1913

Martha J. Witt
Born June 17, 1848
Died - no date

P. J. G. Peoples
Born Mar. 14, 1859
Died July 25, 1934

Lou J. Cannon Peoples
Born March 5, 1860
Died Dec. 12, 1898

David W. Peoples
Born Oct. 25, 1896
Died June 30, 1913

Sm M. Peoples
Born Jan. 30, 1857
Died Sept. 9, 1899

Susan I. Witt
Born Oct. 14, 1854
Died Oct. 21, 1859
"Gone but not forgotten"

Clara M. Walters Peoples
Born 1883
Died 1896

(Hamblen County Witts Cem. P. 10)

J. Nat Peoples
Born 1851
Died 1935

L. E. Peoples
Born 1861
Died - No date

Charles R. Hill
Born Dec. 7, 1848
Died Dec. 11, 1919

Mary Jacobs
Born Feb. 22, 1856
Died April 28, 1888

Rachel Bible
Born June 15, 1840
Died Feb. 10, 1892

William Witt
Born June 28, 1817
Died June 17, 1919

Rose Witt
Born June 20, 1818
Died Dec. 25, 1863

John J. Witt
Born July 26, 1815
Died March 20, 1894

HAMBLEN COUNTY

CONWAY FAMILY GRAVEYARD

Located on the old Conway farm, on a crossroad beteen
Springvale and Lowland pikes, about eight miles south
of Morristown. A sturdy stone wall about three feet
high and at least eightteen inches thick, with a wrought
iron gate, encloses the plot, which is sheltered by
beautiful arbor vitaes.

Copied by Margaret Helms Richardson

May 2, 1938.

The one tombstone bears this inscription:

Dr. Jos. P. Conway
Born in Highland, Highland Co., Ohio
July 23, 1822
Died at his home Hardbargain
Hamblen Co., East Tenn.
June 15, 1884
"He that overcometh, shall inherit
all things"
          Rev. 21- 7

HAMBLEN COUNTY

TIDENCE LANE CEMETERY

Located half mile north east of Whitesburg on the road to St. Clair, on the farm which is now owned by T. O. Hayes, but is known as the Garrett Lane farm. The old graves are in a walnut grove, and are easily seen from the highway.

There are six graves, marked with field stones. The grave of Tidence Lane has the largest stone and a "T" and "L" are still legible.

Copied by Margaret Helms Richardson
March 19, 1938.

HAMBLEN COUNTY

MOORE GRAVE YARD

Situated on the Wm. Carver farm, formerly W. G. Taylor

farm, four miles from Morristown on Valley Home road

south of Morristown.

Copied by Carrie B. Stuart, May 9, 1938

In Memory of Nancy,
Wife of Ephraim Moore
Born July 24, 1792
Died Nov. 30, 1863

In Memory of
Ephraim Moore
Born July 1, 1793
Died Aug. 5, 1875

E. L. Moore
Born Jan. 23, 1836
Died Jan. 18, 1863

Mary C. Moore
Born Aug. 10, 1859
Died Aug. 23, 1859

There are twelve unmarked graves with stones

www.ingramcontent.com/pod-product-compliance
Lightning Source LLC
Chambersburg PA
CBHW081430270326
41932CB00019B/3153